RL

A Taste of the Country

Western Kentucky farm country (courtesy of J. Norman Reid)

A Taste of the Country

A Collection of
Calvin Beale's Writings

Edited by

Peter A. Morrison

A RAND Corporation Book

The Pennsylvania State University Press
University Park and London

Library of Congress Cataloging-in-Publication Data

Beale, Calvin Lunsford, 1923–
  A taste of the country : a collection of Calvin Beale's writings /
edited by Peter A. Morrison.
    p.   cm.
  Bibliography: p.
  ISBN 0-271-00631-5
  1. United States—Population, Rural.   2. United States—Rural
conditions.   I. Morrison, Peter A.   II. Title.
HB2385.B42   1990
304.6'0973—dc 19   87–43183
                                                                    CIP

Contents

Part III   Contemporary Rural America

Preface

Calvin Beale and I first became acquainted in the early 1970s, brought together through a mutual involvement in research for the National Commission on Population Growth and the American Future. My interest in population redistribution out of rural areas (the "places left behind") toward big cities directed me to his extensive writings. That emphasis gradually enlarged to encompass how population settlement patterns were evolving nationally and to include a fascination with the distinct complexions regions acquire through demographic change.

Educated urbanites gain shallow, often fleeting impressions of rural areas and their inhabitants. What Calvin Beale has written can deepen our understanding of them and sensitize us to their diversity.

This volume was prepared with the start-up support of the U.S. Department of Agriculture and with editorial and secretarial costs funded by The RAND Corporation. Thanks go to both for helping to make this book a reality. Special thanks are due to Will Harriss, Helen Turin, Beverly Westlund, and Susan Amatouri of RAND's editorial staff; Constance Greaser, head of RAND's Publications Department; my secretary, Gwen Shepherdson; and two anonymous reviewers whose suggestions enhanced the book's organization.

It is easy to travel the United States and be impressed both with the commonalities of existence that all its residents share and with the diversity that is still imposed by vastness, the wide range of climate and physiography, the residue of history, differences in resources and agriculture, and variations in ethnicity and culture. (1981)

* * *

Outside the small town of Galesville, Wisconsin, a billboard proclaims, "WELCOME TO GALESVILLE, the Garden of Eden, Industry Invited." Here, in a nutshell, the basic modern dilemma of rural America is expressed. On one hand there is the ardent assertion of the idyllic, fulfilling quality that life in a small community can have, but then tempered by the necessity to invite the serpent of industry into the garden if people are to have the means to live there. (1985)

* * *

The Ozark and Ouachita region today finds itself with a mixture of success and problems. The isolation and stagnation of the past are largely gone and more jobs are available. Outsiders evaluate the region as attractive rather than shunning it. Yet, the future of the region creates concern. The population is not dense but some of the lakes are now having pollution problems. Some resort areas have become distinctly "touristy," with commercial attractions that have no relation to the rural charm and natural beauty that give character to the region. Population in small counties is often growing more rapidly than can be readily absorbed. . . . The region is a conspicuous example of a rural problem area of the past that has opened up and developed in an unexpected manner but is faced with a variety of nagging problems created by growth that are different from those of the past, but merit no less attention. (1981)

1

Editor's Introduction

City people began rediscovering rural America in the late 1960s and, in so doing, changed its face. For much of the twentieth century, dwellers in rural areas and small towns had been flocking to the cities. By the 1970s, the tide had turned the other way.

The *McGuffey's Reader* picture of an earlier rural America consisting almost entirely of family farms, and the small towns and villages serving them, was never really true and daily becomes less so. For one thing, we tend to forget that mountain ranges and forests are also rural. So are many mining districts, resort areas,

Wooden trestle bridge in Kentucky (courtesy of J. Norman Reid)

retirement communities, and industries. We will continue to have
farms and towns, but the details of rural life are changing, shifting,
and rearranging as Americans move from place to place. This book
presents some of those details as they have been observed by Calvin L. Beale, the Department of Agriculture's chief demographer
since the late 1950s.

A native of the District of Columbia, Calvin Beale studied geog-
raphy at Wilson Teachers College and history at the University of
Maryland. He then took a master's degree at the University of
Wisconsin, pursuing interests in demography. He was a statisti-
cian at the Bureau of the Census from 1946 to 1953, when he
joined the Department of Agriculture. In 1961, he became head of
the Population Section of the USDA's Economic Research Service,
where he built up its capability for documenting and reporting on
the conditions of rural areas and their inhabitants. He is now
Senior Demographer in that agency.

Beale has devoted his professional career—and also much of his
spare time—to studying rural areas and their inhabitants. He has
been poking about in places that many urban Americans have
never seen and do not know: the Mississippi Delta, the Ozark-
Ouachita Uplands, Appalachia, the Corn Belt, the Cotton Belt, and
the Tobacco and Peanut Belt. "You can't know what's going on in
the country from behind a desk in Washington," he asserts. Com-
bining his firsthand observations with penetrating analyses of statistical data, Beale was the first to detect in some regions that
more people were leaving metropolitan areas than were moving
in—this in the late 1960s, when the government was contemplat-
ing the construction of new cities to handle urban spillover. Small
wonder that his discovery met with widespread skepticism until
massive new evidence bore him out.

Beale has written far more than has found its way into print.
Some of his writings are widely known, but other important pieces
led obscure mimeograph lives. Yet, over the years, his audience
has widened from the Department of Agriculture to encompass
Congressional committees, academic researchers, and popular
writers.

Behind Beale's dignified, somewhat reserved manner lies an
encyclopedic knowledge of—and an endless fascination with—
regions and places and peoples and how they are intertwined. This
knowledge deserves a surer destiny than his scattered publications
might offer, so I have assembled some of his writings on rural
areas and on how the inhabitants earn their keep and live their

Calvin L. Beale (courtesy of Carolyn Riley, U.S. Department of Agriculture)

lives. Complementing these chapters are excerpts from Beale's amusing and occasionally poignant field notes. Together, they present information enriched by the author's perspectives on the transformations of rural America during this century.

Commonalities and Diversity

"It is easy to travel the United States," Beale has written, "and be impressed both with the commonalities of existence that all its residents share and with the diversity that is still imposed by vastness, the wide range of climate and physiography, the residue of history, differences in resources and agriculture, and variations in ethnicity and culture." Those two themes—commonalities and diversity—unify this book and are central to understanding how Beale's insights have shaped and refined the conduct of research.

In the past, researchers had been hampered by the largely undifferentiated measurement of nonmetropolitan population trends. Statistical data on rural America tend to highlight its uniformity, fostering a view that it is all one "type" of place, which it is not. Rural communities lie within broad regional settings that often shape their economic destinies and may also express common heritages.

Beale has elucidated this diversity in several ways, through careful observation and analytic study. At one time or another, he has set foot in well over half of the nation's roughly 2,400 nonmetropolitan counties. The excerpts from his field notes (Chapters 5, 6, 12, and 13) illustrate his model for doing observational studies in hundreds of out-of-the-way places.

Building on his wide-ranging observations, he refined and fostered the use of two analytic schemes for studying the developments under way in nonmetropolitan areas. One is an analytic typology for gauging the susceptibility of nonmetropolitan areas to urban influence. The other is a system of geographic subregions, dividing the nation into twenty-six economically and culturally distinct groupings of counties.

Typology of Nonmetropolitan Areas

Understanding the diversity of rural areas depends on recognizing their widely varying degrees of accessibility to the national metropolitan economy and susceptibility to urban influence. Two kinds of classification schemes now serve this purpose. The first, developed by the staff at the U.S. Bureau of the Census, distinguishes non-metropolitan counties according to the proportion of work force that commutes to a job in a nearby metropolitan area. Such commuting, of course, is a useful index of susceptibility to external metropolitan influence.

The second scheme, refined and updated by Beale and his colleagues at the U.S. Department of Agriculture, distinguishes non-metropolitan counties on a scale of urban influence that reflects the county's degree of urban concentration and its proximity to a metropolitan area. At one end of this continuum lie remote rural counties (such as those found in the Northern Great Plains) whose inhabitants are both sparsely settled and distant from metropolitan centers. Such counties lack cities of any notable size; typically their inhabitants reside in very small towns situated several hours' driving time from a metropolitan area. Their susceptibility to urban economic and cultural influence is minimal; and their remoteness precludes metropolitan sprawl, which is the principal external source of urban influence.

At the opposite end of this continuum are counties that are both densely settled and close to a metropolitan area (such as those throughout much of the industrialized Northeast). The population in such "urbanized and adjacent" counties is clustered in sizable urban centers (generally up to 50,000 inhabitants) near one or perhaps several metropolitan areas. Cities and towns in such counties "borrow" size from neighboring metropolitan centers, enabling the former to function economically as though they were larger cities. Several of the chapters that follow (most notably Chapter 14) illustrate the usefulness of this analytic typology.

Economic-Cultural Subregions

Distinctive regional contexts and settings are also important in understanding the diversity among rural areas. Growth and decline occur in broad regional patterns, but definitions such as "Sunbelt" or "Midwest," which generally are based on state boundaries, mirror this diversity rather poorly. They are too large and loosely defined to be meaningful and thus become conceptual and semantic traps.

Calvin Beale delineated the system of more highly detailed subregions shown in Figure 1.1. These subregions divide the nation into

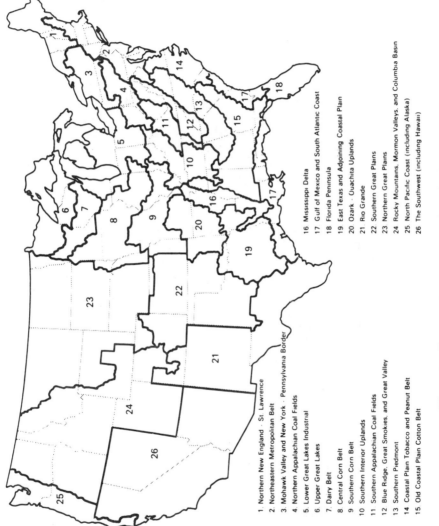

1. Northern New England - St. Lawrence
2. Northeastern Metropolitan Belt
3. Mohawk Valley and New York - Pennsylvania Border
4. Northern Appalachian Coal Fields
5. Lower Great Lakes Industrial
6. Upper Great Lakes
7. Dairy Belt
8. Central Corn Belt
9. Southern Corn Belt
10. Southern Interior Uplands
11. Southern Appalachian Coal Fields
12. Blue Ridge, Great Smokies, and Great Valley
13. Southern Piedmont
14. Coastal Plain Tobacco and Peanut Belt
15. Old Coastal Plain Cotton Belt

16. Mississippi Delta
17. Gulf of Mexico and South Atlantic Coast
18. Florida Peninsula
19. East Texas and Adjoining Coastal Plain
20. Ozark - Ouachita Uplands
21. Rio Grande
22. Southern Great Plains
23. Northern Great Plains
24. Rocky Mountains, Mormon Valleys, and Columbia Basin
25. North Pacific Coast (including Alaska)
26. The Southwest (including Hawaii)

Fig. 1.1. Twenty-six economic-cultural subregions.

twenty-six economically and culturally distinct groupings of counties, regardless of state boundaries (which are often artificial). By grouping counties that are economically and culturally homogeneous, these subregions reflect important differences in resource endowment, economic activity, and the evolution and present form of human settlement. Data analyzed at this scale can reveal patterns that would otherwise be submerged in national statistics. Chapters 7 and 19 contain Beale's sensitive characterizations of these subregions, and other chapters draw on this regionalization to develop certain themes.

Rural America and Its Transformation

The chapters in Part I are chosen to provide some flavor of how Beale characterized and studied particular communities of people defined by common heritage, racial background, or religious affiliation. These communities include various religious groups in the rural Midwest, a mixed racial isolate population of Melungeons in Tennessee, and a company of all-Creole firefighters in Alabama. Together, they illustrate the interplay between Beale's methods of personal observation, historical detective work, and statistical analysis.

Part II focuses on the diverse transformations that have altered rural economies, communities, and populations. Together, they examine various manifestations of the powerful forces that permanently changed the lives and livelihoods of rural people in this century.

Contemporary Rural America[1]

The early 1970s brought new and complex demographic patterns to rural America. In many places, it was a decade of sudden population growth in small, once-stable communities.

This unexpected wave of growth was readily visible at the national scale. Locally, however, subtle features were concealed beneath tabular data on net population shifts. Part of the growth was merely a continuation of the traditional pattern in the vicinity of metropolitan centers; but specialized activities were stimulating

---

1. Portions of this section are adapted from McCarthy and Morrison (1979).

new growth in areas lying outside the immediate sphere of metropolitan life.

Beale's widely cited "The Revival of Population Growth in Nonmetropolitan America," issued in 1975 (and reprinted here as
Chapter 14), illustrates how his melding of personal observation
with statistical data enriched his interpretations of this emerging
development.

The prevailing views on population growth in nonmetropolitan
areas attributed it principally to one or both of *population centrali-
zation* (the growth of freestanding cities at the expense of surrounding villages and towns) or *metropolitan spillover* (the ever-
widening zones of satellite communities springing up on the fringes
of existing metropolitan areas).

These two traditional models could not fully account for the
post-1970 pattern of change, in which some of the most rapid
growth occurred in the *least* urbanized, *most* remote nonmetropolitan counties. Indeed, the repopulation of remote rural areas was
the very antithesis of these two models: Such areas lacked the
urban nodes around which population could be said to centralize,
and they could not be regarded as satellites of any defined metropolitan areas. The accelerated migration into entirely rural nonmetropolitan counties to which Beale called attention signaled the
emergence of a new spatial pattern of settlement. It challenged
prevailing explanations of urbanization.

Beale's perceptive study suggested how multifaceted were the
reasons for this migration reversal. Some people, he noted, were
following the jobs offered by decentralizing industries (as in the
Southeast); others were drawn by the rapid buildup of energy
extraction activities in the 1970s, which generated new growth in
many parts of the West and rejuvenated growth elsewhere. He
also called attention to the emergence of recreation and retirement
as important growth-related (and growth-inducing) activities in
nonmetropolitan areas. People were attracted to areas rich in
amenities for tourism and recreation, as in northern New England,
Upper Michigan, and California's Sierra Nevada foothills; and
retirees were settling in smaller communities, where they could
combine a low cost of living with escape from big-city crime, crowd-
ing, and expense.

Whether people followed jobs or, by their presence, generated
new ones, these changes stimulated a mutually reinforcing cycle of
growth during the 1970s. New jobs helped communities to retain
their existing residents and attract newcomers. Their populations

grew larger and more affluent. The expanding economy attracted the providers of goods and services. Gathering momentum, the process of growth continued, expanding employment and drawing in still more newcomers.

Growth was far from ubiquitous, however. Overall, 19 percent of nonmetropolitan counties failed to grow during the 1970s, and much of the Great Plains, the Central Corn Belt, and the Mississippi Delta continued to experience out-migration and declines in population. For these nonmetropolitan areas undergoing substantial migratory loss, the problems were different but all too familiar: Sustained out-migration typically drains away the young, the educated, and the skilled, leaving behind older workers who are often undereducated and underskilled for contemporary job needs. As a result, the area becomes less attractive to new industries that require a supply of skilled workers, and the area's competitive position erodes further.

Economic Diversification in the 1980s

Beale's most recent work revisits some of his past observations and interprets developments as of the mid-1980s, by which time economic dislocation had replaced the growth and economic vitality of the previous decade. Rural economic stress resulted primarily from a restructuring of the nonmetropolitan economy and its growing integration with metropolitan and global economies. These close ties to national and international economic forces heightened the vulnerability of rural economies to the much broader economic forces operating.[2]

Downturns in agriculture, manufacturing, and mining and energy coincided in the 1980s, producing widespread rural economic distress and decline. Rural job growth slowed, and high unemployment became more pervasive. The generalized decline of population resumed: By the mid-1980s, 1,160 nonmetropolitan counties were losing population, contrasted with only 460 in the 1970s.

Nonetheless, contemporary rural America remains diverse, and most generalizations mask important differences among individual rural areas and their typically specialized local economies. Of the nation's roughly 2,400 nonmetropolitan counties, about 700 specialize in agriculture, nearly 700 more depend principally on manufac-

---

2. See U.S. Department of Agriculture, 1987.

turing, and some 200 depend heavily on mining and energy extraction. About two-thirds of all nonmetropolitan counties, then, were vulnerable to the poor performance during the 1980s of these three important rural industrial sectors. However, areas oriented toward retirement or recreation continued to grow rapidly.

Rural Community Heritages

To the general reader, the most captivating aspect of Beale's writings is likely to be his sensitivity to the *people* of rural America. He was continually fascinated by clusters of people possessing (although not necessarily conscious of) a distinctive common identity. Such an identity might derive from ancestry or shared economic plight. Beale devised procedures to detect these identities—noting common surnames and colloquialisms, for example—where they were submerged beneath present-day consciousness.

He also made sharply focused studies of people who share a common economic or ancestral background and, for that reason, sometimes are common to particular locales. His study of mixed racial isolates reflects Beale's firsthand experiences, such as gained through his 1969 field trip to Hancock County, Tennessee. His work on the high fertility of rural white Midwesterners is a charming examination of the persistence and effect of religious diversity in a region. A common theme is how such identities have translated into distinct spatial patterns (paralleling, for example, Utah's concentration of Mormons) and how those patterns persist or gradually dissolve.

"For generations in our national life, progress was the preserve of cities," he wrote in 1985. "Inventions, standards of services, and social styles and trends lagged in their adoption in rural areas. The countryside was a time machine in which urbanites could see the living past, and feel either nostalgic or superior, as the sight inclined them." An acute and sensitive observer, Calvin Beale continues to travel and write about the countryside, enabling the rest of us to savor its living past.

References

McCarthy, Kevin F., and Peter A. Morrison. *The Changing Demographic and Economic Structure of Nonmetropolitan Areas in the United States*. The RAND Corporation, R–2399–EDA, 1979.

U.S. Department of Agriculture. *Rural Economic Development in the 1980s: Preparing for the Future*, ERS Staff Report No. AGES870724. Economic Research Service, Washington, D.C., 1987.

2
Rural Development in Perspective

How should we view rural development today? If one claims great achievements, there is the risk that the problem will be viewed as solved or nearly so, even if that is not really the case. If the continuing seriousness of problems is stressed, then people may wonder about the effectiveness of remedial programs or the competence of those who ran them.

Certainly both longer-run trends and the current situation have to be examined. Rural trends over time may look good, but the comparative situation with urban areas may still remain poor. Furthermore, one must remember that standards change. Conditions that were deemed adequate yesterday may simply not be thought acceptable today.

When concern over conditions in rural areas first led to major governmental assistance and intervention in the 1930s, these conditions were utterly bleak in comparison with those today. As late as 1940, more than three-fourths of all rural dwellings either needed major repairs or had no bathtub or flush toilet. On farms, 90 percent were in this state, and nearly 70 percent still lacked electricity. Two-thirds of rural adults had never been beyond grade school, and about three-fifths of rural roads were unsurfaced.

All of these conditions are greatly improved today. Yet, housing inadequacies are still more prevalent in rural areas than they are in cities; rural electric cooperatives continue to need credit to maintain their systems; rural areas are still short of college-trained people in an era when post-high-school education has become the standard; and states and localities are puzzling how to maintain deteriorating roads and bridges. Thus, so much is relative to current need and not only to past conditions.

Adapted from a paper of the same title presented at the Professional Agricultural Workers Conference, Tuskegee University, December 9, 1985.

The 1970s were marked by much greater population growth in rural areas and small towns than expected. The revival of growth stemmed from several factors and was very widespread. Nonmetropolitan counties increased in population by about 15 percent during the 1970s, which entailed a net in-movement of about 4 million people. Such growth was a major element of what was intended and desired by public policy at the beginning of the decade—"balanced growth" was the oft-repeated goal. A majority of Americans said then (and still say) that they would prefer to live in a small town or rural area. Therefore, the trends of the decade gave more people a chance to remain in or move to the size and type of community that they preferred.

It would be wrong, then, to label this trend as anything other than broadly beneficial, after decades of rural exodus that seemed impossible to stem. But development and population growth do not solve all rural problems, any more than they cured all ills in urban America. The renewed growth of rural America has occurred selectively and, in some places, excessively. Many mining, resort-retirement, or exurban fringe counties grew by 40 to 50 percent or more in population from 1970 to 1980, especially in the West and Florida. Growth at these rates is next to impossible for a small community to handle effectively and esthetically, particularly if expectations for growth management had been set by a preceding era of decline and comparative stagnation. The impacts of growth on land use, water and sewer facilities, schools, medical and social agencies, crime rates, social pathology, roads, and a variety of other issues and services exceed the capacity of many small local governments to reach timely decisions, make plans, raise money, and make the necessary capital improvements and program changes. Adequate local leadership is often lacking or undeveloped, and some residents may not benefit from growth at all.

On the other hand, acceptance of the notion that economic and demographic growth is now the norm in rural areas may obscure the fact that about 460 nonmetropolitan counties continued to decline in population during the 1970s. These counties typically were heavily agricultural in nature. They lacked alternative sources of employment to offset the reduction of farm jobs as farms continued to consolidate. And, in the South, the losing counties typically had large black populations. In sum, there is such diversity in rural America that almost any generalization is subject to major exceptions.

Since 1980, nonmetropolitan growth has slackened as the farm depression, the loss of manufacturing jobs (especially in the textile industry), and the slump in mining have taken a toll. From 1980 to 1985, about 850 nonmetropolitan counties had population decline, with many more in the lower South than was true in the 1970s.

Nationally, nonmetropolitan America once again is having a lower rate of economic and population growth than metropolitan America. But conditions have not gone back to the pattern of the 1950s and 1960s. So, if the retention of people is a key indicator of the underlying social and economic health of rural and small-town communities, rural conditions today are worse than the 1970s, but better than they were before then.

In one sense the changes that have taken place in rural and small-town areas in the last twenty years or so represent an urbanization of countryside and village life. This is not to imply that most rural towns have grown to urban size. Rather, there is a more thorough penetration of rural life by the amenities, industries, businesses, institutions, communications, programs, laws, styles, family structure, social ills, and stresses and strains that were once regarded as basically urban in nature. It has not been entirely a one-way street. The rise of country music, charismatic religion, and rural-based forms of outdoor recreation represents a penetration of urban life by essentially rural values.

Sometimes the reality of this convergence is hard to accept. For generations in our national life, progress was the preserve of cities. Inventions, standards of services, and social styles and trends lagged in their adoption in rural areas. The countryside was a time machine in which urbanites could see the living past, and feel either nostalgic or superior, as the sight inclined them. And at the heart of it all was farming—with its images of land and animals, planting and harvesting, the cycles of nature, self-sufficiency, and good, hard-working people. God's chosen people, Thomas Jefferson called them.

Yet, one cannot understand rural people and their problems today if "rural" is equated with "agricultural." It is essential to recognize the steadily smaller role that farm work plays in the life of the rural and small-town population. By 1980, only 12 percent of employed rural men worked solely or primarily directly in agriculture. The figure for women was 3 percent.

The modernization of agriculture has been achieved only with drastic reductions in the number of people directly involved in its conduct. Both from local necessity and through changes that fostered decentralization out of the cities, the rural economy has been diversified (and thus urbanized) to the point that more rural people are engaged in manufacturing, in trade, and in services individually than in agriculture. In 1940, agriculture far outnumbered the other three combined in employment. Today, the landscape in rural America is still basically one of farms and forests. But taken as a whole, the people and their pursuits are overwhelmingly part of the nonfarm economy.

It would be equally fallacious, though, to imply that rural and urban distinctions have vanished or are unimportant. People readily offer convictions about preferred community size and list the virtues or disadvantages that they associate with rural or small-town life versus city or suburban life. Most of them regard rural areas as superior in such attributes as desirability for rearing children, friendliness of people, personal safety, lower levels of stress, pollution, and living costs, but inferior in availability of services and economic opportunity. Low density of population and small community size provide a different framework for provision of essential services than is found in larger communities. Economies of scale are often unachievable in rural settings, and certain types of specialized services and occupations are still almost always found in metropolitan centers, where the mass of population needed for their support is present or where proximity to other related businesses is necessary. Most rural areas will continue to be more limited in their industry mix than cities and more limited in the choice of shopping and service facilities.

One of the most obvious consequences of small-scale and dispersed population is the difficulty of providing a focus for rural issues. How does a focus of leadership emerge from 13,000 nonmetropolitan towns and many more thousands of unincorporated communities and rural neighborhoods? How can the unique aspects of rural issues be kept in mind? How can we avoid imposing urban solutions on rural problems in a nation that is three-fourths metropolitan? Or how can we make the public, the press, and the government even conscious of the fact that many of the problems of the day associated popularly with the cities have rural manifestations equally deserving of attention—for example, youth unemployment or chronic poverty?

In a sense, rural areas and rural people as a whole are a minority, in a manner analogous to that of minority racial groups. Rural problems continue to require special focus and tailored programs if their distinctive needs and circumstances are to be addressed adequately, but we must typically rely on special pleading to get the needed support of the urban majority.

Thematically, it has become more difficult to present in a persuasive way the objectives and justifications for rural development. The sure-fire, heart-tugging persuaders of pellagra-ridden children, impoverished sharecroppers, down-and-out rural migrants, gullied fields, and ramshackle housing that were effective in the past are either gone (thankfully) or no longer dominant. Urban self-interest in rural development is also hard to claim, now that the cities are no longer being inundated by poor rural migrants. Rural needs are real, but it is not as easy to appeal to emotion or to traditional notions of need in obtaining support for them.

It seems to me that at least three legitimate rural development objectives for the future can be stated: (1) maintaining the gains that have been made; (2) eliminating remaining conditions of inferior social and economic status in rural America; and (3) maximizing the contribution of rural America to the achievement of national objectives in an era of unprecedented global complexity.

Despite the progress that has been made, we still find that the median income of rural and small-town families is one-fifth lower than that of metropolitan families, that substandard housing and poverty are still disproportionately rural, and that the incidence of chronic illnesses and disabilities is greatest among rural people, as is the frequency of underemployment. And nowhere is the condition of racial/ethnic minorities so far below that of the general population as in the rural setting.

For some functions, such as community facilities and business and industrial development, the federal per capita investment in rural areas and small towns now exceeds that in metropolitan communities (although dwindling in both). But for other functions, particularly employment training, health services, and welfare, the per capita assistance to rural areas is well below that provided to metropolitan areas, despite the higher incidence of need that is often present in the rural communities.

The rural gains that have been made can, in all likelihood, be maintained only if a continued focus on rural conditions and trends exists in the government and in the various private rural-oriented special interest groups and coalitions that have emerged. The investments—both public and private—that have been made in rural facilities, services, education, and leadership provide a much better basis for self-sustained rural development than existed in the past. But, to repeat a point made earlier, such growth and maturation do not solve all rural problems, any more than they do in urban society. Both community and human service needs remain complex, and the diversification of the rural economy increases the variety of rural situations and thus the need to cope simultaneously with conditions of decay, moderate change, and boom as they exist in different regions and situations. In the last few years, however, the seriousness of the farm crisis has understandably consumed the attention of rural leaders.

Nothing seemed to create more potential for a revised view of the role of rural America in national life than the energy crisis. Mining is basically a rural endeavor, and any effort to make the nation more self-sufficient in energy fuels means a renewed role for rural areas, whether in conventional mineral fuels or in sources such as biomass products and geothermal energy. At the same time, much of the country's agriculture is increasingly viewed in strategic terms, whether as a source of exports to balance foreign trade or in terms of growing food needs resulting from world population growth of nearly a billion a decade.

Both these functions—energy production and food—are absolutely essential to the nation's welfare and world position and cannot be served by urban society. Unpredictably (and unfortunately), though, we have seen the short-term and mid-range market for much of American agricultural and mineral output collapse into unprofitability since 1980 from a variety of causes. The long-run need for high American production may be unquestioned, but this is of little consolation to the farmers who find themselves failing today or to the miners who are out of work with no knowledge of when the cycle will turn up again.

The substantial shift of manufacturing to rural and small-town areas has raised the national role of nonmetropolitan communities in industrial production. Indeed, it may be argued that the penetration of foreign-manufactured imports into the American market would be significantly greater than it is had industry not achieved savings by its rural and small-town decentralization. Yet here, too, whatever the advantages of lower wages and other costs are in rural and small-town locations, it has become all too clear by the mid-1980s that they are not enough to withstand the flood of imported goods, particularly given the very high value of the dollar. Some of the jobs being lost were not well paid, but they may have provided the essential margin of income to a two-worker family struggling to get by, or to individuals either lacking or unqualified for other opportunities. In short, several key components of rural economic development in the 1970s are missing now; namely, strong farm income and growth of manufacturing and mining employment. I do not see any of these weaknesses ending quickly.

Outside the small town of Galesville, Wisconsin, a billboard proclaims, "WELCOME TO GALESVILLE, The Garden of Eden, Industry Invited." Here, in a nutshell, the basic modern dilemma of rural America is expressed. On one hand there is the ardent assertion of the idyllic, fulfilling quality that life in a small community can have, but then tempered by the necessity to invite the serpent of industry into the garden if people are to have the means to live there. The end is worthy if rural development is successfully pursued, but it is not easy to retain the gains that have been made, and there is much more to do.

Part I
Rural America in Retrospect

Abandoned farmhouse and smokehouse, western Kentucky
(courtesy of J. Norman Reid)

I asked Collins whether the Melungeon people who moved away from Hancock County went to any particular locality. He immediately said yes, and named Ellicott City, Maryland, and Kokomo, Indiana. He went on to say, "If I walked down the streets of Ellicott City, I would recognize more people than I do here in Sneedville." (From field notes on trip to Hancock County, 1969)

* * *

In Stearns County, Minnesota, some German settlers drifted in during the 1850s and secured a German-speaking Slovenian priest named Francis Pierz. Pierz conducted an advertising campaign in American German Catholic newspapers and also abroad. He left no doubt about the virtues he was looking for, admonishing potential settlers ". . . to prove yourselves good Catholics, do not bring with you any freethinkers, red republicans, atheists, or agitators. . . ." Today, Stearns County is one of the most prominent examples of rural midwestern Catholicism. Within it, forty rural and small-town places have Catholic churches, and the cumulative rural fertility rate in 1970 was 5,024 children per 1,000 women—high enough to far more than double the parental population in one generation. (From "High Fertility in the Rural White Population in the Midwest," Chapter 3)

* * *

She then urged me to go see the old jail. . . . It is an old two-story rectangular brick home of the type in which the prisoners were kept upstairs and the sheriff and his family lived downstairs. She told of going to the jail several years ago to interview the sheriff and of how he was sitting out on the front porch with a big pot belly lapping over his belt, with his feet up on the railing. He took her upstairs and showed her these very miserable cells with shackles on the floor to which recalcitrant prisoners were chained. She asked him if he had much trouble. And he said, "No, when these fellows have done something wrong, they know that I will find them tomorrow if I don't today. So mostly they just come in and say, 'Well, sheriff, here I am!'" (From field notes on trip to Hancock)

3

High Fertility in the Rural
White Population of the Midwest

From the vantage point of a lengthy specialization in rural demography, it has long appeared to me that in the vast attention given to the study of American fertility over the last generation, there has been a failure to understand the importance of rural fertility in total U.S. growth or to notice the extent of truly high reproductive rates in this population. In some areas, high rural fertility is derived from the childbearing of blacks, Indians and Alaskan natives, and Mexican Americans. These are the traditional national racial minorities whose rural condition is often associated with low income, low education, poor housing, and the complex legacy of past social, political, and economic dominance imposed by white society.

In the post–World War II period, however, a major element of high rural fertility was white. I would suggest that the popular conception of rural white families with many children is, aside from the Amish and Hutterites, that of the southern "hillbilly"—be it a mining family from the Appalachian coalfields or the more agrarian population of the Great Smokies and Ozarks. These southern populations did once dominate the high fertility pattern among rural whites. From 1935 to 1940, 157 counties in the United States had period net reproduction rates of 1,750 or higher (per 1,000 white women). Of these, 102, or 65 percent, were rural- and small-town counties of the Protestant Upland South. Only 24, or 15 percent, were in the North Central states, and of these, eight were in Ozark or other southern border locations.

By 1970, the locus of high white rural fertility had shifted radically and the North Central region had emerged as highest. This change resulted both from the exuberant increase of childbearing in certain rural Midwest areas during the postwar years and the

Published here for the first time. Written in 1977, except for the concluding update.

near absence of response in the white rural South to the pronatal-
ism of the period. As measured by cumulative fertility of women
35–44 years old, 266 counties in 1970 had an average of 4,000 or
more children per 1,000 rural white ever-married women. But of
these, 184, or nearly 70 percent, were in the North Central region,
and only 26, or 18 percent, were in the Protestant Upland South.
It is my purpose here to examine the extent and circumstances of
high rural white fertility in the North Central or midwestern
states.

Data Sources

To measure fertility, I tabulated data from the 1970 Census on the
number of children ever born to rural women who had ever married. Tabulations were done separately by race for individual counties within the twelve midwestern states. These data, along with
certain social variables, furnished conventional measures of ecolog-
ical association. To avoid the often dry and substantively deficient
results of this approach, I examined each of the high fertility counties as a case and visited a number of them as opportunity arose.
Further subtabulations by township were used to identify where
the high fertility prevailed within each county.

It quickly became clear that religion promised to be more closely
linked with the fertility rates than were other variables. Accordingly, I obtained estimates of the distribution of church membership for each county.[1]

These church membership data were correlated with fertility,
along with measures of education, female employment, income,
population change, farm residence, size of largest place, and ethnicity. Some other measures, such as density or time of settlement,
were considered but rejected. Counties were combined wherever
there were fewer than 250 women 35–44 years of age.[2]

---

1. The estimates prepared by the National Council of Churches for the early
1950s were favored over those later published for 1971 by the Glenmary Research
Foundation. The former correspond more closely in time to the period of young
adulthood of the cohorts studied and also reveal more of the ethnic background of
counties (since they precede the major Protestant mergers and distinguish more
denominations).

Some modifications were made of the 1950 material in counties where obvious
omissions had occurred. The 1971 material was used as a guide in these cases.

2. Where such composite counties were necessary, as in much of the Great
Plains, care was taken to combine counties of relatively similar basic character, and

A third set of data came from a source of rural information that I have not seen demographers use—namely, the county atlas. Atlases in the form of township plat maps and directories of rural residents are prepared by several private companies and exist for hundreds of counties. After World War II, some of the companies operating in the Midwest enlarged their directories by including personal information for each family, including names of children ever born and religious affiliation. This makes it possible (albeit very tediously) to determine religious composition by township and the average number of children for families of a given religion. The resulting measure is the number of children per family. As a measure of fertility, children per family is crude, for there is no age control on the couples reporting as there is with the cumulative fertility rate for women 35–44. Some of the families are complete, others are still growing, and still others have yet to bear any children. Nevertheless, consistent differences in the results by religion surely reflect the existence of actual differentials in childbearing, not simply differences in age structure.

Religion and Rural Fertility Levels

Comparatively few people, I think, realize the extent of rural Catholicism. The general view of Catholics as an overwhelmingly urban people in the United States is a valid one. For example, estimates of religious affiliation from polls show that 86 percent of Catholics live in urban places.[3] This reality is buttressed by the manner in which the urban-based Italian-, Irish-, and Polish-American populations are portrayed in our culture as our typical Catholic elements.

The white rural Catholic minority, however, is primarily Germanic—a population group with strong Protestant components, and thus not stereotyped as Catholic. In addition, rural Catholics are not evenly distributed nationwide. They are a significant ele-

certain small counties were left uncombined because they lacked similarity with their neighboring counties. An example is Red Lake County, Minnesota, which has a large Catholic French Canadian population, whereas the counties that surround it are strongly Protestant Scandinavian. This procedure yielded 950 counties and composites within the twelve midwestern states, of which 157 recorded high cumulative fertility (i.e., 4,000 or more children per 1,000 rural white ever-married women 35–44 years old).

3. Leo Rosten (ed.), *Religions of America: Ferment and Faith in an Age of Crisis* (New York: Simon and Schuster, 1975).

ment in some areas and comparatively absent from others, such as
the South. Even within the North Central states, there are relatively few Catholics in those areas of Illinois, Indiana, Iowa, Kansas, Missouri, and Ohio that were settled from the South. In other
sections of the region, though, Catholics are common and reach a
majority in some rural counties of each of the twelve states of the
region.

The Protestant "Bible Belt" image of the rural Midwest is
widespread but difficult to document in a formal way. In conversation, a prominent rural sociologist, who had remarked to me that
he had never thought of the rural Midwest as other than Protes-

German grave markers, St. Lucas, Iowa (photo by Beale)

tant, suggested that the absence of any literature on rural Catholicism in itself should be a valid demonstration of my contention that the extent of such Catholicism was not widely known. But one cannot really say that an absence of literature exists. There is a sizable corpus of theses, pamphlets, and even books. However, it is heavily Catholic in authorship and sponsorship and seems to have had little general distribution or impact.

Catholic farming settlements were well established long before the Civil War. The Germans, Irish, and Anglo-Catholics were firmly planted in various places by the 1830s, and even the Poles and Bohemians had some rural footholds before 1860. In the Plains, the German emigrés from Russia of the 1870s and 1880s had a large Catholic component (although it is the small Hutterite minority of this population with its spectacular fertility rates that demographers are more familiar with).

Among Protestants, the groups best known for large families—the Hutterites and the Amish—do not comprise a majority in any county, although they do affect the fertility rates for the counties where they live. Less known to the general public, but much larger in numbers, are the rural Dutch-dominated areas of Reformed persuasion. Three counties are predominantly Reformed Dutch. One of the two largest Reformed churches—the Christian Reformed—has emphasized parochial schools, just as the Catholics, Amish, and Hutterites do.

The township-level data revealed only one other Protestant group to be consistently associated with high fertility: the Apostolic Christian Church, a small denomination of Swiss origin, sometimes known locally (but incorrectly) as the New Amish. Other denominations with a socially conservative Pennsylvania Plain People background, such as the general Mennonite groups and the Brethren Church (Dunkards), tend not to evidence high fertility in the period studied. I have found some exceptions among Russian-German Mennonites, but not for Brethren.

In the northern states of the region, the Lutheran churches are very prominent. They had a majority of all church members in 109 counties. A number of counties that are predominantly Lutheran show high fertility, but many others do not. In the 1950s, the Lutherans were still divided along ethnic origin lines, with the Germans further split by doctrinal views. Based on patterns apparent in the data and a theoretical premise about expected fertility in two Lutheran denominations, I divided the Lutherans into three groups. The heavily Norwegian Evangelical Lutheran Church seemed to predominate in Lutheran counties of high fertility, so it was considered separately. The Missouri and Wisconsin Synod groups of German Lutherans are theologically conservative and also maintain their own parochial schools wherever feasible. Thus, they were combined as a separate class on the premise that their conservative views and educational practices might be associated with larger families in the manner of the Christian Reformed. The remaining Lutheran groups (except for the United Lutherans)[4] were taken as a residual class. They are mainly comprised of Swedes, centrist Germans, Danes, and Finns.

The Evangelical Lutherans have some overall association with high rural fertility, but, within their major states, lower percentages of Lutheranism yield higher rates of county fertility because of the higher childbearing of Catholics, who often comprise most of the rest of the population.

In the case of the Missouri and Wisconsin Synod Lutherans, I find no evidence of high general fertility despite their conservative theology and parochial schools. For example, the rural Missouri Synod Lutheran townships in Perry and Cape Girardeau counties, Missouri, are where the original Saxon refugees, who formed the heart of the present denomination, settled. Yet, the cumulative fertility rate in 1970 was only 3,453 children per 1,000 women, slightly below the regional rural average.[5]

For many counties, atlas data can provide a further indicator of fertility—the number of children per family—that is specific to broad denominational groups. Atlas data are most commonly available in the Dakotas, Nebraska, Minnesota, Iowa, and Wisconsin. I have recorded these data for several entire counties and for selected townships in numerous others. They demonstrate conclusively the higher fertility of the Catholic rural population over the Protestant, and among Protestants document the special situation of the Dutch, Amish, and Apostolic Christian groups mentioned earlier. They also permit comparisons of all Lutherans with other groups (subgroups within the Lutheran population are not separately identified). The following examples illustrate these points.

4. The United Lutheran Church was derived heavily from colonial Pennsylvania Germans and was grouped with other churches of that background. It was also a more urban church than other Lutheran churches.

5. I am not fully satisfied with the data available and remain skeptical that the Missouri and Wisconsin Synod Lutherans are indistinguishable from other Lutherans or most other Protestants in childbearing. If their families are larger, I am satisfied that it is not by much and does not compare with that of rural Catholics.

In Grant County, Wisconsin, Protestants were 62 percent of all households reporting religion.[6] Collectively, the Protestants averaged 3.08 children per family. Lutherans (who were second numerically to Methodists) averaged 3.4 children, which is not meaningfully higher than the Protestant average. However, the large Catholic minority (38 percent of the whole) averaged 4.31 children. The fertility of this Catholic element was sufficiently high to rank Grant County among the 157 midwestern counties with cumulative fertility rates of four or more children per woman in 1970.

In Sioux County, Iowa (one of the few Dutch majority counties), families with Reformed Church affiliations are 64 percent of all families.[7] Whereas those families averaged 3.55 children,[8] the Catholic minority (12 percent of the total) averaged 4.16 children per family. Lutherans (14 percent of the total) averaged 2.76, and all other Protestants averaged 2.72.

Ziebach and Corson counties, South Dakota, form two-thirds of a three-county combination in the Russian-German area. There the Catholic minority (29 percent of the total) averaged 4.46 children, Lutherans 3.04, and other Protestants 3.28.[9] In this area, the Lutherans were below other Protestants.

The data include two counties with Apostolic Christian settlements: Nemaha County, Kansas, and Lyon County, Iowa. Members of this group are not "Plain People" in their manner of living (in the sense of the Amish) and do not have Amish-sized families. They are opposed to birth control,[10] however, and their childbearing appears to be well above that of the general Protestant population, except for members of the Reformed churches. In the northern part of Nemaha County, Apostolic Christian families averaged 3.77 children, according to my data. This level compared with 4.18 for Roman Catholics (a conservative German settlement) and 2.73 for the three leading Protestant denominations present (none Lutheran).[11] In Lyon County, Iowa, the fertility of the rather small community of Apostolic Christians exceeded that of any other group, including Catholic and Reformed.[12]

---

6. *Atlas of Grant County, Wisconsin* (citation not available).

7. *Atlas of Sioux County, Iowa* (n.d.) (Fremont Neb.: Midwest Atlas Company).

8. Four Reformed denominations were present—Christian Reformed, Netherlands Reformed, Protestant Reformed, and the Reformed Church in America.

9. *Atlas of Corson County, South Dakota* (1967), *Atlas of Ziebach County, South Dakota* (1967–68) (Bemidji, Minn.: American Atlas Company).

10. Information supplied by one of the leaders (elders) of the church, 1977.

11. *Atlas of Nemaha County, Kansas* (1964) (Minneapolis: Title Atlas Company).

12. *Atlas of Lyon County, Iowa* (1962) (Fergus Falls, Minn.: Thomas O. Nelson Company).

Although the characteristic high fertility of the Old Order Amish is well known, it is instructive to compare their level with that of other faiths within the same area. I have found atlas information on number of children for only one Amish settlement—one embraced by three townships in Buchanan County, Iowa. For this reputedly very conservative settlement,[13] Amish fertility far surpasses the levels ordinarily found among Catholics or any other group. The Amish averaged 5.89 children per family, compared with 3.84 for Catholics, 3.34 for Lutherans, and fewer than 3.00 for other Protestants.[14] Whether other Old Order groups attain levels as high as this community is not known.

Rural Catholic Settlement

In reading the literature of settlement and the history of Catholic parishes, I am impressed with the extent to which those that were settled as colonies or were served by religious orders or agrarian-minded priests have remained as conservative and large-family-oriented communities today. Often they are distinctive Catholic islands in a larger Protestant sea. A full listing of such cases is not germane here, but some major examples can be offered.

In Dubois County in southern Indiana, a Croatian priest in the 1840s became the leader of a small settlement of German Catholics. He systematically bought land in a compact pattern from earlier southern Anglo-American pioneers. He encouraged other German and Austrian Catholics to settle and also persuaded Swiss Benedictine priests to serve the group and to establish what is now known as St. Meinrad Abbey.[15] About half the county is Catholic now, along with parts of two adjoining counties. In 1970, Dubois County as a whole recorded 4,341 children per 1,000 rural white women 35–44 years old, or fully 1,000 children per 1,000 women above the highest of rates in three adjoining Anglo-Protestant counties.

In Stearns County, Minnesota, some German settlers drifted in during the 1850s and secured a German-speaking Slovenian priest

---

13. Elmer Schwieder and Dorothy Schwieder, *A Peculiar People: Iowa's Old Order Amish* (Ames: Iowa State University Press, 1976).

14. *Atlas of Buchanan County, Iowa* (1966) (Fergus Falls, Minn.: Thomas O. Nelson Company).

15. Albert Kleber, *St. Joseph's Parish, Jasper, Indiana, Centenary, 1837–1937* (St. Meinrad, Ind.: St. Meinrad Abbey, 1937).

named Francis Pierz. Pierz conducted an advertising campaign in American German Catholic newspapers and also abroad. He left no doubt about the virtues he was looking for, admonishing potential settlers "to prove yourselves good Catholics, do not bring with you any freethinkers, red republicans, atheists, or agitators."[16] Settlers soon arrived, and in two years Fr. Pierz acquired German Benedictines to make a foundation in the county, which now includes St. John's University. Bishop John Ireland of St. Paul later called Stearns County "a new Germany permeated to the core with that strong Catholic faith and energy."[17] Today, Stearns County is one of the most prominent examples of rural midwestern Catholicism. Within it, forty rural and small-town places have Catholic churches, and the cumulative rural fertility rate in 1970 was 5,024 children per 1,000 women—high enough to far more than double the parental population in just one generation.

The settlement of Catholics in Carroll County, Iowa, was organized, but of secular origin. In 1868, a railroad company contracted with an agent to settle families on its land. The agent, a Catholic, recruited fellow Catholics from Dubuque County, Iowa, and Grant County, Wisconsin (both counties with high rural fertility today).[18] From this nucleus, Catholic German settlers spread out until they comprised a majority in the county. The community was never dominated by a religious order or any one clerical father-figure, but has remained conservative, with 57 percent of its elementary school children in parochial school in 1970, and 4,385 children ever born per 1,000 rural women aged 35–44.

The largest Catholic farm colonization effort was that conducted by Bishop Ireland of St. Paul.[19] Like some other midwestern priests, Ireland was concerned about the poor conditions among Catholic immigrants in eastern cities and felt that Catholics were neglecting to take advantage of the agricultural opportunities in lands opening up in the western prairies. He was especially concerned about his fellow Irishmen.

Bishop Ireland conceived the idea of using railroad land as a base and ultimately became agent for five railroads. From 1876 to

16. Patrick H. Ahern (ed.), *Catholic Heritage in Minnesota, North Dakota, and South Dakota* (St. Paul, Minn.: Archdiocese of St. Paul, 1964).

17. William P. Furlan, *In Charity Unfeigned: The Life of Father Francis Xavier Pierz* (St. Cloud, Minn: Diocese of St. Cloud, 1952).

18. *Biographical and Historical Record of Greene and Carroll Counties, Iowa* (Chicago: Lewis Publishing Co., 1887).

19. The best discussion of Ireland's work is James P. Shannon, *Catholic Colonization on the Western Frontier* (New Haven, Conn.: Yale University Press, 1957).

1881, he founded ten villages and farm communities in five counties of southwestern Minnesota. Irish settlers were involved in eight of them, but news of the colonies stimulated German, Belgian, French-Canadian, and English Catholics to participate also. The Belgian and German settlements have been particularly persistent in farming, and the areas have been characterized by large families.

A group of a different nature was the Russian-Germans who migrated to the Great Plains. These settlers were from the remotest part of Europe—the steppes of the Ukraine and the shores of the Black Sea. They began arriving in America in the mid-1870s, when conditions for ethnic Germans in Russia deteriorated. Much of the movement was well planned and of a group nature, with agents sent in advance to arrange for land and town sites. The Russian-Germans were not religiously homogeneous. Many were Lutherans, Mennonites, or other Protestants, while a large minority was Catholic. But the individual settlements were traditionally of one faith. The Catholics were particularly strong in western North Dakota and west central Kansas. The Kansas group centered on Ellis County and soon was supplied with German Capuchin monks, who founded a monastery and other Catholic institutions. Research in 1943 showed that members of the community born in 1895 had an average of 8.1 children.[20] The rural women of the county in 1970 aged 35–44 averaged 4,001 children ever born per 1,000.

Conditions in remote western North Dakota did not evolve smoothly, and relations with the church were often turbulent. As a result, the Bishop of Fargo eventually obtained Benedictines from Stearns County, Minnesota, to minister successfully to this distinctive German population.[21] The center for these efforts was at what is now Assumption Abbey at Richardton in Stark County. Fertility in the Dunn-Stark County combination is one of the handful of cases in the entire nation where rural white fertility was above 5,000 children per 1,000 women in 1970.

Judging from township-level census and atlas data, Irish, Polish, Dutch, and Belgian rural Catholic localities also have large families. The population of Czech descent (or Bohemians, as all of the settlement records refer to them) is the only one that shows fertil-

20. Mary Eloise Johannes, *A Study of the Russian German Settlements in Ellis County, Kansas*, Catholic University Studies in Sociology (Washington, D.C.: Catholic University of America, 1946).

21. Elwyn B. Robinson, *History of North Dakota* (Lincoln: University of Nebraska Press, 1966).

ity below that of other primarily Catholic rural groups. Some individual Czech Catholic communities have high fertility rates very like their German counterparts, but others do not. The one predominantly Czech Catholic county (Colfax, Nebraska) had a fertility level of 3,558 children per 1,000 women, which was little different from the average of 3,531 for all rural white women in the North Central Region as a whole.

It seems possible that the notably free-thinking and anticlerical views of many of the immigrant Czechs may still have a lingering cultural reflection today in somewhat distinctive childbearing patterns. The settlement history of the nineteenth century shows repeatedly that the Czechs were often the bane and despair of the Catholic clergy.[22] Many Czechs of nominal Catholic background were individual dissenters. They provided an organized proselytizing alternative to religion with their *sokols* and fraternal organizations. The virus not only produced nonbelievers and defections to Protestantism but infected Catholic Czech parishioners as well, who were regarded as less financially supportive or willing to assist the priests than were other nationalities.

Update

After the mid-1960s, childbearing rates declined rapidly throughout the United States, and the rural Midwest is no exception. By 1980, there were only five midwestern counties in which rural ever-married white women 35–44 years had averaged better then 4,000 children per 1,000 women, compared with 184 such counties in 1970. The overall number of children ever born in the region per 1,000 rural ever-married white women of this age fell from 3,531 in 1970 to 3,016 in 1980.

To determine the degree and trend of linkage between Catholicism and rural white fertility, correlations were run at the county level between fertility rates and the percentage of Catholics in the population. The correlation between Catholic presence and the cumulative childbearing of rural white women 35–44 was .54 in 1980, just moderately below the .62 value of 1970.[23] Catholicism

22. H.W. Casper, *History of the Catholic Church in Nebraska,* vol. 3, *Catholic Chapters in Nebraska Immigration* (Milwaukee: Bruce Press, 1960).

23. In 1970, the data used were percentage of Catholics among religious adherents and cumulative fertility of women ever married. For 1980, the correla-

continued to have a stronger association with rural fertility than did four other factors traditionally viewed as influential in determining family size—income levels, female labor force participation rates, education levels, and the extent of male employment in farming.

Among younger women 25–34 years old, the picture is very different. In this group, the correlation of Catholicism with midwestern rural white fertility in 1980 was just .19, far below that of .47 found in 1970. A somewhat lower correlation of religious affiliation with fertility for women 25–34 years than for those 35–44 is understandable, for the higher cumulative fertility of Catholics might not express itself until the latter half of the childbearing years. However, the radically lower correlation among the younger women in 1980 seems to confirm that the importance of Catholicism as a determinant of rural midwestern family size is waning.

---

tion was between the percentage of Catholics in the total county population and cumulative fertility of all women. Thus there is not total comparability of data between the two years, but the difference is not thought to impair the conclusions drawn.

4

An Overview of the Phenomenon of Mixed-Racial Isolates in the United States

In about 1890, a young Tennessee woman asked a state legislator, "Please tell me what is a Malungeon?" "A Malungeon," said he, "isn't a nigger, and he isn't an Indian, and he isn't a white man. God only knows *what* he is. *I* should call him a Democrat, only he always votes the Republican ticket" (Drumgoole 1891:473).

The young woman, Will Allen Drumgoole, soon sought out the "Melungeons" in remote Hancock County and lived with them for a while to determine for herself what they were.[1] Afterward, in the space of a ten-page article, she described them as "shiftless," "idle," "illiterate," "thieving," "defiant," "distillers of brandy," "lawless," "close," "rogues," "suspicious," "inhospitable," "untruthful," "cowardly," "sneaky," "exceedingly immoral," and "unforgiving." She also spoke of their "cupidity and cruelty," and ended her work by concluding, "The most that can be said of one of them is, 'He is a Malungeon,' a synonym for all that is doubtful and mysterious—and unclean" (Drumgoole 1891:479). Miss Drumgoole was essentially a sympathetic observer.

The existence of mixed-racial populations that constitute a distinctive segment of society is not unique to the United States—needless to say. But this nation must rank near the top in the number of such communities and in their general public obscurity. I refer in particular to groups of real or alleged white–Indian–Negro mixtures (such as the "Melungeons") who are not tribally affiliated or traceable with historical continuity to a particular tribe. It is also logical to include a few groups of white-Negro ori-

Reprinted in slightly condensed form from *American Anthropologist* 74:3 (June 1972).
    1. I have used the modern spelling, *Melungeon*, except where quoting Drumgoole.

gin that lack the Indian component. The South in particular is rich
in such population strains, with all states except Arkansas and
Oklahoma having such groups at present or within the twentieth
century. (And I would not be surprised to be contradicted on my
exception of those two states.)

They are found in the Tidewater areas, the interior Coastal
Plain, the Piedmont, the Appalachians, and in the Allegheny-
Cumberland Plateaus. They may be Protestant or Catholic, of
Anglo provenance or French-Spanish. Their mixture may have
originated in the area of residence, or they may have come in as racially mixed people. Some are landless, some landed. But they are
all marginal men—wary until recently of being black, aspiring
where possible to be white, and subject to rejection and scorn on
either hand.

Many themes classically connected with racial marginality occur
repeatedly in the history of these groups, such as (to repeat
Drumgoole only in part): illegitimate origin; the use of stigmatic
group names by the general society; proscription from social inter-
course with others on terms of equality; and, in particular, barriers
to upward out-marriage or attendance at white schools; a reputation for violence, drunkenness, and crimes of passion within the
group, and for petty thievery against outsiders; the ascription of
beauty and sexual attractiveness to the women of the group when
young; a reputation for laziness, illiteracy, poverty, and inbreeding;
a relegation of settlement to the least desirable land (hilly, sandy,
swampy, backwoods); and a preference to withdraw from public
attention. These are stereotypes, of course, and exceptions to their
validity as public images occur, especially with respect to the
mulatto or colored Creole groups of the Gulf Coast.

At least a few of the groups clearly originated in the period well
before the Revolution—even in the seventeenth century in Maryland and Virginia. They do not seem to be viewed in public records
as communities or elements in society until after the Revolution.
Gradually during the nineteenth century, and continuing to the
present day, they came to local public notice in one way or another
as individual groups, but usually with no recognition of the fact
that such communities have been a common phenomenon
throughout the East and South. Questions relating to legal racial
status, jury service, voting, taxation, schools, inheritance, census
enumeration, civil disorder, crime, and health have been prominent among issues that have brought public attention. Some
examples from different times and places follow.

In 1791, the "Turks" of South Carolina petitioned the legislature to be recognized as white and not as free Negroes. Somewhat later, their right to sit on juries was challenged and their patron, General Thomas Sumter, vouched for them, in particular by publicly shaking hands with one (Kaye 1963:10).

In 1823, another South Carolina group with such classic triracial surnames as Locklier, Oxandine, Chavis, and Sweat was reported as delinquent in taxes but difficult to find because "of the peculiar situation of their place of residence" (Price 1953:153).

In Mobile, a Creole Fire Company was organized in 1819 and remained independent well into the present century.[2]

In 1840–41, North Carolina legislative papers describe how "the County of Robeson is cursed with a free colored population that migrated originally from the districts around about the Roanoke and Neuse Rivers. . . . Having no regard for character they are under no restraint but what the law imposes. They are great topers, and so long as they can procure the exhilarating draught seem to forget entirely the comfort of their families."[3]

In 1842, a member of a group in present-day Vinton County, Ohio, that I have heard referred to only as "the half-breeds," sued the township trustees for refusing him the right to vote because he was partly of Negro ancestry. He lost his suit at the county court level but won a reversal in the state supreme court (*Thacker* v. *Hawk*).

In 1856, voting by the free colored people (present-day "Red Bones") of Ten Mile Creek Precinct in what is now Allen Parish, Louisiana, became a source of public concern. Several were tried for illegal voting—for free Negroes did not have the franchise—but they were acquitted when their colored ancestry could not be proven and the judge would not permit the jury to evaluate them by their appearance (Shugg 1936).

In 1857, Frederic Law Olmsted noted and publicized in his book *Journey Through Texas* the skirmishes and murders that took place in the Sabine country of east Texas between the "Moderators" and "Regulators" based on friction with the local mixed bloods of Louisiana "Red Bone" origin (Olmsted 1959:164–66).

In 1860, the census taker in Calhoun County, Florida, noted, "The Free Negroes in this county are mixed blooded, almost white, and have intermarried with a low class of whites. Have no trade,

---

2. Information from present-day Creoles.
3. Manuscript North Carolina Legislative Reports (Robeson County).

occupation, or profession. They live in a settlement or town of their own. Their personal property consists of cattle and hogs. They make no produce except corn, peas, and potatoes and very little of that. They are a lazy, indolent, and worthless race" (Free Inhabitants Census 1860). This was the Dead Lake or Scott's Ferry group, of South Carolina triracial origin.

During the Civil War and Reconstruction, Henry Berry Lowry, a folk-hero of the group now known as Lumbee Indians, led a band of fugitives and outlaws in Robeson County, North Carolina. Disorder requiring federal troops continued for some years until Lowry and others were killed (Rights 1947).

In the mid-1880s, this group was provided with separate schools and Indian status by the state—beginning a procedure that spread to several other groups (ibid.).

In 1930–31, the Virginia Registrar of Vital Statistics endeavored to prevent mixed bloods from being accepted as Indians in the U.S. Census. The bureau declined to change the original returns, but footnoted the published results of the Virginia census in four counties to note that the count of Indians "includes a number of persons whose classification as Indians has been questioned."[4]

During the 1950s, the "Wesorts" of southern Maryland came to the attention of physicians and dentists in the Washington area because of one of the most serious and varied complexes of genetic diseases and anomalies ever recorded.[5]

In September 1969, a number of Indian ("Brass Ankle") parents in Dorchester County, South Carolina, were arrested for attempting to enroll their children in a public school other than the small segregated one that had traditionally been provided them.[6]

The establishment of separate schools for the racial isolates was a major factor in maintaining group identity. Typically, the mixed bloods were denied enrollment in white schools and declined to attend Negro schools. In some states, separate public schools were provided for them. This was particularly true in North Carolina, where the ultimate in triracial school systems was created—one that included a separate college. In other areas, only the operation of mission schools by churches provided any educational facilities

4. Correspondence files of the Bureau of the Census; see also "Indian Populations of the United States," 1937:20.

5. Various published studies of the research work led by Carl J. Witkop, Jr., of the National Institutes of Health.

6. See the *Charleston Evening Post*, various issues beginning September 19, 1969.

at all. Disputes over the racial background of children attempting
to enter either local white schools or the separate schools were
common.

So long as segregated public schools were permitted, and so long
as small rural elementary schools were common and high school
education was not often sought, the separate school pattern was
feasible. But in recent decades, the school situation of the mixed-
blood communities has changed rapidly, sometimes through
lawsuits, sometimes without. Most of the mission schools have
been closed or made a part of the public system. Most of the rural
one- and two-room schools have been consolidated into larger
integrated schools. Conditions have changed so steadily that
without an up-to-the-minute survey it is impossible to speak
definitively about the extent of separate schooling that still exists.
Essentially, it is no longer a characteristic of mixed-racial communities.

Where separate schools have been closed, the church is usually
the only formal social arrangement that continues to reflect the
existence of a mixed-racial community, and that reinforces the
endogamous marriage patterns of the past. Church separatism has
never been complete and is probably declining, but there are still
many examples of congregations comprised entirely or largely of
the mixed-racial populations.

Interest in the racial isolates by anthropologists began in the
late nineteenth century, stimulated, I should say, by the emergence
of the Robeson County, North Carolina, people as Croatan Indians
and the suggestion of their descent from the Lost Colony. At the
Smithsonian, James Mooney conducted a mail inquiry through
postmasters in 1889 in Delaware, Maryland, Virginia, and North
Carolina seeking information on people of reputed Indian descent.
He received responses that related not only to the Powhatan tribes
that seem to have been his principal interest, but that also
identified the "Wesorts," the "Guineas" of western Maryland, the
Amherst County "Issues," and the group that later emerged as the
North Carolina "Haliwa." It is unfortunate that someone could not
have followed up all of Mooney's leads at the time, for it was more
than half a century later before Gilbert produced the first scientific
inquiries into the "Wesorts" and "Guineas," and another ten years
before I and others visited the "Haliwa." Mooney's replies, inciden-
tally, are still on file at the Smithsonian.

Frank Speck followed in the 1920s and later with extensive
inquiry into the eastern Virginia groups—usually regarded as

Negroes locally—who appeared to show authentic evidence of Indian origin through cultural survivals. But perhaps because of the tribalized Indian focus of American anthropology, very little later anthropological work dealt with the mixed-racial isolates. Sociologists, educators, journalists, geographers, and local historians gave some attention to the groups, and more lately genetic research and accounts by members of the isolates themselves have appeared.

In terms of today's research needs, it is already a generation too late to pursue some of the questions that would have been relevant earlier. Some of the smaller groups have for all practical purposes disappeared. The practice or knowledge of handicrafts or of distinctive food habits, hunting practices, or folkways is gone or rapidly disappearing. Increasing outmarriage makes meaningful genetic studies less feasible. And the abolition of legal segregation reduces the likelihood of the groups continuing as separate and readily identifiable elements of local society.

But there is still worthwhile research to be undertaken, whether one is satisfied with knowledge for its own sake or insists on socially significant inquiries. I would suggest the following topics relating to southern groups as relatively untouched by research or in need of a modern appraisal:

(1) The Goins family. Beyond a doubt, the surname Goins (with its many variations in spelling) is the most widespread and one of the oldest and most reliably indicative surnames of triracial origin in the United States. I have documented its existence among mixed bloods in more than thirty-five counties of seven states. The Goinses were mixed in Colonial days in Virginia and both of the Carolinas. The name is found today among the Lumbee, the "Melungeons," the "Smilings," the "Red Bones," the Ohio "Guineas," and in various other parts of Ohio, Tennessee, and North Carolina, where none of these terms is used. Some are white, some Indian, and some Negro, in current status. An investigation of the Goinses, their origins and traditions, their dispersal through the South and the old Northwest Territory, and their status today would touch almost the whole fabric of the triracial phenomenon.

(2) Sociopsychological studies of the mixed-blood people. The precarious social acceptance of the mixed bloods by the white, Negro, or Indian elements of society has created problems of psychological insecurity for many of them that the average person never experiences. Berry touches on this issue in his work, but a study focusing on it is needed (Berry 1963:212).

(3) Gulf Coast Creoles. Other than Horace Mann Bond's valuable article of nearly forty years ago (Bond 1931), I have not seen work on the Creole populations of the Gulf Coast (Mississippi, Mobile Bay, Pensacola). These people of French-Spanish and Negro origin have an interesting history, a comparatively high degree of social stability, and respectability in the eyes of the whites; and considerable documentation is available on their origins and social history. A general research treatment on any one of these groups would be both interesting and useful.

(4) The Tennessee groups outside Hancock County. Most all work relating to Tennessee has focused on the Hancock County "Melungeons." But there are a number of other areas in Tennessee where unstudied triracial groups are found—sometimes related in the past to the Hancock County people and usually derived from mixed-blood origins in the Carolinas or Virginia. In addition, an unrelated Tennessee group of white and Indian descent known as the Upper Cumberland River Cherokee has surfaced in the last several years in Scott County and adjoining McCreary County, Kentucky, asserting its Indianness in a rather vigorous way to officials in Washington.

(5) The "Red Bones" of Louisiana and Texas deserve research attention. Given the number of people and counties involved, it is surprising that they have not received more. Or perhaps it is not surprising, in view of the sensitivity of the population to the subject of origins.

(6) The "Smilings" of Robeson County, North Carolina, are of particular interest, for their interplay is not only with the white and Negro populations but also with the surrounding Lumbee people, from whom they appear not to have received full acceptance. The group had an antebellum origin in Sumter County, South Carolina, but migrated to Robeson. What were the circumstances that impelled this long-established population to leave, but that did not affect the Sumter County "Turks" similarly?

I have not mentioned specific studies of a more conventional anthropological nature, such as Indian cultural survivals or linguistic studies, but here, too, there are still positive results to be obtained, if I may judge from the recent fieldwork in several groups by Claude Medford (personal communication), or Everett's study of language among the Clifton "Red Bone" community in Louisiana (Everett 1958).

In 1950, I estimated the triracial isolates in their rural and small-town settings to number 75,000 people. I do not think the number is less today, primarily because of the growth of the Lumbee. But many of the isolates, particularly those of non-Indian status, can be said to be in a process of decline or even dissolution. They have with a few exceptions been rural communities, and in the last half a century have experienced the same heavy out-migration to a variety of urban destinations as have rural people in general. Thus, despite typically high fertility, many of the isolates have dwindled in size. The special racial status is not generally transferred in a group context to urban environments. Also, the frequency of out-marriage and assimilation into either the white or Negro populations has greatly increased. I have found this in every group whose marriage records I have examined.[7] Harte has rather thoroughly documented it for the Maryland "Wesorts" (Harte 1959:218).

Given this trend, I think the odds are against the survival of groups that do not have a concentrated core of at least several hundred members and that are no longer distinctly different in appearance or status from the local white or Negro populations. Both severe lack of local economic opportunity or rapid local population growth seem to militate against group survival. In the first instance, the population disperses to seek opportunity elsewhere, and in the latter case, the intrusion of other people or changes in employment and residential patterns facilitate a breakdown in cohesion.

It will be interesting to observe the fate of the Lumbee in the future, for in this case, the local numbers of people involved are large (26,000 in Robeson County in 1970, and 7,000 in nine nearby counties). The local tobacco economy is under some strain, but with an acceptable official social status as Indian, a large pool of potential marriage partners, a fair amount of nonagricultural job opportunities, and a fund of history and legend in which to have some pride, this group—along with several others—may well continue indefinitely in its local setting, although surely not without change.

---

7. I refer to groups such as the "Pools" of Pennsylvania, the Amherst and Rockbridge County "Issues," the "Shifletts," the Poquoson and Skeetertown groups of Virginia, the Dead Lake group in Florida, the Cane River "Mulattoes" and Natchitoches "Red Bones" of Louisiana, and the Mobile area Creoles.

References

Berry, Brewton, 1963. *Almost White*. New York: Macmillan.

Bond, Horace Mann, 1931. "Two Racial Islands of Alabama," *American Journal of Sociology* 36:552–67.

Drumgoole, Will Allen, 1891. "The Malungeons," *The Arena* 3:470–79.

Everett, Russell I, 1958. "The Speech of the Tri-Racial Group Composing the Community of Clifton, Louisiana," Master's thesis, Louisiana State University.

Free Inhabitants, 1860 Census, Florida 1860, National Archives 1:129.

Harte, Thomas J., 1959. "Trends in Mate Selection in a Tri-Racial Isolate," *Social Forces* 37(3):215–21.

"Indian Populations of the United States and Alaska 1930." Washington, D.C.: U.S. Government Printing Office, 1937.

Kaye, Ira, 1963. "The Turks," *New South*, vol. 18, no. 6, June.

Olmsted, Frederic Law, 1959. *The Slave States*. New York: G. P. Putnam's Sons.

Price, Edward T., 1953. "A Geographic Analysis of White-Negro-Indian Racial Mixtures in Eastern United States," *Annals of the Association of American Geographers* 43(2):138–55.

Rights, Douglas L., 1947. "The American Indian in North Carolina." Durham, N.C.: Duke University Press.

Shugg, Roger W., 1936. "Negro Voting in the Ante Bellum South," *Journal of Negro History* 21(4):357–64.

Thacker v. *Hawk*, 1887. *Ohio Reports* 11:377.

5

Notes on Visit to Hancock County, Tennessee

On July 12, 1969, I visited Hancock County, Tennessee, which has the principal settlement of Melungeons. I drove from Oak Ridge, where I had just participated in a seminar on Urban Decentralization at the Oak Ridge National Laboratory, to Sneedville, the county seat of Hancock County, with the specific purpose of attending an outdoor play about the Melungeons to be given that night.

Along the way, I went through Grainger and Claiborne counties, which also have part of the Melungeon population. The countryside is a mixture of mountains and valleys. I went into Hancock County from Claiborne County following a road up the Clinch River Valley. This valley I found very beautiful, with a bottomland of perhaps one-sixth to one-quarter mile wide that is cultivated in corn and tobacco. Sneedville is a small town of just about 800 population occupying a fairly level area but surrounded by hills. The courthouse occupies a small square, which was filled with many men lounging around on the wall and the steps in the old-time southern Saturday afternoon courthouse manner. There were a good many men in bib overalls, a style of work clothes not much seen anymore.

A young woman at the theater box office agreed to try to find a place for me to stay. I then asked whether anyone was available to drive with me around the countryside for a while during the afternoon. She took me up to one of the school administration buildings and we found Mr. Claude Collins there, who is one of the men whose picture was shown in a recent article on the Melungeons published in the *Louisville Courier Journal*. Collins is thirty-three years old, according to the article, and is the librarian of the school and also does certain administrative work for the school system. He agreed right away to act as my guide. This was a very for-

Published here for the first time.

tunate circumstance for me because he is not only a Melungeon but one of the comparatively small number who are well educated, being a college graduate and having a very objective view about the group and its history.

Collins is white, yet there is something different about his appearance. He has very black hair, very dark eyes, and a somewhat sallow or slightly tan complexion, which is his natural color and not the result of sun. He was easy to talk with and we got along well together right away.

First we drove over Newman's Ridge to the valleys that lie beyond, and turned southwestward into an area known as Snake Hollow. Collins said that he would show me Snake Hollow and then by contrast the Vardy Valley. As one might almost imagine from the name, Snake Hollow is a narrow hollow several miles long with a one-lane gravel road. It primarily contained poor people of lower social economic status. There was almost no flat land. Some land was still in cultivation, but other tracts of hilly land had been taken out of cultivation and were growing up in brush. Many families, however, still had their small allotment of burley tobacco, which Collins said was still very highly valued as a source of income by numerous families in the county, white and Melungeon alike.

Snake Hollow contains one of the four remaining one-room schools in Hancock County. There are only eight left in the entire state. We stopped at the school, which is known as the Ramsey School. It is simply an old one-room wooden building with old-fashioned desk-and-chair units, in which one person's chair is attached to the desk of the person behind him. There was an old coal stove and a pile of coal outside of the building. The building has electricity but no running water. The kids have to use a privy about seventy-five feet away. All or nearly all of the children are from Melungeon families. The county once had fifty schools. As a result of consolidation this is now down to fourteen and there is only one high school. However, Collins said that Ramsey School could not yet be discontinued because of lack of sufficient space in the school in Sneedville to take more elementary pupils. He said that he had been asked whether he would teach the school and told the person who asked him that the first thing he would do if assigned to teach that school was to set a match to it and burn it down. He felt that strongly about the inadequacy of education that the Melungeon children could get in this little school. At least one other of the four one-room schools in the county is attended primarily by Melungeons, I gather, for the name of the school is the Lawson School, and that is essentially a Melungeon name.

We left the school and proceeded up the road further into the Hollow. As we came around a slight bend in the road, a car suddenly appeared from the opposite direction. I put on my brakes and stopped immediately, but the fellow driving the other car did not see us right away and eventually had to slam on his brakes and turn to one side as best he could. He was quite surprised when he finally saw me. The incident was nobody's fault. The road is a one-lane road and there are only certain places where people can pass. The only way to avoid this type of incident was to drive at a reasonable speed. But he gave us a very hard glare. It was obvious that he considered us at fault, although he was the one who had not been watching and had not seen us until the last moment. Collins didn't know the man and said to me, "Well, I guess he is going to cuss us out." The fellow straightened his car in the road but he would not back up, although it was far easier for him to go back to a wide place than for me to do so. So to avoid trouble, I backed up as best I could, practically in the ditch, and he finally inched past and went on.

We then drove on up the Hollow perhaps for another three-quarters of a mile or so heading for the home of a man named Bell. Collins was acquainted with him and felt that we could stop and talk and I could get a chance to see some of the people. Along the way we passed two other families by the name of Bell, most of whose members were of very dark complexion. By that I mean that they were people who were distinctly brown in color and who would under no circumstances be taken as being of unmixed white ancestry. However, these people did not have negroid features. Eventually we came to where the family lived that Collins wanted to see and we found them all out in the road near the house. There was a husband about fortyish who was the darkest person and who did have rather tightly curled hair, but without negroid facial features; his wife who was lighter and who was barefoot; his son who was probably about ten years old and fairly dark; and a somewhat lighter man who might have been his father. The husband had once taken an adult education class that Collins had taught, and Collins had become friendly with him in this connection.

When we pulled up and stopped, Collins became very animated in his manner, in a way that rather surprised me, for he had been somewhat mild mannered and even a little feminine in his personality. Apparently one way of dealing with these families was on a jocular basis. Collins had a freshly lit cigarette in his hand and after he had greeted Bell, he said to him, "Gimmie a couple of cigarettes." Bell started to say, "I don't have none." But then he noticed Collins with his cigarette and said in a very rapid manner of speech, with a thick mountain accent, something like, "God-damn, here this man just lit up a cigarette and he's trying to bum one off of me." But this successfully set a tone of banter between the two of them. Bell then took over and started joking Collins. Collins was wearing a pair of shorts, checked shorts at that, and Bell said something like, "Look at this man with a pair of girls' shorts on. Come on, get out of this car here and let me see what those things look like." He tried to open the door to the car on Collins's side. Collins started fending him off saying, "Get away from me now, get away from me." Collins then sort of pointed to me, I guess after Bell had asked what we were doing up there, and said, "I brought the law along. We want to know who's making liquor up here." I thought this was an outrageous way to introduce me and would queer the conversation for sure. But apparently it would have been such an unthinkable thing for Collins to have brought the law in that Bell didn't for a moment believe that I was the law, and he joked right back. Collins said, "We want to know if you're making any whiskey up here." Bell said no, that he wasn't making any but he could get us some. Collins said, "Who's making it?" Bell said, "Ain't nobody making it up here." Collins said, "Where you getting it from?" "Bringing it in from Claiborne County."

So apparently moonshining isn't dead. In fact, Collins had told me as we went up Snake Hollow that the Hollow had been well known for its moonshining over the years. In kidding Collins, Bell then told me of an incident that had happened down at the school when Collins was teaching the adult education class. Although I think that I have a fair ear for accents, I really could not understand more than half of what Bell was saying, even though he was right in front of me and I could see him when he spoke. His speech was very rapid and staccato in manner. The gist of the story was this (as Collins filled me in on it later): One day at the school, Bell and several of the other men jacked Collins's car up and put cinder blocks under the rear axle, just enough to lift the rear wheels off the ground and yet not be very visible. Then when Collins got ready to go home, he started up his car and the engine ran beautifully but the car wouldn't move. Collins couldn't imagine what was wrong, and the Melungeon men just about died laughing. They enjoyed themselves thoroughly at his expense. Collins took it all good naturedly and the Melungeons then had the effrontery to charge him twenty-five cents apiece for them to jack the car back up again and take the blocks away. They thought this was a great joke on him.

During the time we were talking, I suddenly realized that Bell was carrying a gun in his arm. It was pointed down toward the ground and I could not see all of it and hadn't sensed at first that it was a gun. I thought he just had a stick or shovel in his hand. When I looked a little further, there was his wife with either a rifle or shotgun in her hand. Bell said to us, "Did you meet (so-and-so) on the road back there?"—meaning, as it turned out, the man with whom we had almost had the head-on accident. We said yes. Then Bell said, "He shot at my feet up here a few minutes ago." He proceeded to tell how the man in question, whose last name we did not catch, but which was not a Melungeon name, was angry about something that Bell's son had done, and came there with a gun, apparently wanting the boy to be corrected in some way and threatening to shoot Bell if he didn't do so. Bell had told him that he might just as well shoot and kill him because he wasn't going to do anything. The man then fired his gun near Bell's foot. Bell rushed at him before he could do anything else and wrestled the gun away from him. I suppose in the meantime Mrs. Bell had run into the house and gotten their own gun. They had then forced the man to leave his gun and to go away. It wasn't until this part of the story that Bell said rather casually, "He's married to my sister." So it was a family fuss with guns, and I think nothing typifies better the traditional, passionate mountaineer nature of this rather isolated community of Melungeons.

After we had retraced our route out of Snake Hollow, we entered the Black Water Creek Valley or, as it is more often called now, Vardy Valley. I think the little stream that runs through Snake Hollow empties into Black Water Creek. The people in this valley are of a higher income and social-economic status, and some of them are not Melungeons. The valley is wider, there is more level land, it is a more open area, and has a well-paved road. Vardy was the first name of the original Collins in the area, who came in the post–Revolutionary War era and obtained a very large tract of land. Collins told me that the valley extended for four miles up to the Virginia border. Not too far up the valley is the Vardy community center. This is a former Presbyterian mission center, which was the focus of the life of the people in the valley during

Claude Collins's youth. The school is now operated as a part of the Hancock County school system and has thirteen rooms and fifty-five students, with the enrollment rather steadily declining now. In addition, there is a Presbyterian church there, and a rather substantial building in which the mission staff used to live.

Near the community center was a cemetery, a fairly nice one with a mixture of old gravestones that were simply native stones and rather broken, with no identifications on them, plus much more conventional tombstones. There were a few non-Melungeon families in this cemetery, but most of the names were Melungeon—Collins, Gibson, Mizer, and Johnson—the latter name not being a name that I knew, but which is apparently a fairly extensive name that has entered into the group in the male line through a white Johnson who intermarried. Claude Collins also pointed out a spot in a cornfield where Vardy Collins is buried. They are going to clear this spot and put a marker on it.

After traveling up the valley a mile or so, we came to a little bridge over the Black Water Creek and a rather rough and now poorly maintained road that led up onto Newman's Ridge. Newman's Ridge was the center of the principal Melungeon community in years past. It was where Mahala Mullins lived, the very fat Melungeon woman who was for many years a moonshiner but who could not be arrested and taken to jail because she was too large to leave her cabin. It is a matter of record that when she died, weighing somewhere between 400 and 700 pounds, according to various stories, part of the chimney of the house had to be dismantled in order to get her body out. In approximately the last twenty years, however, *all* of the Melungeon families have left the Ridge. There is only one non-Melungeon family now left up on the Ridge. Some of the houses still remain vacant, others have fallen down. There are at least two cemeteries up on the Ridge, one known as the Goins Cemetery, but we did not visit either of these.

I asked Collins whether the Melungeon people who moved away from Hancock County went to any particular locality. He immediately said yes, and named Ellicott City, Maryland, and Kokomo, Indiana. He went on to say, "If I walked down the streets of Ellicott City, I would recognize more people than I do here in Sneedville." Two of his brothers live there, his mother lived there for a period, and he himself taught school in Edmonston, Maryland, near Ellicott City, for a short period of time after losing his teaching position in Hancock County two or three years earlier when the school board administration changed.

I asked Collins the extent to which he was aware of the term *Melungeon* as he grew up. Much to my surprise, he said that he had never heard the word, ever. He did not know of the term until he went to college. The word was never mentioned in his family or in the Melungeon community, and no one in the white community ever called him by this name. I don't think this is necessarily typical, but it illustrates the extent to which the term may be of more historical significance than of actual current usage. I then also asked him whether he heard the tradition of Portuguese ancestry as he was growing up, and he said yes, that in his family he had heard that the family was of partial Portuguese ancestry. He commented to me on the highly varying color of the Melungeon people, and stated that either a grandfather or great-grandfather of his was a Bell, and that although this man was light complexioned, his brother was definitely very dark (I assume like the Bells that we saw up in Snake Hollow). He also confirmed that the word Portuguese was pronounced "Port-a-gee" by the Melungeons.

I then asked him about a number of family names that had not come up in the course of our conversation to that point. Collins knew of the Goins family historically, but he did not know of any who were left in the area. I noticed that there was just one in the Sneedville telephone book.

Collins knew about Melungeons in neighboring Grainger County and Hawkins County and also up into Virginia (certainly Lee County, which Hancock borders). I do not know whether he knew how extensive they are in Virginia. However, he knew nothing about Melungeons or similar types of people in either Campbell County or Claiborne County, and when I told him about the existence of such people and of some of the names, this was news to him.

Collins had never heard of the Lumbee Indians of North Carolina. Nor did he know of the Rockingham, North Carolina, people who are named Goins and Harris and who used to include Gibsons (all relevant Melungeon names), nor of any of the other Goins communities along the Virginia–North Carolina border, although he knew that the Melungeons had originally come to Tennessee from the Carolinas and Virginia. My point is, he did not know of the existence of present-day communities in those states where some Melungeon names are found. Nor did Collins know of the English ancestry of the Mullins family that I found in the 1880 Census. He was quite interested to learn of this.

After we finished our tour of Snake Hollow, Vardy Valley, and Newman's Ridge, we headed on back to Sneedville and stopped off at Collins's house to have a cold drink and talk a little bit. He has a very nice, modern suburban home. His wife is not a Melungeon, but is a local girl. She looked a few years younger than he. He showed me a genealogical chart that he had started to fill out on his parents, but said that he had sort of stopped because his parents were first cousins. I'm not sure what he meant by this; it sounded as though he meant there just wasn't much to look up since they both had so much of the same ancestry. He showed me several photographs of previous generations in his family, including the grandfather or great-grandfather who was a Bell. In all of the several photographs that he showed me, the people looked to be white.

There was a rather nice drugstore in the town and, before the play that evening, I went there to get something to eat. While I was at the drugstore, an older women came up to me and asked me if I was from out of town. I said yes. She wanted to know from where and whether I had come to see the drama and how I had heard about it. She then told me that she wrote a column for a newspaper. I don't know what paper it is that she writes for, although it is not a local paper. She asked me if I thought she looked like a Melungeon. I told her that I had learned that Melungeons could look like almost anyone. She then said that she had some Melungeon ancestry, that she did not live in Sneedville, but that she liked to come up here. She went on to say that the community was losing much of its older charm, and told me how at one time it used to be called Greasy Rock instead of Sneedville.

She then urged me to go see the old jail, which she said was probably the oldest building in town. I later did so. It is an old two-story rectangular brick home of the type in which the prisoners were kept upstairs and the sheriff and his family lived downstairs. She told of going to the jail several years ago to interview the sheriff and of how he was sitting out on the front porch with a big pot belly lapping over his belt, with his feet up on the railing. He took her upstairs and showed her these very miserable cells with shackles on the floor to which recalcitrant prisoners were chained. She asked him if he had much trouble. And he said, "No, when these fellows have done something wrong, they know that I will find them tomorrow if I don't today. So mostly they just come in and say, 'Well, sheriff, here I am!'"

That evening at about 7:30 I went to the open-air amphitheater where the play was to be held. When I entered the amphitheater to take my seat, the young man who was taking tickets looked at me and asked, "Are you Mr. Beale?" I said yes. Then he said, "Well, we have a seat for you in our dignitary section." So I guess Collins had tipped them off to watch for a stranger with a mustache and a slightly receding hairline. At any rate, my dignitary status got me a seat in the middle of the center section.

The play, which is called "Walk Toward the Sunset: The Melungeon Story," is in two acts. The first act, set in the early 1780s, portrays the Melungeons as settled along rich bottom lands of the Holston River, and living a rather prosperous and middle-class frontier life—if such an expression could be applied to frontier living. However, they were not regarded as white people and their origins were unknown. White settlers were given title to their lands, but nonwhites were not considered eligible to own land. According to the plot, the Cherokee Indians were sympathetic with the Melungeons and helped them to move to the lands in what is now Hancock County, which were at that time under control of the Indians. I don't know how much truth there is to any of the events

Sneedville, Tennessee, jail, c. 1969 (photo by Beale)

in the first act. Its purpose, I infer, was to show the injustices that
had been suffered by the Melungeons, to account for their present
location, and to say something about their mysterious, unexplained
background. It also served to picture them as reasonably prosperous and cultivated people at this earlier period.

In the second act, the scene changes to the year 1870, and the
principal characters are descendents of characters portrayed in the
earlier period. The plot of the second half revolves around the
desire of white people in Sneedville to get the Melungeons to sell
off their timber land. The key Melungeon figures in the story did
not want to do so, claiming the promoters involved were not offering them nearly as much as the land was worth and that this was
just another chapter in the historic exploitation of the Melungeons
by the general white population.

A love story is then presented between the daughter of the key
Melungeon figure and the son of the principal Sneedville business-
man who was involved in the effort to purchase their lands and cut
the timber. The author then rather skillfully attempts to show the
violence and tragedy that result from the longstanding distrust
between the two groups. The play ends, of course, with the marriage of the white boy and the Melungeon girl, and lo and behold,
the timber company comes around and doubles its offer for the
Melungeons' lands.

This sounds rather trite, but the second half was skillfully done
and it absorbed the interest of the audience. In fact, there was
hardly a dry eye in the place. What the playwright has done is to
demonstrate to the whites the rather mindless racial prejudice that
they have had against the Melungeons, and the injustice that the
Melungeons have suffered as a result. But, in the second half of
the play, he very distinctly and deliberately portrays the Melungeons as having gone downhill socially and culturally in the previous hundred years. They are pictured as being for the most part
barefooted hillbillies given to moonshining and quite disinclined to
work for a living. His message to the Melungeons is that "the
world was passing them by" and that despite the injustices of the
past, they could not simply continue to retreat to the mountain
ridges. Their youth would get nowhere anymore without an education and it was necessary for them to change their attitudes if they
were not to completely degenerate.

Today, another century after the setting of the play's final act,
some of the older isolation and mode of living remains. But an
enormous amount of material and social progress has been made in

the last generation. The play has been well received by most of the Melungeon element of the population. Bell of Snake Hollow said that he had seen it, enjoyed it, and planned to go again. The act of sponsoring the play and thus confronting publicly the mystery of their origin and their inferior status in the past seems to have been liberating in itself.

6

Visit to Creole Company No. 1, Mobile City Fire Department

Years ago, I read in one of William Gilbert's articles that the Creoles of Mobile City, Alabama, had their own fire company.[1] Here, unlike Louisiana, the term *Creole* refers only to colored Creoles. While visiting Mobile in January 1963, I decided to see if I could document this and determine the fate of the company. At the public library I found an excellent collection of Mobile City directories, which extend with a few breaks back into the 1830s. It did not take long to verify the existence of the company, which was generally listed as the "Creole Steam Fire Company No. 1. Instituted in 1819."

From the directories, I found that the city organized its own fire department in 1889. For some years thereafter, the Creole company continued to be listed as a valued, private company partly supplied by the city. It remained at 13 North Dearborn Street—where it had been since at least the 1870s—until 1941, then was gone.

While working in the library one evening, the only other occupant of the local history room could not contain his curiosity and asked me what I was doing. I was glad he did, for when I told him I was interested in the Creoles, he immediately mentioned that the No. 1 city fire company was Creole, and gave me the address.

On Sunday, January 20, 1963, I visited the company. They were on Spring Hill Road at the corner of Ann Street, less than a mile from the old location. I had a long talk with a driver named Woods, who was acting captain that day, and we were later joined by another member named Petite. They were quite congenial and were pleased to talk with someone interested in the company.

Published here for the first time.

1. William H. Gilbert, Jr., "Surviving Indian Groups of the Eastern United States," *Annual Report of the Smithsonian Institution, 1948* (Washington, D.C.: Government Printing Office, 1948), pp. 407–38.

The gist of the story is this. When the Creole company became part of the city department, the city agreed to let the company have the right to continue to choose its own members. This means exclusively Creoles who are descendants of former members. The company may also discharge members if it wishes. In other respects, the company is part of the city system. It consists of one truck and ten men, working in twenty-four-hour shifts of five men each. Both shift captains are Treniers (brothers). Other members have the names of Trenier (cousin), Woods, Petite, Wright, Weeks, Bush, Hafler, and Reid.

The immediate neighborhood is largely black, but the company is also called out on fires in other districts. Both the white informant at the library and Mr. Woods claimed that the company has a very good reputation for its service and efficiency, and that people like to see it called. Woods related with relish how, at a recent fire, another company had been unable to get the fire plug open! Finally, someone said, "Call No. 1," and when the Creoles arrived they opened the plug immediately. Woods stated that as outlying fires develop, the Creole Company gets ready because they are often called for additional alarms, even though closer companies are not.

If they have a good reputation, it is not reflected in the equipment, however. The engine is old, Woods says that the steering is very bad, and the truck was secondhand when they got it. The last time the company had a new engine was when they were independent and bought their own. The company still has its last horse-drawn pump, which had a greater pumping capacity than the motor truck they now are furnished.

Woods said that all the crew members are related to one another. Despite some Anglo-Saxon names, they may all have French or Spanish backgrounds. Woods had a "tante" who spoke French, or "that Gumbo" as he called it. I asked whether there was any Creole police unit, but he said no. According to him, the Mobile City Creoles still tend to marry one another, but they are spread out and no longer as concentrated in location as before. The former Creole Social Club and all other organizations except the fire company have ended.

Woods knew of the Pensacola Creoles and of the name Pons. He said some years ago he and other Mobile Creoles had been on picnics with the Pensacola people. The Mobile City people socialize with the Fowl River and Bellefontaine groups. And he knew of the Baldwin County group, for one of the firemen is a Weeks who is either from Baldwin or descended from Baldwin Creoles. Woods did not seem to draw any distinctions between the Creole groups. He said they were not related to the Cajans, who stayed to themselves.

The Creole fire company was organized in 1819 and is considered the oldest in Alabama. In earlier days there had been white members also. (This seems verified by the city directory, which shows T. S. Bidgood as Captain in 1861 and 1873. Bidgood was white.) The fire company possesses many of its old records, presently kept by one of the captains. Woods spoke of a recent visit by the company's old secretary, a man named Instant. Woods knows of no history or even brief article written about the company—despite its uniqueness. Neither he nor Petite know of any other Creole companies in other cities, such as New Orleans or Pensacola.

At the end of the visit, the front door of the station was opened so that I might take a photograph of the old steam pump. At this time, a third member came down, but the other two remained upstairs in the living quarters throughout the hour or so that I was there.

The Creole fire company brings together people from all of the Mobile-area Creole communities—the city, the Fowl River group south of Mobile, the Chestang group north of the city, and the Baldwin group across the bay. In Mobile, members of the company obviously accept a black status in the larger society—none of the three I saw could have passed for white or Indian. Yet, in Baldwin County, the Creoles insist on a separate school and are treated as white in restaurants and other public places and are white in the census. In Fowl River, the Creoles call themselves French, have their own church, and are listed in the census as Creole. I don't know the situation in the Chestang area, except that many of them were listed as a separate race in the 1950 Census. Thus, the landed Creoles in the country attempt to perpetuate a nonblack or even white racial status, which the city Creoles have given up.

The old Creole fire hall is still standing on North Dearborn Street at the corner of St. Francis. The lower floor is occupied by a business. The building is brick, and above the second story a brick design spells out "1 CREOLE 1."

Part II
Economic and Demographic Transformation

Downtown Watkins Glen, New York (courtesy of J. Norman Reid)

The central fact of American agriculture is the increase in its output despite the loss of three-fifths of its labor force in forty years. (1983)

*　　*　　*

Given the fact that since 1940 two-thirds of all Negro farm youth have left the farm before reaching age twenty-five, and considering that the current birth rate among Negro farm families is much more than double that needed to replace the population, it seems appropriate to suggest to a group devoted to the welfare of farm people that encouraging and preparing the majority of farm youth for a nonfarm life in the future is as great a service as can be rendered to them. (1956)

*　　*　　*

Manufacturing has led the way to alternatives to farming in many rural communities, and other sectors—such as trade and services—are now picking up the slack as the growth of manufacturing lessens. One of the major contributions of manufacturing has been to provide jobs for women, which otherwise were so lacking in farming areas. Such second household incomes—even though usually not large—have been instrumental in permitting many small-scale farm families to remain on the land who otherwise would probably have had to leave. (1980)

*　　*　　*

In one sense, the changes taking place in rural and small-town areas today represent an urbanization of countryside and village life. This is not to imply that most rural towns have grown to urban size. Rather, there is a more thorough penetration of rural life by amenities, industries, businesses, institutions, communications, programs, laws, styles, family structure, social ills, and stresses and strains that were once regarded as basically urban in nature. It has not been entirely a one-way street. The rise of country music, charismatic religion, and rural-based forms of outdoor recreation represents a penetration of urban life by essentially rural values. (1981)

7

A Characterization of Types
of Nonmetropolitan Areas

It is easy to travel the United States and be impressed both with the commonalities of existence that all its residents share and with the diversity that is still imposed by vastness, the wide range of climate and physiography, the residue of history, differences in resources and agriculture, and variations in ethnicity and culture. The purpose of this chapter is to ensure that in the necessary course of generalizing a nonexistent sameness is not assumed. Procrustean policy beds, of the one-size-fits-all variety, are all too common in public affairs. Therefore, a characterization is provided here of some of the principal sociodemographic and economic subregional situations that are found in rural America today. These areas are for the most part well recognized and reasonably distinctive. No effort is made to encompass the entire country.

Interstitial Rural Areas in the Northeastern Metropolitan Belt

Around the belt of major metropolitan areas that stretches from southern Maine to northern Virginia live more than 3 million nonmetropolitan people. This is the most densely settled nonmetropolitan population in the United States, averaging about 140 persons per square mile, but outnumbered 12 to 1 by the central city and suburban population. Most of the rural and small-town communities are within reasonable commuting distance of metropolitan areas and are quasi-metropolitan in character and orientation. All the nonmetropolitan counties are used to some degree for second-

Adapted with minor changes from Appendix to chapter 1 in Amos H. Hawley and Sara Mills Mazie (eds.), *Nonmetropolitan America in Transition* (Chapel Hill: University of North Carolina Press, 1981).

home and recreation purposes by the massive nearby urban population in the Boston, New York, Philadelphia, Baltimore, and Washington areas.

Although there are some fringes of good farming country—as in the Delmarva Peninsula—agriculture is quite subordinate to manufacturing and the large service-oriented economy. The population of the nonmetropolitan counties has been growing steadily for several decades (18 percent just from 1970 to 1978) despite metropolitan losses. In the process, some counties are gradually changing character and becoming added to the suburban ring. Income levels are good.

An analogous situation exists along the Hudson River–Mohawk Valley–Lake Ontario corridor, dominated by Albany, Syracuse, Rochester, and Buffalo. But the densities of rural and small-town population are somewhat lower, incomes are lower, and no net in-movement of people occurred in the 1970s, although out-movement has become negligible.

Northern New England–St. Lawrence Area

This entirely nonmetropolitan subregion does not have a particularly large population (1.6 million), but has been receiving a substantial amount of publicity, and has a very self-conscious rural and small-town culture. An in-movement of people has developed (66,000 from 1970 to 1978) into what was widely regarded not very long ago as a classically depressed area. There are the new gentry—people of professional skills and good incomes—and what might be called the new peasantry—"homesteaders" inclined to self-sufficiency and simple living. There is widespread interest in environmentalism, conservation, alternative fuel sources, rural esthetic values, home food production, and local self-government. Centers, institutes, journals, and supportive philosophies of life abound. Manufacturing is still the main strength of the economy, but there has been an increase in tourism and other service industries.

The megalopolitan population to the south is so large, especially the 25 million people in the Boston to New York axis, that further spillover into the Northern New England–St. Lawrence area seems inevitable, so long as even a small fraction of people become disaffected with the big cities and attracted to the vision of a more satisfying neorural life.

Lower Great Lakes Industrial and Agricultural Subregion

From Cleveland through southern Michigan and around to Green Bay is the midwestern equivalent of the Northeastern Metropolitan Belt. Chicago, Detroit, Cleveland, Milwaukee, Indianapolis, and lesser cities provide large metropolitan populations separated by nonmetropolitan areas. There are many small nonmetropolitan industrial cities, but the flat, open, rural hinterland is uniformly committed to a highly productive agriculture. Corn Belt and assembly line exist in close proximity. Four million nonmetropolitan people reside in the subregion. Agriculture is vital, but manufacturing, which is heavily oriented toward metal products, is not primarily farm related.

Unlike the Northeastern Metropolitan Belt, the nonmetropolitan population here is not experiencing much growth (5 percent from 1970 to 1978), and this large subregion is unique as the only one in the nation that does not show improved retention of nonmetropolitan residents in the 1970s. Some of the nonmetropolitan manufacturing towns are like northern metropolitan centers in miniature, in the sense of heavy dependence on an older manufacturing economy that is experiencing losses to other regions. Without resorts, retirement attractions, energy development, or other common sources of nonmetropolitan population growth, the combined dominance of an older manufacturing economy and agriculture has produced a small increase in out-movement from rural areas and small towns. But the level of living is good.

Upper Great Lakes Area

The territory around the Upper Great Lakes resembles northern New England in being a previously depressed, resource-based rural area on the periphery of a densely settled metropolitan belt. However, the cultural setting is different. The set-piece New England village image is replaced by the Paul Bunyan logging and mining camp tradition. Rapid growth has come in the 1970s after an earlier start in the 1960s. Second homes, recreation, and retirement are supplemented by some increase in manufacturing, but agriculture is now negligible—mercifully curtailed in the last generation.

The area is an archexample of the propensity for modern rural growth to come in open country areas and unincorporated settlements rather than in the small cities and towns. Some growth rates are high—in the northern half of the lower peninsula of Michigan, for instance—severely testing the ability of sparsely settled counties to cope with rapid and seemingly inexorable development. Natural lakes abound, both small and large, and are the basis for much of the amenity-based attraction of the area and for the policy issues of land and water use and control that the area faces.

Southern Coastal Plain

The Coastal Plain from eastern Virginia to the Mississippi Delta has more than 7 million nonmetropolitan people. No area has changed more greatly in the last generation. One has only to read the economic and social literature of the 1930s to be aware of how impoverished in every way the rural communities of this region were, and of how dependent the mass of people, many landless, were on unmechanized cotton and tobacco farming. Central to any consideration of the region, too, was the segregated and subordinate position of the black population.

In the three decades from 1940 to 1970, a vast outpouring of people from this region took place as agriculture was mechanized and blacks went to the North. In the 1950s alone, a net of 1.7 million people left the nonmetropolitan counties, a majority of them black. Despite the disproportionate out-movement of blacks, a majority of Southern Coastal Plain counties still had 30 percent or more blacks in their total population in 1970, and in eighty-seven counties better than 50 percent of the people were black.

Substantial introduction of manufacturing has taken place, although not to the extent found in the Piedmont. There are a number of small- to middle-sized metropolitan areas scattered around (such as Richmond, Norfolk, Raleigh, Columbia, Macon, Montgomery, Jackson, and Memphis), but this is still a part of the country in which the nonmetropolitan population outnumbers the metropolitan, and in which the bulk of the nonmetropolitan people are not adjacent to a metropolitan area. There is still much rural and small-town poverty, partly associated with the low socioeconomic status of blacks, but also derived from low wage scales and insufficient economic development.

Like most parts of the South, the rural population is widely distributed. The open country portions contain many residences, stores, other business places, churches, schools, and even factories, unlike the more concentrated settlement pattern of the Corn Belt, Great Plains, and West. Government outside of incorporated places functions almost entirely at the county level. Township government does not exist, nor are there generally independent school districts. Agriculture is still important, but its occurrence is spottier than in the Midwest, with many more wooded areas. Cotton is now of minor importance except in the Mississippi Delta. Tobacco and peanuts continue to be planted, and soybeans claim much of the old cotton land. The tenant system of farming is greatly reduced, and no more than 10 percent of nonmetropolitan blacks are associated directly with agriculture. Since 1970, out-movement and in-movement in the region have been almost in balance. Few counties are growing rapidly, but except in the Mississippi Delta, few are declining in population. A number of people who left in earlier decades are now moving back in retirement, but there are few retirement or resort-recreation communities as such.

Southern Piedmont

Inland from the Southern Coastal Plain and stretching from central Virginia to eastern Alabama is the Southern Piedmont, a more rolling area in topography characterized by its reddish-orange soil. The Piedmont, with its water power, became the cradle of southern industrialization in the late nineteenth century. The emphasis was and still is on textiles, but much diversification has occurred and the degree of concentration on manufacturing in the economy is often startling. Forty-six percent of the entire nonmetropolitan working population was employed in manufacturing in 1970, a percentage rarely reached in metropolitan areas. (Only 4 percent worked in agriculture.) Labor-force participation rates for women are the highest in the United States. Factories may be in towns of every size or in the open country.

It is difficult to say that this area has any particular inherent advantage for manufacturing today because water power and locally produced cotton (for raw material) are no longer important. But the historic industrial base has been successfully added to in the modern period. In the last two decades, the minority black population has finally gained access to the mills, and a variety of products beyond the staples of textiles and furniture has been introduced. Atlanta, in the southern end of the area, has emerged as the leading metropolis of the Southeast, with far-reaching influence. Piedmont wage scales tend to be somewhat higher than in the Coastal Plain and, with high labor-force participation by women, family income levels are better.

The black population averaged a little more than one-fifth of the total in 1970 but reached a majority in only seven counties. Most of the farmland of fifty years ago has either reverted to forest or been placed in pasture. Rural settlement densities tend to be high, although not at the level of the Northeastern Metropolitan Belt. The visual context of most of the area is rural and small town, but the economy is the most exclusively dependent on production of manufactured goods of any rural area in the country.

Florida Peninsula

In both the 1960s and the 1970s, the Florida Peninsula was the most rapidly growing subregion of the United States, in metropolitan and nonmetropolitan areas alike. In that part of the state south of St. Augustine and Gainesville, the nonmetropolitan population doubled from 1960 to 1978 while the metropolitan areas increased by about 85 percent. In the 1970s, nearly all of this growth came from people moving in from other states. There is little excess of births over deaths because so much of the in-movement consists of people of retirement age. Better than one-fourth of the nonmetropolitan residents of the peninsula are now sixty or older.

There are about 7 million people living in the semitropical part of Florida today—that part where citrus fruits can be grown. Not more than one-eighth of them are still officially nonmetropolitan because rapid growth has created six new metropolitan areas just since 1970, in addition to the somewhat older ones. However, the metropolitan areas frequently contain many rural people and much of the best agriculture. In this sense, Florida farming is analogous to that in California, with vegetables and fruits dominating a highly specialized agriculture based on large operations and extensive use of ethnic-minority hired labor in a frequently metropolitan setting. There is the climatic capacity to produce crops not generally growable elsewhere, especially in winter. But the runaway growth of population coming into the peninsula for retirement, recreation, or the warm climate is putting increasing pressure on the supply and cost of farmland.

As the southern and central parts of the peninsula have filled, growth has moved farther north into areas that are not frostproof and do not have idyllic palm-fringed beaches. Still, they are relatively attractive to people from colder regions. One county, Citrus, grew by 185 percent with the addition of about 35,000 people in just the ten years from 1970 to 1980, despite having more deaths than births. In such a situation—or anything remotely approaching it—many problems of rapid growth appear, although one seldom hears the alarm in Florida that attends much smaller booms in the energy areas of the West, where communities are unaccustomed to it.

Although the retirement phenomenon exists in an unparalleled way in Florida, it must not be thought that most of the newcomers are retired. About 70 percent of the in-movement to nonmetropolitan parts of the peninsula consists of people less than sixty (and their children), who for the most part are in the labor force. However, the distinctive reality for most of the area is the dominance of recreation and retirement, and the supporting service industries. The future of the rural and small-town areas of the Florida Peninsula is hard to picture if growth at recent rates continues. Although many parts were thinly settled thirty and forty years ago, this is no longer true. Living costs have risen greatly, but the potential population wanting to settle in the area, especially in retirement, is huge. The peninsula's total population has become larger than that of all but eight states, and except for a minor segment, all of its rural and small-town people now live in or adjacent to metropolitan counties.

Corn Belt and Great Plains

If there is an idealized type of the agrarian and small-town image in America, it surely belongs to the Corn Belt and the Great Plains—the land of the Homestead Act, frugal, hard-working farmers, Garland's *Son of the Middle Border*, Rolvaag's *Giants in the Earth*, Lewis's *Main Street*, Inge's *Picnic*, Willson's *Music Man*, and Grant Wood's *American Gothic*. A land of struggle—not always rewarded—and even occasional strife, but without the degrading legacy of slavery, sharecropping, grinding poverty, and soil depletion that has overlaid the rural South.

The visual reality of agriculture is overwhelming in an area of 750,000 square miles. At least 85 percent of the land surface is in farms. The open fields and ranges extend to the horizon with level to rolling terrain and few woods. The rural population of the region has gone through an extended period of open country decline, and small-town and city concentration, lasting longer than that elsewhere. Goods and services tend to be absent from the countryside, as compared with the South. Many farmers have relocated into town and commute to work, although the majority still live on their farms, except in some areas of the High Plains.

The region is indisputably the grain and meat basket of the nation. Except for some minerals, there is little to the economy of the plains part of the region other than agriculture, but farming is highly commercial and family operated. The ratio of farm operators to hired farm workers is typically 2 to 1 (in contrast to the Southern Coastal Plain, for example, where it is generally less than 1 to 1).

Because of its greater rainfall, the Corn Belt part of the agricultural heartland has smaller farms and greater productivity per acre, with an emphasis on soybeans, corn, pork, and fed beef. In addition, there are relatively more small towns and a moderate infusion of manufacturing activity, some of which is related to agriculture.

In the Great Plains, the average density of people is just eight per square mile, barely one-fourth that of the Corn Belt. Metropolitan centers are few and small, except for Denver, and most of the region lies beyond convenient accessibility to urban centers. As a result, smaller cities often serve functions not found in places of comparable size in the East or the South. For example, towns tend to acquire such facilities as television stations or airline service at a smaller size than is common in more densely settled areas. With some exceptions, the physical size of counties in the plains is not exceptional as it so often is in the West. When combined with the low density, this produces an average population of only 11,000 people per county, the lowest of any major part of the country. Thus, local units of government are small, lack economies of scale in furnishing services, and are confronted with the social costs of space.

Except where irrigation prevails, most Great Plains and Corn Belt counties have declined in population for several decades, because of farm consolidations and lack of other job opportunities. Considerable distortion of the age composition has resulted, with an undercutting of the young-adult and young-child groups. Widespread introduction of irrigated farming, spreading up from the Texas Panhandle to western Kansas, has developed areas with high-yield production of corn and sorghum and even new crops such as sugar beets. However, depletion of the underground aquifer threatens a short life for these practices and a difficult readjustment to dry farming.

At present, the Corn Belt has about 6.25 million nonmetropolitan population and the Great Plains subregion has a little less than 5 million. The Corn Belt as a whole is still having some net out-migration. In the plains the degree of turnaround in population trend in recent years is greater than in the Corn Belt, but much of the difference is accounted for by growth around those cities now reaching metropolitan status, such as Fort Collins, Greeley, Rapid City, and Bismarck.

Parts of the northern Great Plains encompass the zone of recent and potential coal development. The affected communities are as yet few in number—not more than ten or so. However, the potential effect is larger if and when coal-gasification plants become a reality and as more mines and mine-mouth generating plants are built. The coal communities lack the size, experience, or confidence to deal with these developments and are now legally entitled to special impact assistance.

Southern Appalachian Coalfields

Probably no other rural region has had a more unfavorable stereotyped image in the public mind than the more isolated parts of the Southern Appalachians. The hillbilly, moonshiner-revenuer, Li'l Abner image has been accompanied by the picture of the coal-blackened underground miner and the violence of mine strikes. This was about the last area of the United States to be modernized in terms of electricity, telephones, highways, and housing. Yet, no other rural region has had a greater degree of nonmetropolitan turnaround in population trend since 1970 than the Southern Appalachian coalfields. The area—broadened to include the non-mining parts of the Cumberland Plateau—has about 1.7 million rural and small-town people, all but a comparative few of whom are white highlanders of colonial stock. The heart of it is characterized by the most dissected topography in America. Narrow, winding creek valleys with their tributary hollows often comprise

the only level land. In an intensely rural region, level land suitable
for home sites, schools, industrial parks, or any purpose is actually
in short supply. Only one-sixth of the population is urban, and
except in West Virginia, there are still no towns of even 10,000 people.

Fewer than 5 percent of the people are engaged primarily in
farming, and those who do are generally in small-scale operations.
Coal mining is the main single source of income. On any map of
wage rates, the coal counties look very good—well above the
national average. But the intermittency of work, the high frequency of work-limiting health conditions, the relative lack of
employment for women, and the residual influence of long years of
isolation and underemployment create conditions of social dependency and poor levels of living that are incongruent with unionized
work and miners' pay scales. Outside the mining counties wage
rates fall to some of the lowest in the nation.

The region was an area of heavy out-movement of people in the
1950s and 1960s as coal mining and agriculture declined. Since
1970, the population has been increasing as quickly as it declined.
Mining jobs have revived (although not to the extent expected), a
number of people who had left in earlier years have returned
(many with pensions), and improved highways and industrial job
development programs have brought some broadening of the
economy. Conditions are changing, but the topography and cultural heritage will continue to make the area distinctive. Many
problems related to mining, employment, living conditions, and
small-scale farming remain to be handled.

Lower Ohio Valley–Southern Interior Uplands

The subregion described here is not as distinctive or popularly
recognized as some others with more familiar names. Perhaps it is
best described as bounded by better-known areas such as the Corn
Belt on the north, the Southern Appalachians to the east, and the
Southern Coastal Plain on the south and west. Basically the
subregion includes the Lower Ohio Valley and the lower courses of
the Tennessee and Cumberland rivers. It contains 3 million nonmetropolitan people. It is all southern or border southern. Some
sections of it are reminiscent of the white highland culture of the
Appalachians; others have black minorities but were never charac-

terized by the plantation system of the Coastal Plain or a predominantly black population.

Within the Lower Ohio Valley and Southern Interior Uplands are some prosperous agriculturally well-endowed areas such as the Kentucky Bluegrass and the Nashville Basin. However, there are many poorer areas, such as the Highland Rim country with its hills, poor soil, and legacy of white poverty. A characteristic feature of all but the southern part of the subregion is the presence of thousands of small tobacco farms, which produce most of the country's burley, snuff, and chewing tobaccos. Labor-saving procedures have come slowly to this industry, yet the system of allotments and price supports used in tobacco farming has created a relative tenacity in the persistence of such farming despite the often tiny allotted acreages that a family may have.

Cincinnati, Louisville, and Nashville have long provided islands of metropolitan activity and employment, and in one section of Kentucky there is coal mining (the western Kentucky coalfields). However, a high dependence on small-scale farming led to heavy rural out-migration at mid-century. Today much of the subregion continues to be intensively rural, but the development of the Tennessee and Cumberland rivers changed the power supply, created large reservoirs, and, together with general modernization, stimulated manufacturing and other activities.

So rapid has been the economic transformation of the subregion that from 1940 to 1970 employment in agriculture dropped from 50 percent to just 8 percent of all nonmetropolitan workers, while manufacturing jobs increased from 10 percent to 30 percent of the total. This reflects consolidation of farms, some abandonment of farming, and, in part, the large-scale entry of women into manufacturing and other nonfarm work. A majority of counties now have manufacturing as the leading source of income, although not with the intensity of the Southern Piedmont. The factories are rather diverse in character, ranging from small sewing operations to large aluminum mills.

Much of the potential agricultural displacement from the Lower Ohio Valley–Southern Interior Uplands had been completed by 1970. In the 1970s, a net in-movement of 176,000 people took place through 1978, as former out-migrants returned and new in-migrants entered. This contrasts with the Southern Coastal Plain, where the "rural turnaround" up to this point consists essentially of a stemming of the previous large outflow of people, especially blacks, with no net in-migration occurring.

Ozark and Ouachita Uplands

The west-of-the-Mississippi version of the southern highlands is, like its eastern counterpart, an area of distinctive conditions and notable changes. Southern Missouri, northern and western Arkansas, and eastern Oklahoma have a nonmetropolitan population of about 1.8 million living in a rolling-to-hilly plateau (the Ozarks) and a ridge-and-valley mountain area (the Ouachitas), separated by the valley of the Arkansas River. With the exception of some mining activity in Missouri (mostly lead), the area was long one of small-scale farming and timber work, with a pattern of poor transportation, low income, and relative isolation, settled primarily by white southern highlanders.

After 1940, a period of population loss ensued, lasting until about the mid-1960s. Farming began to be abandoned or consolidated, and many people moved elsewhere. However, the area became a major locus for dam building, especially on the White and Osage rivers, having only moderate significance for electric power, but producing a series of reservoirs in a woodland setting. Resorts and the in-movement of retired people developed quickly—despite a low level of service facilities for older people. Furthermore, a variety of manufacturing (mostly low wage) began to develop in the area. Population increased in several places, and since 1970 the growth has spread to all but one of the 85 nonmetropolitan counties (the one exception being a military county). Some of the newcomers are returnees, some are midwesterners of urban origin, and others are back-to-the-land types who buy small farmsteads. And some growth stems from less out-movement of natives. Many counties have now returned to their former population levels, and outright rapid growth is not uncommon.

The Ozark and Ouachita region today finds itself with a mixture of success and problems. The isolation and stagnation of the past are largely gone and more jobs are available. Outsiders evaluate the region as attractive rather than shunning it. Yet, the future of the region creates concern. The population is not dense but some of the lakes are now having pollution problems. Some resort areas have become distinctly "touristy," with commercial attractions that have no relation to the rural charm and natural beauty that give character to the region. Population in small counties is often growing more rapidly than can be readily absorbed. (The average annual growth of rural and small-town population has been about 2 percent in the region as a whole, rising to 5 percent in some counties.) The region is a conspicuous example of a rural problem area of the past that has opened up and developed in an unexpected manner but is faced with a variety of nagging problems created by growth that are different from those of the past, but merit no less attention.

Rio Grande Valley and the Southwest

The Rio Grande Valley and the rest of the Southwest are as distinctive for the composition of their rural population as they are for their climate and landscape. The land—defined here as Arizona, most of New Mexico, and the Rio Grande portions of Colorado and Texas—is a mixture of arid to semiarid plateaus and mountains, and key river valleys. Of the 1.67 million nonmetropolitan residents in 1970, about two-fifths were of Mexican-American origin and one-tenth were Indians. Only in the Southern Coastal Plain are there such large ethnic minority rural populations. The living situation of Mexican-Americans and Indians, similar to blacks in the rural South, is often associated with low income, poor housing, large families, low education, limited labor-force participation, and other social problems.

The region described here has well over 300,000 square miles, but a nonmetropolitan population density that averages only about six persons per square mile even with the rapid growth that many sections have experienced since 1970. Crop agriculture is essentially impossible without irrigation. Where water is available, there are productive districts where cotton, vegetables, and citrus products are raised. Cattle and sheep ranching extend over wide areas. But much of the land was never taken up under any settlement scheme and (except in Texas) about three-eighths of it remains in federal ownership.

Besides farming, scattered mining activities (copper, uranium, and oil and gas) and tourist attractions (for example, Grand Canyon and Carlsbad Caverns) are the major economic functions. In Arizona and southern New Mexico, retirement areas are attracting increasing numbers of people. Many counties have none of the common rural goods-producing activities (agriculture, mining, and manufacturing) as the leading source of income. The combined effect of the federal presence (much of it through landownership), ethnic minority populations with high social-service needs, plus the growing retired population, has caused transfer payments and income from employment in public administration and professional services to become the leading sources of income and growth of income in a majority of counties.

Central Valley of California

In a slight arc stretching from north to southeast, the Central Valley of California extends for 400 miles. There is no area of comparable size on which Americans are as dependent for food supply, but it is quite different from the good farm areas of the Midwest. As the Corn Belt and the Wheat Belt epitomize the domain of the independent family farmer providing most of his labor, the Central Valley reflects large-scale corporate farming and family farms engaged in crops that require large amounts of seasonal hired work.

Farming has changed over the years in the valley, but from the first period of American settlement it has been conducted on a large and capital-intensive scale, always on the leading edge of innovations in machinery, techniques, new crops, and marketing. With extensive irrigation, productivity is high. In 1978, the Central Valley produced more than $5 billion worth of farm goods for sale, as much as the combined total of Alabama, Mississippi, and Tennessee. The output is highly varied, with commodities such as cotton, rice, grapes, barley, tomatoes, sugar beets, peaches, plums, oranges, almonds, walnuts, cattle, milk, and eggs all being produced in major quantities. A great deal of employment is generated in packing and processing and the servicing of farms.

Here much of the agriculture is metropolitan. Sacramento, Stockton, Modesto, Fresno, and Bakersfield are in the valley and serve agricultural functions. Only in the northern part are metropolitan centers not within accessible distance to rural people.

About one-sixth of the nonmetropolitan and rural metropolitan population was Mexican-American in 1970, with an additional 4 percent of blacks and Asians. But these percentages do not reflect the real degree of ethnic aspects of agriculture in the daily life of the valley. Resident hired farm workers alone outnumber farm operators by better than 2 to 1, but among Mexican-Americans the ratio of hired workers to farm operators is 10 to 1. Thousands of migrant seasonal workers are also used who come into the area from other U.S. areas or from Mexico. The Central Valley, along with other similar California farm sections, such as the Coastal

Valleys and the Imperial Valley, is the center of farm labor unionization efforts, land-redistribution movements (160-acre irrigation limitation), and legal challenges to the thrust of land-grant university research policies. In sum, there is a much greater degree of social activism relating to agriculture and rural ethnic divisions than is common in most other regions.

In addition to farming, there are oil and gas fields in the southern part of the valley and a number of military bases that add to rural employment.

The Mormon Country

Several subregions of the West lend themselves to characterization as distinctive rural environments other than the Central Valley of California and the Rio Grande Valley and Southwest. In the case of the Mormon Country, the unifying theme is not so much physiographic and economic as cultural.

After the Latter Day Saints, or Mormons, made their trek to the Salt Lake Basin in 1847, they soon began a systematic series of settlements in other parts of Utah and in southeastern Idaho. Except for mining developments, most later settlers crossing the continent bypassed the Mormon areas. The result today is that in an area embracing almost all of Utah and southeastern Idaho, plus smaller neighboring portions of southwestern Wyoming and eastern Nevada, the great majority of the population is actively Mormon or of Mormon background.

This fact has secular significance in several ways, especially in regard to social conservatism and rural demography. If there is a Mormon ethic, it surely includes self-reliance, hard work, education, and the importance of the family. It also manifests itself in political conservatism, a somewhat negative view of the role of federal government and of labor unions, a conservative view of the societal role of women, and abstinence from tobacco and alcoholic beverages. Some of these traits are not necessarily different from those of many other non-Mormon westerners in the Mountain states, but they seem to be stronger among the Mormons.

The most striking demographic feature of the Mormon areas is the relatively high birthrate and the near immunity of this population from the substantial reductions in childbearing that almost all other segments of rural and small-town America have made since the early 1960s. The nonmetropolitan Mormon counties (with a population of about 600,000) have as many births as they did in 1961, when the national number of births peaked, and have three-and-a-half times as many births as deaths, with about 1.8 percent annual natural increase. The nonmetropolitan U.S. population as a whole had an annual natural increase of only .6 percent in the 1970s, whereas births have decreased by one-fourth since 1960, and the ratio of births to deaths is only 1.5 to 1. The Mormon areas, therefore, have a youthful age structure with a large potential for natural growth, even without in-migration. In consequence, they have a much greater need for continued job development if they are to avoid the necessity of exporting their youth to other areas as they enter the labor force.

The economy of this subregion has been basically agricultural, with a mixture of ranching, dairying, irrigated crops, and dry farming. But there has been a surge in mining, particularly fuels—coal, oil, gas, and uranium. This industry brings in outsiders, as it did in the past at the older copper and coal mines. In addition, there is a growth of recreation business in the unique scenic areas of southern Utah (e.g., Lake Powell, Zion National Park, and Bryce Canyon National Park) that attracts many people from other regions. Altogether, the Mormon Country had a net in-movement of nearly 50,000 people from 1970 to 1978, a factor that leads to a gradual dilution of the cultural homogeneity of the population. When combined with the high rate of retained natural growth, the Mormon Country has had a near explosive nonmetropolitan growth of 25 percent in the years from 1970 to 1978, with every part of the area affected. Overall density is still low, for there are vast, nearly uninhabited arid areas, but the impact on the environment and culture is high, especially when the likelihood of further similar growth rates is considered.

North Pacific Coast

Large-scale timber industry is the most characteristic feature of the western portions of Washington and Oregon and northwestern California. This area, containing only 3 percent of the nation's land surface, has two-fifths of all the growing stock of softwood timber and one-half of the national volume of softwood sawtimber that is cut. The mountains and hills of the Coast Ranges and the Cascades are covered with fir, spruce, hemlock, and (in California) redwood, made especially verdant by the moist and comparatively mild marine climate. The combination of topography, location, climate, and forests has produced a distinctive regional setting.

The Willamette River Valley and Puget Sound Lowlands provide an axis of settlement, farming, and transportation in an otherwise difficult terrain. Some of the subregion's 2 million nonmetropolitan people have access to the large Seattle–Tacoma and Portland metropolitan areas, but about one-half are in distinctly distant and self-contained rural and small-town communities. The timber industry of the Northwest has suffered from periodic recessions and the closure of smaller operations. Despite sustained-yield forestry practices, imbalances of supply, demand, and mill capacity still occur, producing local or more general bouts of unemployment and underemployment. Such a trend is now officially predicted for sizable areas of Oregon in coming years.

Nevertheless, the nonmetropolitan population of the subregion has been growing rapidly—with a 22 percent increase and 260,000 in-migrants from 1970 to 1978. Some of the increase is stimulated by economic growth, but some is an excellent example of the infusion of metropolitan people into a rural and small-town area for noneconomic style-of-life considerations. For example, many urban Californians have moved into southwestern Oregon, despite their inability to avoid some unemployment or to earn as much as they did formerly. Many have the desire to shift from former wage and salary work to self-employment.

Some of the rural areas are attracting retired people, such as the islands and shore areas of Puget Sound, the valleys and coastal areas of southwest Oregon, and even localities on the drier eastern side of the Cascades. Probably no state has made so plain its desire not to attract in-migration and rapid population growth as has Oregon, and environmental concerns about growth are generally high throughout the North Pacific Coast. But the subregion is growing nevertheless, and with its "Cloud Belt" status it exemplifies the fact that Sunbelt is a very imperfect synonym for population growth.

8

Nonfarm Rural America

There was a time when rural Americans were overwhelmingly agricultural in their livelihood. When the first inquiry into occupations was made in the Census of 1820, 72 percent of all employed people in the nation worked directly in farming. In rural areas the figure was at least 75 percent. Many of the other one-fourth were in jobs that directly served farmers, such as blacksmiths, wagonmakers, harness makers, millers, or drovers.

Over the years the rural economy gradually diversified. Mining and timber industries developed. The industrial revolution brought manufacturing into rural towns, especially where there was waterpower. Resorts began to flourish, particularly after the coming of the railroad and, later on, the automobile. As life modernized and subsistence living declined, trades and services flourished that were supported by the agricultural economy of rural communities, even though they did not provide goods or services directly related to farming, for example, housewares, clothing, recreation, and community services in health and education. With the coming of the automobile and the interurban railway, urban employed people began to settle in rural areas, foreshadowing the extensive commuting of today.

Although such changes gradually took place, rural people remained primarily agricultural until World War II, well after the time when the farm population reached its peak number during World War I. However, in the 1940s, the number of farms and farm people began to decline at a rapid rate. Except in the Dust Bowl, people had been somewhat backed up on farms during the depression years of the 1930s. With the immense recruitment of people into urban-located defense industries and into military service during World War II, a vast outpouring from rural areas

Adapted from *Farm Structure: A Historical Perspective on Changes in the Number and Size of Farms*. Congress of the United States (96th Congress, 2d Session, Committee Print). Committee on Agriculture, Nutrition, and Forestry. U.S. Senate. April 1980, pp. 36–48.

occurred. Some return to farms took place immediately following the war, but the sustained high level of economic activity in the cities, coupled with rapid strides in mechanization and enlargement of farms, soon produced a resumption of out-movement. In the single decade of the 1940s, a net of 11.4 million persons left farms or lived on places where farming operations were ended during that time. By 1950, farm residents no longer comprised a majority of all rural people. A turning point in American rural life had been passed.

In general, farm people dwindled because of (1) the rapid reduction in man hours of work required in farming caused by adoption of modern technology, (2) the near abandonment of the tenant system of row-crop farming in the South, (3) the pressures on farmers to consolidate other farms into their own as profit margins narrowed and high volume production became essential, (4) the movement of a majority of farm laborers to off-farm residences, (5) the decline in the birth rate among farm families after 1960, and (6) the irresistible attraction of urban or nonagricultural jobs to farm people looking for higher and steadier income and shorter working hours.

Where few alternatives to farm work were available, the loss of farm people led to an extensive decline in total rural population. This was true in hundreds of counties in the Great Plains, the Corn Belt, and the Southern Coastal Plain. Some areas lost half of their people in thirty years. Elsewhere, however, the rural population often grew where agricultural dominance was not so overwhelming and where nonfarm sources of employment thrived. The result was a total rural population level that changed very little nationally, but that reflected a complex pattern of regional losses and gains.

Public perception of the changing economic base of many rural communities lagged behind the reality. It has been my experience that well into the late 1960s many people requesting information from the Department of Agriculture equated "rural" with "agricultural," and that the full extent of nonagricultural sources of employment and income in rural and/or nonmetropolitan areas is still not commonly appreciated.

Concepts

In assessing the extent and nature of nonfarm activities in rural America, a word about definitions is necessary. Rural areas as defined in the census of population consist of open country and of places that have fewer than 2,500 people and lie outside of the urban fringe of metropolitan cities. This is a useful and time-honored statistical definition. However, some government programs that are labeled rural—such as those authorized in the Rural Development Act of 1972—use other, more liberal definitions. In rural housing and community facilities programs, towns are rural so long as they have fewer than 10,000 people. For purposes of business and industrial loans, cities of up to 49,999 population are rural if they lie beyond the "urbanizing zone" of a city of 50,000 or more. There is no one standard program concept.

Another popular way of looking at areas along size and density lines is by metropolitan status. In general, metropolitan areas are established wherever a central urban nucleus of 50,000 or more people can be defined. The area is then generalized to county lines, and adjoining counties are added if they meet certain tests of metropolitan character and worker commuting. The nonmetropolitan residual contains a majority of the rural population of the country, plus a substantial number of cities of 10,000 to 49,999 people. This concept omits a number of rural people living in the outer parts of metropolitan areas but has an advantage in that a variety of information is available for counties annually, and thus can be compiled by metropolitan status. In contrast, rural data are only obtained once each decade in the decennial census and are therefore often out of date. Both concepts will be used here, as necessity dictates. Neither is fully adequate in policy terms, but both give a reasonable picture of trends in rural areas.

Population and Settlement Patterns

In 1970, nearly 85 million people lived either in the rural areas of the United States or in urban places of fewer than 50,000 people that lay outside of metropolitan urbanized areas (Table 8.1). This population amounted to nearly 42 percent of the total U.S. population and is the largest number that could be considered "rural" under a definition that includes persons living in small cities. Fifty-four million of the 85 million lived in nonmetropolitan areas. The other 31 million were officially metropolitan, living in a variety of circumstances ranging from small commuter suburbs lying just beyond the urbanized area to outlying farm, ranch, or mining districts of metropolitan counties whose boundaries extended far

Table 8.1 Metropolitan and Rural Population (in thousands)

Year	Metropolitan	Nonmetropolitan	Outside Urbanized Areas			
			Total	Places of 2,500 to 49,999	Open Country and Places of Fewer than 2,500	
					Nonfarm	Farm
1978	157,946	60,122	—	—	—	8,005
1970	148,880	54,424	84,765	30,878	44,175	9,712
1960	127,191	52,132	83,474	29,420	38,419	15,635
Percent change:						
1970 to 1978	6.1	10.5	—	—	—	−17.6
1960 to 1970	17.1	4.4	1.5	5.0	15.0	−37.9

Source: Various reports of Bureau of the Census and Department of Agriculture.

beyond the limits of central city influence. Some 54 million of the 85 million were residents of the open country or of towns and villages of fewer than 2,500 people. The remainder lived in places of 2,500 to 49,999 population. Quite by chance, the nonmetropolitan and rural populations were almost identical in size (54 million) in 1970, but they only partly overlap one another.

The nonfarm rural population is located somewhat differently by region than is the farm population (see Table 8.2). For example, a higher percentage of the nonfarm rural total is in the northeastern states, where the farm population is relatively small. In contrast, the West North Central states, with their highly commercial farming, contain a much larger proportion of farm people than they do of rural nonfarm residents. At the broadest level, one can identify a contiguous belt of twenty northeastern and South Atlantic states, lapping over into the most industrialized part of the Midwest (Ohio and Michigan), each of which contains a greater part of the nation's nonfarm rural population than it does of the farm population. In total, these states have 54.5 percent of all rural nonfarm people compared with 30.8 percent of the farm group. Therefore, even when one considers matters relating only to open country and village areas, exclusive of small urban places, this large block of states is much more affected by nonagricultural trends, conditions, and programs than it is by agricultural concerns. Its rural nonfarm population exceeds the farm population by 8 to 1.

On the other hand, one can add most of the South Central states and several western states to the bulk of the Midwest to define

Table 8.2 Regional Location of Rural and Small-Town/Small-City Population, 1970

| | Rural | | | | | | Places of 2,500 to 49,999[a] | |
| | Total Rural | | Farm | | Nonfarm | | | |
Area	Number (thousands)	Percent Distribution	Number (thousands)	Percent Distribution	Number (thousands)	Percent Distribution	Number (thousands)	Percent Distribution
United States	53,887	100.0	9,712	100.0	44,178	100.0	30,878	100.0
New England	2,798	5.2	128	1.3	2,670	6.0	1,517	4.9
Middle Atlantic	6,793	12.6	571	5.9	6,222	14.1	3,138	10.2
East North Central	10,161	18.9	2,053	21.1	8,108	18.4	5,455	17.7
Mich., Ohio	4,948	9.2	720	7.4	4,227	9.6	2,278	7.4
Ill., Ind., Wis.	5,213	9.7	1,333	13.7	3,881	8.8	3,177	10.3
West North Central	5,930	11.0	2,252	23.2	3,678	8.3	3,565	11.5
Iowa, Minn., Mo.	3,885	7.2	1,421	14.6	2,464	5.6	2,101	6.8
Kans., Nebr., N.Dak., S.Dak.	2,045	3.8	831	8.6	1,214	2.7	1,464	4.7
South Atlantic	11,147	20.7	1,357	14.0	9,790	22.2	5,215	16.9
Del., Md., W. Va.	2,136	4.0	172	1.8	1,964	4.5	800	2.6
Ga., N.C., S.C., Va.	7,690	14.3	1,073	11.0	6,617	15.0	3,081	10.0
Fla.	1,321	2.5	113	1.2	1,208	2.7	1,334	4.3
East South Central	5,816	10.8	1,329	13.7	4,487	10.2	2,778	9.0
Ky., Tenn.	3,153	5.9	836	8.6	2,317	5.2	1,380	4.5
Ala., Miss.	2,663	4.9	493	5.1	2,170	4.9	1,398	4.5
West South Central	5,292	9.8	1,069	11.0	4,223	9.6	3,980	12.9
Ark., La.	2,197	4.1	388	4.0	1,809	4.1	1,285	4.2
Okla., Tex.	3,095	5.7	680	7.0	2,415	5.5	2,695	8.7
Mountain	2,227	4.1	446	4.6	1,781	4.0	1,879	6.1
Idaho, Mont., Wyo., Colo.	1,256	2.3	319	3.3	937	2.1	1,039	3.4
Ariz., N.Mex., Nev., Utah	971	1.8	127	1.3	844	1.9	840	2.7
Pacific	3,723	6.9	508	5.2	3,215	7.3	3,352	10.9

Source: Various reports of Bureau of the Census and Department of Agriculture.
[a] Places outside of urbanized areas.

another contiguous block of twenty states which contain a much larger percentage of the rural farm population (61.3 percent) than they do of the national nonfarm rural population (33.7 percent). Even in these states, however, nonfarm rural people outnumber those on farms in every state even though farming is high in relative importance. The overall ratio of rural nonfarm to farm people was 2.5 to 1 in this region.

The population living in places of 2,500 to 49,999 residents that are not in metropolitan urbanized areas is somewhat more evenly distributed than either the rural farm or nonfarm populations. The one major exception to this is the West. In most western states, plus Texas, there is an above-average concentration of people in small towns and cities, as distinct from the open country and villages. The dry nature of much of the region, the limited degree of agriculture in some areas, and the large acreages required per farm or ranch in others have contributed to a greater propensity to settle in towns than is generally true in the Midwest, South, or East.

Economic Activity of Nonfarm Rural and Small-Town People

Many people who do not operate farms or live on farms are dependent on farming. Most directly, there were 1.1 million hired farmworkers in 1977 who were not farm residents. Some of them lived in metropolitan cities and commuted to the fields, but most were rural and small-town residents. Beyond this group, however, it is difficult to be specific about the number or proportion of nonfarm rural and small-town people whose fortunes are tied to agriculture. There are many whose work is fully related to agriculture, such as those in agricultural machinery manufacturing and sales, fertilizer production and distribution, grain elevators, livestock markets, irrigation services, custom land preparation or harvesting work, farm finance, commodity hauling, canning and packing, agricultural research and teaching, or veterinary services. Then there are others in a variety of trade, service, and manufacturing businesses whose activities are partly agricultural or whose customers make their living from farming.

Some of these categories could have been measured by 1970 census data if detailed industry tabulations had been made by a rural-urban or other residential breakdown. Unfortunately, they were not. Generally speaking, in the heart of the Great Plains (North and South Dakota, Nebraska, and Kansas), where farming most dominates the economy without significant competition from other basic activities, farm employment averaged one-third of all rural employment in 1970. In such areas, then, about two other rural jobs (at the most) were supported for every one farm production job. This is in a highly commercial and productive agriculture. If one assumes that a similar average ratio applies elsewhere, then about 6.7 million rural employed people were in farm or farm-dependent jobs in 1970 (two times more than the number in farming only). This number would have been 36 percent of the total number of employed rural people, suggesting that the remaining 64 percent had little or no dependence on farming as a source of direct or semidirect livelihood. The degree of dependence in small towns and cities would have been considerably less. Although there has been a reduction in dependence on farming over the years, this does not imply any reduction in farm output nationally, but rather reflects the enormous increase in agricultural productivity per worker that has taken place.

Manufacturing

The most notable employment substitute for farming in rural areas has been manufacturing. Even in the strictly rural population, excluding towns of 2,500 population or more, two and one-third times as many people were primarily employed in manufacturing industries in 1970 as in agriculture. In Piedmont North and South Carolina, and to a lesser extent in Alabama and Georgia, there are a number of multicounty economic areas where more than half of all employed rural people have manufacturing jobs. Such a manufacturing concentration is not found in metropolitan areas, and its counterpart in direct agricultural employment is not found even in rural areas of the Great Plains. In the Piedmont South, rural manufacturing is based on textiles but has diversified into many other products in recent decades. Although the raw material for textiles was originally southern-produced cotton, a majority of it now comes from polyester or other synthetic fibers not derived from farming.

Textile manufacturing is now basically a rural industry. Other manufacturing industries in which the bulk of at least the larger plants are located in nonmetropolitan counties are logging, pulp, paper, and other wood products (except furniture), primary aluminum, and poultry processing. These activities tend to locate near rural-based raw material sources, or, in the case of aluminum, near locations with large quantities of water and power. A disproportionate nonmetropolitan location of large manufacturing plants also occurs in farm machinery, meatpacking, canned and frozen foods (all directly related to agriculture), man-made fibers, plastic products, and inorganic industrial chemical industries.

In addition, hundreds of plants have been introduced into rural and small-town areas in recent times that produce items that are still primarily centered in metropolitan areas but are increasingly dispersed. For example, this is true of plants producing a wide variety of nonagricultural machinery and other metal products, such as primary metals, automotive equipment, industrial machines and tools, hardware, heating and refrigerating equipment, electronic products, and consumer goods. Nonmetropolitan employment in these plants is second only to textile industries and is important in many northern areas as well as in the upper South.

Industrialists offer a variety of reasons for locating or expanding plants in rural and small-town areas. Many of them involve aspects of labor force, such as untapped supply, lower wage scales, work-oriented attitudes, and less unionization. Other perceived advantages of these locations include ample space, lower site costs, less pilferage, lower taxes, improved highway connections, community receptivity, and economic concessions. Manufacturing employment nationally is essentially stationary, and thus is a diminishing sector of the total economy. However, rural areas have continued to attract a larger fraction of it.

The lack of national growth may limit the future amount of employment increase that manufacturing can offer to rural areas. Indeed, rural areas already have trouble retaining some of their industries in the face of competition from abroad. The shoe industry is an example. But manufacturing has led the way to alternatives to farming in many rural communities, and other sectors, such as trade and services, are now picking up the slack as the growth of manufacturing lessens.

One of the major contributions of manufacturing has been to provide jobs for women, which otherwise were so lacking in farming areas. Such second household incomes, even though usually not large, have been instrumental in permitting many small-scale farm families to remain on the land who otherwise would probably have had to leave. From 1960 to 1970, there was a net growth of more than a half million in the number of rural women employed in manufacturing work.

Mining

Mining has long been a key rural activity, although it is not necessarily thought of as such. We have no rustic terms of imagery associated with mining comparable to the rural images conveyed by agricultural words such as "agrarian," "pastoral," or "bucolic." Yet, a majority of mining takes place in rural and small-town communities. Nearly three-fourths of all people employed in mining in 1970 lived in rural areas or in small cities outside of urbanized areas. However, like agriculture, mining employment peaked in the period between World War I and the economic crash of 1929. It averaged between 1.0 million and 1.2 million persons during this time.

Thereafter, mining employment began to fall. Most of this loss came in coal mining, as mechanization, the shift to strip mining, and the switch to other fuels cut manpower needs in the industry. From the early 1920s to the end of the 1960s, the number of production workers in soft coal mining dropped from more than 550,000 to about 110,000, a loss of four-fifths. The proportionate loss in hard coal was even greater, although the absolute numbers were smaller. Certain other types of mining increased in employment, especially oil and gas, and stone, sand, and gravel. However, overall mining employment drifted down to barely 600,000 workers by 1970, just one half as many as fifty years earlier.

Since 1970, the drop in mining employment has been halted and reversed. This is largely the result of increased efforts to produce mineral fuels. Coal employment has about doubled, and oil and gas activities have also increased. Some of these increases have gone into older production areas. For example, the Southern Appalachian coalfields have had substantial increases in rural population after several decades of rapid decline. But others represent new developments, especially in the western states, where mining boom conditions have come to certain areas of Alaska, Montana, Wyoming, Colorado, and Utah. By 1978, total mining employment had risen above 0.8 million, despite the coal strike of that year.

Wood Products Industries

The third of the three major rural extractive industries is wood products. Here, as with mining and agriculture, the industry was a motive of settlement from the early colonial days, as tracts of the best trees were sought and reserved for naval uses, reflecting the shortage in Europe. For generations wood industries had a shifting aspect, in which large rural districts were cleared of their timber in a manner as complete as mining an ore deposit. If farming was a logical successor to logging, then well and good. But often areas with little agricultural promise were despoiled and abandoned in a manner that only made sense in an era when other virgin stands were still available. Today, with sustained yields as the objective, there is comparative stability in the timbered areas, although some cyclical aspects of employment are still present.

Introduction of modern labor-saving techniques and loss of certain markets for wooden products gave the wood products industry the same problems of job loss as experienced in farming and mining. This was particularly true in the 1950s, when one-fourth of all jobs in logging and in the making of lumber and wood products, exclusive of furniture and paper, were lost. These were the jobs most likely to be located in rural and small-town areas. They dropped from an average of 824,000 in 1950–51 to 605,000 in 1960–61. The decline then stopped and a partial recovery to about 642,000 jobs had occurred by 1977. Logging, sawmills, planing mills, millwork, veneer, plywood, and wooden containers are the major types of rural wood industries, together with the basic forest-management activities that sustain the timber resource. There are also a number of rural paper mills and furniture plants. The paper industry offers the highest pay of these generally low-paid industries, but it is primarily located in metropolitan areas.

Timber resources are primarily found in the southeastern and northwestern parts of the country, with areas of lesser importance in New England and the Upper Great Lakes area. Timbered areas have consistently offered more in the way of alternative job opportunities for rural people than have the prairies and plains of the center of the country. In substantial parts of the Southeast, large amounts of land that were used for farming only one or two generations ago have either been planted in trees or allowed to revert to forest. In fact, in a majority of southern states, less than half of the land is now in farms, whereas a majority was in farms as late as 1950. Roughly 75 million acres of southern land were removed from farms from 1950 to 1974. Not all of this has gone into timber, but a substantial majority of it almost certainly has.

Although mining and wood industries have long been important nonfarm sources of livelihood in rural areas, it is important to note that both were declining in employment during the same years when major farm adjustments were taking place. This compounded the conditions of economic stress felt in rural areas. Rural-to-urban migration patterns were often interpreted as though they stemmed solely from farm displacement, but lack of opportunity in the two other major extractive industries was also important.

Other Employment

In 1975, 24 million employed people lived in nonmetropolitan America. Of this number, 23 percent worked in manufacturing plants, 20 percent were employed in wholesale and retail trade, and 18 percent were engaged in providing professional services. At a considerably lower level of frequency, 9 percent were in agriculture. The rather high percentage in professional services is dominated by health care and education, especially work in hospitals, doctors' offices, nursing homes, and schools. Employment in these fields has increased greatly in the last generation, and in particular has been a source of work for rural and small-town women. In 1975, nearly one-third of all employed nonmetropolitan women worked in a business providing a professional service. Among men, manufacturing ranked in first place, employing 26 percent, followed by trade (18 percent), agriculture (13 percent), and construction (10 percent).

During the 1960s, manufacturing was the only industry in which employment increased at a faster rate in nonmetropolitan counties than in the metropolitan areas. But a measure of the strength of the economic revival in rural and small-town areas in the last decade is found in the fact that since 1970, nonfarm wage and salary employment has increased more rapidly in every industry group in its nonmetropolitan setting than in the metropolitan areas (see Table 8.3).

In the aggregate, nonmetropolitan wage and salary jobs rose by 34.6 percent from March 1970 to March 1979, compared with a 22.1 percent increase in metropolitan areas. Jobs in nonmetropolitan service-performing industries increased at nearly twice the

Table 8.3 Nonfarm Wage and Salary Employment by Residence
for the United States, 1979 and 1970 (in thousands)

Residence and Industry Group	Employment (March)		Change, 1970–79	
	1979	1970	Number	Percent
Metropolitan[a]	65,018	53,249	11,769	22.1
Goods-producing	17,965	17,285	680	3.9
Manufacturing	14,760	14,654	106	0.7
Construction	2,903	2,422	481	19.9
Mining	302	209	93	44.5
Service-producing	43,200	32,431	10,769	33.2
Private sector	31,753	23,393	8,360	35.7
Trade	14,693	11,372	3,321	29.2
Services	13,063	8,957	4,106	45.8
FIRE[b]	3,997	3,064	933	30.5
Government	11,447	9,038	2,409	26.7
TCU[c]	3,853	3,533	320	9.1
Nonmetropolitan	23,041	17,120	5,921	34.6
Goods-producing	7,747	6,260	1,487	23.8
Manufacturing	5,978	5,110	868	17.0
Construction	1,146	749	397	53.0
Mining	623	401	222	55.4
Service-producing	14,160	9,946	4,214	42.4
Private sector	9,334	6,160	3,174	51.5
Trade	4,912	3,323	1,589	47.8
Services	3,585	2,307	1,278	55.4
FIRE[b]	837	530	307	57.9
Government	4,826	3,786	1,040	27.5
TCU[c]	1,134	914	220	24.1

Source: Unpublished data from Bureau of Labor Statistics, Employment
Security, developed by Claude Haren, USDA.
[a] Includes 225 mostly larger standard metropolitan statistical areas
designated through December 31, 1977. Excludes some smaller SMSAs
and some SMSA fringe counties.
[b] Finance, insurance, and real estate.
[c] Transportation, communications, and utilities.

rate of those in goods-producing work (42.4 percent versus 23.8
percent). Remarkable gains of better than 50 percent in nine years
were shown in finance, insurance, and real estate; personal, business, repair, and professional services; as well as in construction
and mining. This illustrates the rapid broadening of the employment base in rural and small-town areas. Rural areas are supporting a greater variety and depth of trade and services, as well as

acquiring a greater ability to serve as the location for service businesses whose clients are metropolitan.

Recreation and Retirement

In rural areas endowed with attractive features for resort and recreation purposes, considerable economic development has occurred in the post–World War II period. In addition, a distinct rural retirement trend has emerged, a fair amount of which is found in the same areas that have recreational districts. Several factors have stimulated the growth of rural recreation, such as general prosperity, more leisure and vacation time, improved access to rural areas, the rise in popularity of skiing, the development of travel-home and other recreational vehicles, the proliferation of reservoirs and public parks, and a generally greater interest in outdoor rural recreation resulting as a by-product of the environmental-ecological movement.

Some of the places that have had rapid growth of rural and small-town population based on recreation include the Aspen and Vail ski areas in Colorado, Sun Valley in Idaho, the Lake Tahoe area in California and Nevada, the Outer Banks of North Carolina, the outer islands of Hawaii, and Cape Cod and Martha's Vineyard in Massachusetts. Since 1940, the United States has added at least 13,000 square miles of inland waters (exclusive of Alaska), largely in the form of reservoirs created by dams. Whatever the primary purpose of the dams, they have usually attracted people for both recreation and permanent living. The effect has been particularly great in those inland states that lacked natural lakes. For example, in Oklahoma, Missouri, Arkansas, Kentucky, and Tennessee, there was a 133 percent increase in inland water area from 1940 to 1970, compared with less than 25 percent in the rest of the United States. The great majority of counties with major dam reservoirs in these states have had rapid population growth.

When retired people move, about twice as many of them leave metropolitan areas and settle in rural areas and small towns than move in the opposite direction. Movement of older people into rural areas that were not established Sunbelt retirement centers became apparent in the 1960s. It accelerated in the 1970s. This trend affects many sections of the country. Rural retirement districts are found in the Ozarks, in the central Texas hill country, around the Upper Great Lakes, along several sections of the

Atlantic Coast, in the southern Blue Ridge Mountains, in the Sierra Nevada foothills, around Puget Sound, and in ever-widening areas of the Southwest and the Florida Peninsula. Furthermore, in some hundreds of counties elsewhere, smaller numbers of retired people have migrated to or returned to rural areas that do not have a pronounced retirement aspect to them. It seems correct to say that we did not foresee the extent to which the growing number of older people would include many people with (1) retirement incomes large enough to make them mobile, (2) the option of retiring at a comparatively early age, and (3) a desire to choose a rural or small-town setting for their retirement despite the poorer quality of medical and community services that many such areas have.

The combined impact of the growth of rural recreation and retirement has stimulated business and employment in many rural areas that until recently had been rather stagnant in population and economy. Often the impact has been just as explosive as that of mining booms. If one examines the list of nonmetropolitan counties that have had rapid population growth since 1970, more of them prove to be recreational-retirement areas than mining boom developments.

The rapid growth of a nonagricultural economy in rural areas in this century—and especially since 1940—is both a consequence of changes in the structure of farming and a force that exerts further pressure for change on farmers. As farms were consolidated in good farming areas and as farming itself dwindled in less favored areas, rural communities were faced with drastic declines in population, employment, income, and community life if new sources of work were not developed. Some, indeed, did not attract a new economic base, and these counties and towns have seen the majority of their young people leave even if agricultural production has remained high. Where this has happened over several decades, the average age of the population has risen dramatically. Many farm counties in the Great Plains and Corn Belt now have more deaths than births because there are so few young adults to bear children compared with the much larger number of older people at ages where most deaths occur. In several hundred such counties more than one-sixth of the total population is sixty-five and over, and more than one-fifth are this age in numerous farm counties of Texas, Kansas, and Missouri. This is the direct result of the prolonged and continuing shift to fewer and larger farms.

Only by diversifying their economy have other areas been able to avoid this condition. Industrial plants and other nonfarm businesses do not bring utopia to the countryside any more than they have to the cities. If they lack competition for labor force, they may be exploitative—offering low wages and benefits. If they are branches of absentee corporations, there is a loss of local control over the economy. The public expenditure burdens that they induce may not be matched by growth of tax revenues in affected communities. In other cases, growth has been brought about by forces either unsought or so powerful that development is too rapid for the community to absorb effectively. This is often the case with mining or recreational-retirement developments.

On the other hand, nonagricultural development of rural areas has stemmed the flow of people to the major urban areas, and this was a major goal of public policy in the years between about 1965 and 1975, culminating in the Rural Development Act of 1972. Repeated public-opinion surveys since the mid-1960s have made it clear that millions of people living in the metropolitan cities and suburbs have lived there only from economic necessity. Residents of rural and small-town communities have consistently reported the highest ratings on residential satisfaction in such surveys. The increase in job opportunities in these communities has given many more Americans the opportunity to live in the type and size of community they prefer. As time passes, many of the revitalized rural areas see their economies broaden. The quality of the industrial mix improves. Plants requiring substantial capital investment or higher levels of technology arrive. The quality and quantity of modern services available increases. Slowly but surely the relative gap between metropolitan and nonmetropolitan family income levels has narrowed. These are desirable social outcomes.

The impact of these changes on agriculture itself has not been adequately assessed, although a major federal effort is now under way to examine the question of agricultural land supply. Beyond doubt, where substantial nonagricultural population growth has occurred in commercial farm areas, it has increased the demand for nonfarm use of land. One clear trend, even in midwestern farm areas, is for more town and city workers to want homes in the countryside on plots of land. Many an old 160-acre quarter-section of farmland is now 155 acres, as a 5-acre corner has been sold for residential use, perhaps even with the former farmhouse included. These moves not only pinch off quantities of farmland, they help distort the value of farmland. In areas with recreational appeal, the effect is magnified.

The infiltration of nonfarm people into farming areas also always has the potential of increasing pressures on farmers for control of noxious smells, noise, dust, or farm chemicals. Vandalism is a growing threat. Each year there is more insistence on land-use regulations or special tax provisions to encourage the uncompromised continuance of farms. In short, farming in localities where most of the people no longer are farm people—even in rural areas—adds one more dimension of complications to a business that has become increasingly technical, large scale, and specialized in so many other ways.

Yet, there is surely no turning back. The peaking out of large-scale urbanization is occurring in other advanced nations—for example, in northern and Western Europe—just as it has in the United States. It is not something transient, readily altered, or caused by peculiarly American circumstances. If it were somehow possible to channel American agriculture into a large number of smaller but viable farms and ranches, then the growing imbalance between the role of agriculture and nonagriculture in rural areas might lessen somewhat. But the die is essentially cast. The modernization of the countryside through electricity, water supply, roads, communications, and education, coupled with growing disenchantment with mega-scale urban areas, creates favorable conditions for further nonagricultural and demographic growth in rural and small-town areas.

It is well to stress again that major regional differences exist in the role of agriculture in rural areas, but all parts of the country have seen a greater part of their employment and income stem from nonfarm businesses in recent years. One may debate the balance of benefits versus social costs that have resulted from this trend. There is no debate about the essential and inevitable nature of the trend, once farm employment began to decline and rural areas become attractive for other industries or for residential purposes.

9

Subregional Variations in Population Change Within the Nonmetropolitan South

One can generalize about a region as large and diverse as the South only at the risk of giving false impressions about some parts of the region. Within this qualification, I think the most important aspect of recent population trends in the nonmetropolitan South is the greatly diminished extent and amount of net out-migration and population decline. The societal lag in awareness of the extent and impact of southern out-migration has left an impression not yet dispelled that out-movement was at its peak in the 1960s. The peak of out-movement had in fact passed before extensive public attention to rural out-migration and questions of population distribution surfaced in the mid- and late 1960s.

During the 1960s, private nonagricultural wage and salary employment increased by 50 percent in the predominantly rural counties of the South, compared with a growth of 45 percent in the predominantly urban counties. A view of the nonmetropolitan South based on past conceptions of universal agricultural and mining dependence and decline, unrelieved by growth of manufacturing or service industries, is by 1972 outmoded and unrealistic.

It is too late to "save the cities" by stemming rural out-migration, as rural fundamentalist-oriented statements still seem to urge, for the bulk of the potential displacement has taken place. By the same token, it is too late to continue to talk in urban fundamentalist terms, which imply that southern nonmetropolitan areas either are beyond hope of development, or do not need it anyway if people will only commute, or should not really want the kinds of development that they do get. Demographically and economically,

Adapted from "The Nature and Significance of Recent Population Trends in the South, With Particular Reference to Nonmetropolitan Areas," prepared for the Office of Economic Opportunity, dated July 1972.

the actual situation is mixed in character—always an unpopular condition. Out-migration *is* still significant, but without currently being critically high in its national impact. Nonmetropolitan economic growth is increasing and varied, although not yet sufficiently great or diffused to absorb all national population increase.

It is valid to say that average wage rates are below national norms in the southern areas where decline has ended and growth resumed. For example, in the northwestern half of Arkansas, the wages paid to nonagricultural workers covered by the Social Security Program averaged just $4,533 per worker annualized, based on the first quarter of 1970. In the west central Kentucky turnaround area, the figure was $4,972. By comparison, wages in the United States, exclusive of the thirty largest metropolitan areas, averaged $5,990 annualized in the same quarter. The differences are substantial even if one assumes somewhat lower costs of living in the rural/small-town areas compared with the U.S. average.

Because of such wage differentials, the population growth in nonmetropolitan areas associated with nonagricultural development sometimes is deprecated as undesirable, with the implication that local residents are not really wise to remain in the rural area for the sake of such jobs and might be better advised to move to a higher-wage urban area. But the recent population growth of the Ozark–Ouachita region or the lower Tennessee Valley does not stem only from natives remaining in these areas rather than migrating. Much of it is due to net in-migration, and includes many people of prime labor-force age.

For example, in the Ozark–Ouachita area there was at least a 25 percent net in-movement during the decade of persons who were twenty-five to twenty-nine years old in 1960 and thirty-five to thirty-nine in 1970. These people are still young, but old enough to be married, to have children, and to have finished their education. As migrants, they have been elsewhere and apparently have found elsewhere lacking in comparison with the totality of living conditions that they perceive in this redeveloping rural and small-city area, below-average wages notwithstanding. It is not a choice that can be casually dismissed or judged only in income terms.

So far as the southern black population is concerned, however, it is just as obvious that the improved nonagricultural job opportunities in nonmetropolitan areas have not had any major impact as yet on the propensity of blacks to remain in such areas. Given the low economic position of nonmetropolitan blacks and their high natural increase, economic development is essential to their ability to continue to live in the nonmetropolitan South, but it clearly is not sufficient. Scattered surveys indicate wide differences in the residential preferences of rural southern white and black youth, with a majority of blacks stating a preference for the city, in contrast to whites. In addition, the vast majority of southern blacks have contacts with close family members or friends in large cities that provide a ready network of migration auspices and supportive services, both economic and sociopsychological. It may be easier and more sustaining of self-esteem and peer group respect for a young black to move from the Carolina Coastal Plain to Washington or New York than to go the much shorter distance to the industrial Piedmont, where contacts may be lacking, or stay in his rural county.

The potential for further out-migration from the South or its nonmetropolitan areas is shaped by the extent of past migration and the underlying fertility of the population, as well as by employment opportunities and residential preferences. The number of children in the nonmetropolitan South has fallen from both the out-migration of young adults of childbearing age and a reduced birthrate among those remaining.

The decline in number of children has been especially noticeable in the Southern Appalachian coalfields. The number of children under five years old dropped by 40 percent in the heart of the coalfields in the 1950s and again in the 1960s. Thus, the supply of potential young adult migrants from this area is now rapidly falling and will continue to drop for at least the next twenty years. In addition, the decline in coal-mining employment finally stopped between 1969 and 1970. Adjustment to new safety regulations is creating problems in the operation of some of the smaller underground mines, but a number of large new mines are under construction and a shortage of qualified younger miners has actually developed. Thus two of the main forces that impelled outmovement from the Southern Appalachians (fertility and loss of mining jobs) are no longer operative in the way they were. Outmovement has slowed and will almost certainly recede further.

In the major counties of the Mississippi Delta and the Carolina flue-cured tobacco areas, there was very little drop in number of young black children from 1950 to 1960, but a decline of about three-eighths took place in each of these areas during the 1960s. Therefore, we can see the onset of a reduced number of black outmigrants from these areas by the late 1970s, unless the already high percentage rate of out-movement were to increase. It seems unlikely that it could increase in the Delta, where it has been very high during the cotton mechanization period. In the tobacco areas, however, the economy now stands in roughly the same relationship to labor-saving technology and slackened demand for the product as cotton did fifteen years ago. There is substantial potential for further displacement of people—particularly blacks—from the flue-cured tobacco areas. Much of this out-movement in the past has flowed up the Atlantic Coast to the major eastern cities (Washington, Baltimore, Philadelphia, New York, etc.). It is conceivable that the out-movement rates could increase in this decade as the mechanization and other crop changes proceed, thus offsetting the fact that there is a somewhat lower base population from which to draw migrants.

In the Lower Rio Grande Valley, it is only in the last ten years that a decline of births has occurred. Fertility remains high and the proximity of Mexico constantly augments the local Mexican-American population, which is the principal locus of poverty and source of out-movement. The potential for further out-migration would seem to be high for at least another fifteen years.

In the South as a whole, the potential for improved population retention in nonmetropolitan areas would seem to be good, at least east of the Great Plains. This assumes that growth of nonagricultural jobs in nonmetropolitan areas would continue to be as good as it was in the 1960s. But one must caution that much of the job growth was associated with the availability of a comparatively untapped and undemanding female labor supply whose entry into employment retarded out-migration by bolstering the income of many families. The mix of new nonmetropolitan jobs must contain a reasonable proportion of jobs for men if greater general population retention is to be attained. To affect the migration of the population groups that give receiving cities or regions the most concern, there would have to be greater entry of blacks and Mexican-Americans in particular into the nonmetropolitan southern economy.

10

Quantitative Dimensions of Decline and Stability Among Rural Communities

Our country is dotted with the remains of towns that reached their zenith generations ago—some before the Revolutionary War. Their decline has not gone unnoticed. (A century ago, for example, the

Adapted from chapter 1 in Larry R. Whiting (ed.), *Communities Left Behind: Alternatives for Development* (Ames: Iowa State University Press, 1974).

The author is grateful to Vera J. Banks, Judith A. Zelan, Dorothy A. Hull, Manuel L. Goldberg, Anna E. Lane, Gloria J. Jackson, and Peggy A. Colbert for assistance with the material presented.

Deserted farmstead, Hand County, South Dakota, c. 1974 (photo by Beale)

historian Charles Jones wrote a book-length study called *The Dead Towns of Georgia*.) Recognition of the attendant problems in declining communities, however, has been slow to develop.

Communities may decline for various reasons: natural disasters, exhaustion of natural resources, loss of transportation advantages, and loss of political status, for example. But community decline, as measured by population loss, has been at a maximum only since declining manpower needs in agriculture occurred simultaneously with forces that acted to relocate and centralize many business and community functions into larger units. Since World War I, we have had the paradoxical situation that the faster our national population has grown, the faster and more extensively our small communities have declined.

About 31 percent of all counties in the nation declined in population during the 1930s, when national population growth was low because of low birthrate and lack of immigration. As national population growth revived in the 1940s, and went even higher in the 1950s, the number of declining counties actually rose. Despite the much higher potential for growth as a result of the high birthrate of the period, 49 percent of all counties decreased in population in the 1950s as a widespread exodus to the cities occurred. Furthermore, the rate of loss among the losing counties rose. In the 1930s, less than one-third of the losing counties declined by as much as 10 percent in the decade, but in the 1950s, over half of the losers had losses of 10 percent or more. Thus, although losses occurred in many counties earlier in the century, both the extent and depth of the losses increased after the Great Depression. It is only natural that awareness and concern about the matter should emerge.

In this chapter, I consider both towns and counties, focusing generally on the North Central states and especially the West North Central ones. Although rural communities everywhere have had difficulty retaining population in modern times, the trends have by no means been identical by region.

The term *dying small town* is a common cliché. The phrase, with its sense of hopeless finality, has permeated the national consciousness, but it hampers comprehension of the problem by professional research workers, the concerned public official or layman, and the general public. Certainly there has been considerable misunderstanding in Washington over the years about the actual trends in small communities. Part of the problem is that the term *small town* lacks precise meaning. One person may use it who has in mind the grain elevator, creamery, and railroad-siding hamlet of his Corn Belt youth, and his listener may be a big-city native to whom any place of fewer than 50,000 people is a "small town." The distinction is critical, because small towns of different sizes have fared differently, and variations of even several hundred in average population are associated with differences in retention of population. These variations in turn are almost certainly related to the increased variety of services and employment available in communities as population exceeds typical threshold levels at which the support of particular services and businesses becomes feasible.

Of course, the stereotype of "the dying small town" has its kernel of truth—as most stereotypes have—but when used indiscriminately as a description of all (or even most) small places, it becomes badly misleading.

Population Change in Towns and Counties

In a cooperative project with the Economic Research Service, Glenn Fuguitt of the University of Wisconsin has compiled data on the population changes of nonmetropolitan towns. The North Central region has nearly 5,600 incorporated towns of fewer than 2,500 population located in nonmetropolitan counties. This is 30 percent of all incorporated places of all sizes nationwide. Of these rural North Central towns, 49.6 percent increased in population from 1960 to 1970 and 50.4 percent decreased. Despite a small majority of losers, the overall population in the towns increased by 4.8 percent, because the gaining towns tended to grow by larger amounts than the declining towns lost (see Table 10.1). Some 3.5 million people lived in the region's rural towns in 1970, and contrary to a general impression, the number had grown by about 160,000 in the previous ten years. Inspection of the data by size of rural place, however, shows considerable contrast between the largest places— those of 1,000 to 2,499 population—and the smallest—those of fewer than 500 population. About 64 percent of the largest places had population increases, compared with just 41 percent of the group with fewer than 500 people.

A further look at the data for towns of fewer than 1,000 people (grouped by size intervals of only 100 population each) shows that the likelihood of population retention or loss is sensitive to very small differences in population size (see Fig. 10.1). From fewer than 100 people up to 800 people, each increment of 100 population

Table 10.1 Population Change in Nonmetropolitan Rural Towns, North Central Region, 1960–70

Size of Town 1960	Number of Places	With Population Loss, 1960–70		Total Population		
	Total 1960	Number	Percentage of Total	1970 (thousands)	1960 (thousands)	Percentage Change 1960–70
All towns under 2,500 persons	5,566	2,803	50.4	3,498.4	3,339.3	4.8
1,000–2,449	1,063	383	36.0	1,750.5	1,640.1	6.7
900–999	150	50	33.3	148.8	142.5	4.4
800–899	217	91	41.9	190.5	183.7	3.7
700–799	261	101	38.7	205.6	195.5	5.2
600–699	289	118	40.8	203.7	186.9	9.0
500–599	334	146	43.7	188.9	182.3	3.6
400–499	505	241	47.7	233.6	227.0	2.9
300–399	605	324	53.6	212.9	210.6	1.1
200–299	828	493	59.5	205.8	204.4	.7
100–199	933	599	64.2	134.2	140.4	-4.4
Under 100	381	257	67.5	23.9	25.9	-7.7

Source: U.S. Census data by Department of Rural Sociology, University of Wisconsin, and Economic Research Service, U.S. Department of Agriculture.

Note: Nonmetropolitan status as of 1963. Incorporated places only. Excludes places that were incorporated or disincorporated during the decade.

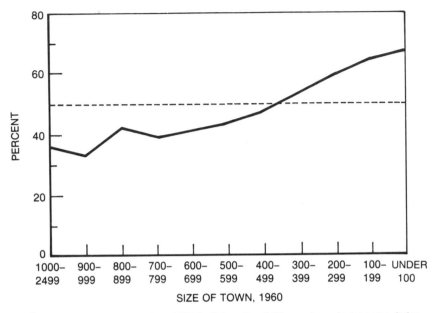

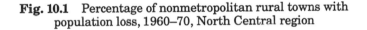

SOURCE: Unpublished data from USDA–University of Wisconsin project on population change in nonmetropolitan towns.

Fig. 10.1 Percentage of nonmetropolitan rural towns with
population loss, 1960–70, North Central region

reduces the probability of a town losing population. Among incorporated towns of fewer than 100 residents, 67 percent declined. With each additional 100 people, 3 or 4 percent fewer places declined. Only among places of fewer than 400 people were losses more common than gains. In the 400–500 size group, 48 percent lost; from 700–800, just 39 percent lost; above that point, places of just 800 to 1,000 people were only a little more likely to lose population than cities of 10,000 or 25,000 people.

Places of fewer than 1,000 in the West North Central states had a higher probability of loss than those in the East North Central group. And among West North Central towns, declines were more numerous than gains in places with fewer than 500 population.

There was no increase in the 1960s in the percentage of rural-size towns in the North Central states that lost population. The proportion losing, 50.4 percent, was remarkably similar to that in the 1950s, 50.6 percent. And places of fewer than 500 people actually showed some reduction in incidence of loss in the 1960s. East of the Mississippi River a decentralizing trend into the nonmetropolitan countryside was evident, as open country areas shifted from a 4 percent loss of population to an 8 percent gain. Such a gain means that many of the rural towns of the East North Central division have more populous trading-zone hinterlands than before. In major contrast, the open-country population of the West North Central states declined by 10 percent, nearly as large a decrease as that of the 1950s (12 percent). Although there is a sense of decline in many of the West North Central towns, the more substantial loss of population has been occurring in the open country. There has been a relative drawing-in of the West North Central rural population into the towns.

Quite aside from the reality of decline in many of the small towns of the North Central region is the fact that the decline is more visible because those states have had a much greater propensity to incorporate their rural towns than have most other states. This is particularly true in the seven North Central states west of the Mississippi River (Minnesota, Iowa, Missouri, North Dakota, South Dakota, Kansas, Nebraska). In that area, in 1960, there was a ratio of only 1,647 total rural people for each incorporated rural town. By contrast, the ratio of rural people to rural towns was 3,739 to 1 in the East North Central states, and 6,720 to 1 in the twelve southern states east of the Mississippi River. In California, the extreme case, there were more than 37,000 rural people for every incorporated rural town.

Many states simply have not incorporated small towns. In such cases, there is no measurement of population change available from the census and no formalized structure of local municipal government to experience decline and discouragement. The comparative lack of incorporated towns elsewhere is particularly true of places with fewer than 500 people. The twelve southern states referred to have three times as many rural people as the West North Central states but less than half as many incorporated places of under 500 population. The Midwest, especially in the Plains and western Corn Belt, has a much larger inventory of communities that are accustomed to an organized corporate life and therefore more sensitive to decline when it occurs.

There appear to be fourteen counties (six in Missouri, five in Kansas, and one each in Indiana, Nebraska, and Ohio) that have had consecutive population decline in every census since 1890, showing how long and unremitting an adjustment of population to

changed circumstances can be. But the more important losses that
continue to shape everyday life are probably those that have
occurred since 1940. In general, they are the heaviest declines and
have taken place since the end of the rather atypical period of the
Great Depression.

A comparison of county population changes from 1940 to 1970,
without regard to intermediate changes, shows the concentration of
the heaviest losses in the West North Central division (see Table
10.2). A handful of counties have declined by more than half in
thirty years. About 97 of the 619 counties in the West North Central region have lost 35 percent or more of their 1940 population,
but they are not closely grouped. They include most of the Flint
Hills grazing area in Kansas, the southern Sand Hills in Nebraska,
the Corn Belt margin counties along the Nebraska-Kansas border
and the Missouri-Iowa border, and many counties in western North
Dakota. Very few of the counties with heaviest losses are east of
the Mississippi River.

In general, the higher the rate of loss, the smaller the initial
average county size. Those decreasing by 35 percent or more had a
1940 average population of 10,200, those with up to 10 percent loss

Table 10.2   Population Change of Counties, 1940–70, and Average
Initial Population, North Central Region

Population 1940–70 (percent)	Number of Counties			Average Population 1940 (thousands)		
	Total	ENC	WNC	Total	ENC	WNC
Total	1,056	437	619	38.0	60.9	21.8
Loss	547	120	427	17.0	22.4	15.5
−35.0 or more	104	7	97	10.2	12.3	10.1
−20.0 to −34.9	190	29	161	16.9	19.2	16.4
−10.0 to −19.9	136	41	95	18.7	23.6	16.5
0.0 to −9.9	117	43	74	21.3	25.2	19.1
Gain	509	317	192	60.5	75.5	35.9
0.0 to 9.9	101	49	52	22.9	22.4	23.3
10.0 to 19.9	78	41	37	26.1	30.4	21.4
20.0 to 29.9	65	42	23	35.4	40.0	27.1
30.0 to 49.9	96	71	25	129.4	157.1	50.7
50.0 or more	169	114	55	69.5	76.7	54.5

Note: ENC is East North Central division, WNC is West North Central
division.

averaged 21,300 people initially, and those that gained by more than 50 percent averaged 69,500.

In the course of a decade, out-migration rates are highest for persons reaching age twenty during the period. In counties of most severe overall population loss—say, where it has dropped by 20 percent in just ten years—the net out-migration rates are often 50 percent or more for young adults. However, they are much lower for persons over thirty. In less extreme cases of loss, the out-movement of young adults will be 35 to 40 percent and that of persons over thirty will be less than 10 percent. With some exceptions, the rural communities of the North Central region are not suffering from rapid out-movement of established families but from continued loss of young adults. And this loss, extended over several decades, leads to progressively smaller numbers of established families and children.

The pattern of out-migration by age is illustrated in Figure 10.2. Part of the data relates to all counties in South Dakota that did not

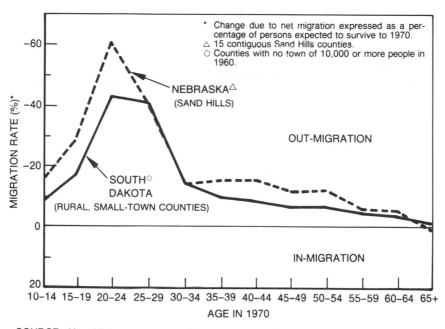

SOURCE: Unpublished data from USDA-University of Georgia net migration project.

Fig. 10.2 Net migration rates, by age, for selected Nebraska and South Dakota counties, 1960–70

have a city of 10,000 or more people in 1960. These counties experienced an overall decline of 6.6 percent in population from 1960 to 1970. For contrast, Figure 10.2 also shows migration rates for a block of fifteen counties in the Nebraska Sand Hills that averaged 15.2 percent population decline in the same decade.

In the rural and small-town counties of South Dakota, out-migration was nearly 15 percent for the 1960 population surviving to 1970. It was 43 percent for those who reached age 20–24, but less than 10 percent for all groups aged 35–39 or older.

In the Sand Hills counties, overall net out-movement amounted to nearly 20 percent. The rate reached majority proportions among youth attaining age 20–24, where 60 percent left during the ten years, and remained above 10 percent for all age groups up through persons reaching age 50–54. In this area, it is the minority of youth remaining behind who are probably most selective in character, rather than those who leave. Active displacement of population extends to people well up into middle age, where considerable personal strain may attend a move made that late in life.

Factors Inducing Population Loss

The most important factor behind the decline of population in rural areas of the North Central region has been dependence on industries with declining manpower needs—farming in particular and mining to a lesser extent. One farmer can handle a great increase in acreage with modern technology, and farmers need high volume to counteract eroding profit margins, so a major reduction in the number of farms has resulted from these forces. Mining activity has experienced the same reductions in manpower from mechanization as has farming, and in addition has had employment losses from exhaustion of deposits.

If the counties of the North Central region are grouped by degree of dependence on farm and mine employment in 1960, the association between such dependence and population retention is very clear (see Table 10.3). In the region as a whole, ninety-four counties had more than 50 percent of employed workers in agriculture (farm production work) or mining. All but six of them decreased in population during 1960–70. There were 159 counties where 40 to 49 percent of all workers were in agriculture and mining, and all but fifteen decreased in population. Only where farm and mine work dependence was less than 30 percent did half of the

Table 10.3 Population Change, 1960–70, of Counties, by Percentage of Workers Employed in Agriculture and Mining, 1960, North Central Region

Workers Employed in Agriculture and Mining 1960 (percent)	Number of Counties with		Population		
	Population Increase 1960–70	Population Decrease 1960–70	1970 (thousands)	1960 (thousands)	Change 1960–70[a] (percent)
Total	526	530	56,575.0	51,617.5	9.6
50 and over	6	88	466.8	536.1	−12.9
40–49	15	144	1,578.1	1,733.4	−9.0
30–39	64	138	2,827.2	2,870.5	−1.5
20–29	105	97	4,062.8	3,953.1	2.8
Less than 20	336	63	47,640.2	42,524.5	12.0

[a] The relationship between percentage change in population 1960–70 and percentage employed in agriculture and mining 1960 is $Y = 17.36 - .56X$ with a coefficient of determination (r^2) of .37. On the average, there was a .56 percentage-point decline in population change for every percentage-point increment in employment in agriculture and mining.

counties avoid population loss, and only where such work was less than 20 percent of all work did growth occur in the great majority of counties.

The nature of this relationship creates very different patterns of population change between the West North Central states and the East North Central states. Nearly all counties where agricultural and mining dependence were over 40 percent were in the western half of the region. Such levels of dependence make any population growth very unlikely. New jobs in other industries can rarely be developed fast enough under such conditions to offset decline in the traditional work.[1]

The Plains tier of states in the West North Central division has suffered not only from the heaviest dependency on extractive industries but also from the least relative success in obtaining alternative employment. These states (the Dakotas, Nebraska, and Kansas) had higher nonagricultural job growth in the predominantly urban counties rather than in the rural ones, contrary to the national pattern; and the growth rate of the rural counties was only 25 percent, compared with 41 percent east of the Mississippi River and 51 percent in the South. The Plains tier of the West North Central states has not been able to obtain significant rural job development, despite the modest absolute increase that would be needed to produce rapid percentage gains from a small base.

Unlike large areas of the South, the out-movement from the small communities of the North Central region is not generally associated with poverty or race. Except from Indian communities and parts of southern Missouri, the out-movement generally comes from areas of high educational standards, good median incomes, and reasonable housing conditions. In effect, the rural areas of the Midwest have avoided poverty by exporting their youth.

---

1. In the United States in general, the more rural counties did succeed in obtaining the highest growth rate of private nonagricultural wage and salary jobs during the 1960s. For example, the entirely or predominantly rural counties of the United States as a whole had a 43 percent increase in such jobs, compared to a growth of 34 percent in the predominantly urban counties. Rural nonagricultural job growth was especially high in the South, where the rural counties averaged better than 50 percent growth in these jobs in just ten years. Nonagricultural job growth levels in the East North Central states resembled those of the United States as a whole, with the more rural areas having rapid growth. West of the Mississippi River, the average nonagricultural growth rates were lower, and the comparative advantage of higher growth in the more rural counties was absent. As a result, a county with a given level of agricultural or mining dependence was less likely to decline in the East North Central states than in the western group.

However, the pressures on the supply of jobs within the region have not been equal. There are substantial differences in child-bearing patterns that in turn produce different potential rates of labor force increase. In some areas, such as northern Missouri, southern Iowa, or southeastern Kansas, people have had comparatively small families. In such areas, only a moderate rate of job growth is needed to cope with the oncoming labor force. But some other areas of different cultural and religious background have childbirth rates sufficient to double the population each generation. In these counties, the labor force would grow by more than 25 percent in the 1970s if none of the young people left. Even a partial slowdown of the out-migration rate would soon result in local population gain.

Effects of Decline

Data that measure the effects of decline on rural communities are not regularly reported and therefore not easy to quantify. But several things can be said. As noted earlier, the typical process of decline is for young adults to leave the community in large proportions as they finish high school and not return. As successive classes of young people leave, the average age of the community rises and the age structure becomes rather distorted. Eventually, people in their fifties or sixties may come to outnumber those in their twenties or thirties. The birthrate begins to fall because of the shortage of young adults, and the population then ages even faster. If the median age of the population passes thirty-five years, deaths are likely to begin to exceed births, and a condition occurs in which the community declines in population both from migration and because there are more deaths than births.

The average age in hundreds of midwestern rural towns is now over forty years, and in many it is over fifty years.[2] Where the latter figure applies, towns are usually small hamlets of just several hundred people, but median ages of over forty occur in many larger places and in some entire counties. The median age of the entire U.S. population, by contrast, is twenty-eight years.

2. In the three North Central states for which age data of small towns are published—Wisconsin, Minnesota, and South Dakota—ninety places had populations with a median age of fifty years or more in 1970. Nine of these had populations with a median age of over sixty years. All of the latter were places of fewer than 200 population.

Where the median age is up into the mid-forties, the proportion of people who are sixty-five years old and over is one-fourth or more of the total population. This is a far higher proportion of older people than is normal, and it has far-reaching effects on the context of life in such communities—for both the old and the young.

With the relative absence of families of childbearing age, the average number of people per household (or per occupied housing unit) is somewhat low. For example, the nonmetropolitan towns of fewer than 1,000 population in Wisconsin, Minnesota, and South Dakota have an average household size of 2.87 persons, compared with 3.21 persons in those states as a whole. But more significant than this is the fact that average household size is declining generally, even in towns without population loss. People live longer, so we have more older husband-wife families where the children have grown up and left. People are more financially independent in old age now and are less likely to move in with their children after retirement or even after widowhood than in the past. And in the younger age groups, people are less likely to remain in the parental household until marriage. The result of these factors is that small average household size requires more occupied housing units than before to accommodate a given population. Nationally, households are increasing at a more rapid rate than total population, so a community that is decreasing in population is not necessarily decreasing in numbers of households.

It might come as a surprise to many to learn that although the towns of fewer than 1,000 population in Wisconsin, Minnesota, and South Dakota had an overall decline of 0.7 percent in population from 1960 to 1970, they had an increase of 5.3 percent in the number of occupied housing units. And whereas 62 percent of them had population declines, only 42 percent had household declines. Even among towns as small as 300–399 people, the average trends of population and household change were in opposite directions. These differences are not extreme, but they do have significance. The housing function—and the goods and services that it supports—has held up better in the small communities than total population changes would indicate.

It is widely assumed by locals and outsiders alike that many of the brightest young people leave. It is certainly true that the bulk of those leave who seek a college education or specialized occupations. Some return after college; many do not. Many of the careers open to college graduates are disproportionately located in urban areas. Throughout the Midwest, the major current educational difference between urban and rural adults younger than fifty is the proportion who have gone to college, not the proportion who have completed high school. High school enrollment rates for sixteen- and seventeen-year-olds are generally higher in rural areas than in urban ones.

But the out-movement is not limited to the more ambitious. It has taken so large a proportion of young people, especially west of the Mississippi River, that all economic and ability classes are represented. In addition, it is clear that the educational attainment of rural populations has risen rapidly, regardless of the effects of out-migration. As an example, in Iowa the median education of the rural population in 1960 was 1.5 years less than that of the urban; by 1970 both medians had risen, but the difference had been reduced to 0.1 year by the more rapid rural rise.

Further, it cannot be said that decline of population has prevented income increases. Grouping counties in the West North Central states by population change shows that those losing population had lower average family incomes than those gaining population (see Table 10.4). This accords with the typical heavy dependence on agriculture of losing counties and shows an income rationality in the population movement. But as a class, the declining counties experienced more rapid rates of income growth from 1959 to 1969 than did those where population was increasing. The reasons for this are not clear from the information available. The comparative returns from the 1959 and 1969 crop and livestock years could be a factor. So could the increase in employment of women in rural areas, or the shifting of the adult population in de-

Table 10.4   Median Income of Counties in West North Central States, 1960 and 1970, by Population Change, 1960–70

Population Change 1960–70	Number of Counties	Median Family Income		
		1970 (dollars)	1960 (dollars)	Change (percent)
Total[a]	619	8,985	5,154	74.3
10% gain or more	77	10,696	6,239	71.4
0–9.9% gain	127	8,835	5,237	68.7
0–9.9% loss	209	7,652	4,278	78.9
10–14.9% loss	108	6,877	3,766	82.6
15% loss or more	98	6,531	3,760	73.7

[a]Total includes St. Louis City. Values are partly estimated for counties with 15 percent loss or more.

clining counties toward middle ages, where income is typically at its peak. Whatever the factors, counties with decreasing population typically have an income disadvantage relative to those with increasing population in the same region. But the demographic decrease has apparently not prevented progress in attaining higher incomes and narrowing the relative income gap.

The Future

In one sense, the 1970–80 decade is the last chance that many small communities will have in the immediate future to stabilize their populations. Despite the overall population loss, most small communities in 1970 had fairly large numbers of youth ten to nineteen years old as a result of the high birthrates of the 1950s. In both the East and West North Central divisions, there are more rural youth of this age than there were in either 1960 or 1950.

However, the out-migration of rural adults who would now have children under ten years old, coupled with the decline in the birthrate of the 1960s, has greatly undercut the number of very young children. In 1970, there were only 76 percent as many rural children under five years old in the East North Central states as there were in the ten-to-fourteen age group, and only 67 percent as many in the Plains Tier of the West North Central states. The rapid decrease in the birthrate since 1970 is further reducing these proportions. Thus, once the present cohorts of rural youths now ten years and older are out of school, the subsequent groups leaving school will be successively smaller for many years to come. If those youths reaching adulthood in the 1970s do not feel any greater attraction to remaining in the rural and small-town environment than did those in the 1960s, population declines in the Midwest, especially in the western half, could become more widespread, because there will be fewer births to offset the out-migration.

In the West North Central states, the proportion of jobs that are agricultural (plus mining) continues to be high in many counties. Even after the farm consolidations of the 1960s, more than half of the West North Central counties still have more than 30 percent of their workers in farm production work. Under the pattern of economic development in recent years, such a proportion is usually too high to permit any population increase. Although I would expect somewhat faster nonextractive industry and business growth in the 1970s in these counties, it is unlikely to occur at a pace sufficient to avoid further population declines in counties or towns that are already low in population. If the statistical relationship between extractive industry employment and population change observed in the region in the 1960s were to persist in the 1970s, about 280 West North Central counties might expect to decrease in population in the 1970s. This would be less than the 415 that decreased in the 1960s. The interplay of nonextractive development trends and the birthrate will determine whether the actual number proves to be larger or smaller than this projection.

The East North Central states no longer have high exposure to population decline from lowered agricultural and mining manpower needs. Only 7 percent of the counties in this division now have even one-fifth of their workers in farm or mine work. Some areas in this division will be susceptible to population decrease, but it is just as likely to be from problems with their manufacturing mix or movement out of central city counties as from agricultural or mining trends.

Many rural areas of the North Central region that have extensive districts unsuited to agriculture and well suited to recreation or retirement have been attracting population rapidly. This is especially true in the Missouri Ozarks and the Lower Peninsula of Michigan, and it is partly true in northern Wisconsin and Minnesota. This trend has reversed long-standing population declines in many counties and small towns. Given the increasing prevalence of steady retirement incomes among growing numbers of older people, plus the increased emphasis on recreation activity, this trend will almost certainly spread to additional areas, particularly where there are lakes—natural or otherwise—and cheap land. This is a force that is bringing many urban natives and former rural people back into rural areas, but it cannot be expected to affect all rural areas equally or materially.

The forces of population spread and redistribution that characterize most midwestern metropolitan cities affect villages of fewer than 500 people to some extent, just as they do places of several thousand. Such places may become attractive for cheap housing or as a commuting refuge from urban congestion. But away from the metropolitan perimeters, I foresee a continuation of the existing pattern of predominant population loss among very small places. Even as early as 1951, Chittick found that half of the towns in South Dakota with 250 to 500 population did not have drugstores, fuel dealers, or household appliance stores; two-fifths lacked banks;

and one-third had no eating places.[3] Such communities may be
incorporated and have a sense of identity and a desire for per-
petuation, but they are not generally centers with an adequate
minimal range of urban services. Their origin was often the product of a limited span of years in between the railroad and automotive eras. They typically have little to attract industry. Their prospects for active survival may be dim except to serve as satellite
residential and retail nodes, dependent economically on larger
towns.

But by the same token, I am impressed with the ability of a
majority of places of more than 500 people to retain their population. The forces that impelled metropolitan concentration of industry have been weakened, especially for manufacturing. There are
many factors persuading firms to seek nonmetropolitan locations, if
not for their headquarters then at least for branch plants. The
cities have lost some of their urbanity and the rural areas have lost
much rusticity. Especially among people who have finished the
wandering and questing period of post-high school youth, there is
an increasing willingness—if I interpret both polls and events
correctly—to live in smaller-scale communities. This may be most
difficult to translate into economic feasibility in the West North
Central states. But the potential for demographic stability after
the present inevitable period of transition to lower population levels is evident in many areas.

<hr>

3. Douglas Chittick, *Growth and Decline of South Dakota Trade Centers,
1901–51*, Bulletin 448, Agricultural Experiment Station, South Dakota State College, Brookings, May 1955, p. 44.

11
Rural Minority Populations: Their Growth and Distribution

The racial and ethnic composition of rural and small-town America has never been an exact replica of urban America, but the nature of the differences between them has gradually changed. The tenor and origin of most of the eastern seaboard settlements was English, but with a leavening of other people well before the Revolutionary period. Some were also British, such as the Welsh or Scotch-Irish who came in through Philadelphia. Others, such as the Dutch of New York or the Swedes in the lower Delaware Valley, had settled independently before the British had extended their hegemony. French Huguenots were common in South Carolina, and many Germans were attracted to Pennsylvania, from which they fanned out into the Great Valley and parts of the Piedmont. Among them were the conservative Mennonite, Old Order Amish, and Brethren groups with their strong attachment to agriculture. The French were firmly planted in Louisiana, and in the southwest, the Spanish had moved far up the Rio Grande and the California coast. Simultaneously, from the early years of European settlement, blacks from Africa had been brought in, usually as slaves. With the exception of minor numbers in the Hudson Valley and southern New Jersey, their use in farming—and thus their rural location—was southern.

In the wave of mid- and late nineteenth-century immigration, large numbers of German agriculturalists permeated the Midwest and were joined by Scandinavians and western Slavs. Given the reputation of the Catholic Irish as city dwellers today, there were surprisingly large numbers of Irish farm settlements. Rural and small-town mining districts attracted a wide variety of nationali-

Adapted from the chapter "Race and Ethnicity," in Glenn V. Fuguitt, David L. Brown, and Calvin L. Beale, *Rural and Small Town America*, a volume in the series *The Population of the United States in the 1980s*. Copyright 1988, forthcoming, The Russell Sage Foundation. Used by permission of The Russell Sage Foundation.

ties, including southern Slavs, Hungarians, Finns, Italians, and Cornish, as well as most of the other groups mentioned above. And throughout the period there were the indigenous Indian peoples, some of whom were settled and in close contact with the white population, while others led traditional lives and were not even counted in the census until 1890. All but a few were rural.

By World War I, the period of rural settlement was essentially over. There were few suitable unoccupied lands still to be cultivated and the era of uncontrolled immigration had nearly ended. Rural population exceeded 50 million for the first time in 1920 and has not yet reached 60 million. Racially, 85 percent of rural people were white in 1910, shortly before the slowdown in rural growth occurred. All but a small fraction of the rest were black. Slightly over half (52 percent) of all whites lived in rural areas as of 1910, but blacks were still heavily rural (73 percent).

Rural Blacks

In a manner perhaps unexpected at the time, the black rural population reached its peak size of 7,143,000 in 1910 and then began to diminish. The lure of urban jobs during World War I, the early depredations of the boll weevil on cotton farming, and increasing erosion of older cotton lands were factors leading to an out-movement from rural areas that lowered the black rural population by about a quarter million by 1920. The rural white population, however, gradually increased.

These patterns continued until 1940, when a pell-mell exodus of rural blacks began. Initially, that exodus was associated with war-time job opportunities, but it was fostered thereafter by the radical modernization of southern farming, the abandonment of the former tenant farming system that had long been the main support of rural blacks, and the sheer momentum of the movement away from the poverty and social suppression that was the common black experience in the rural south. As a result of these trends, the rural black population had declined to only 3,901,000 by 1980 and made up only 6.5 percent of the total rural population, compared with 14.3 percent in 1910. In part because of black out-movement, whites had risen to 90.8 percent of the rural total by 1980, compared with 80.4 percent in urban areas.

The regional location of rural blacks is still essentially what it was after the Civil War. In 1880, 94 percent of rural blacks lived in the South; in 1980, 93 percent still did so. The vast migration of blacks out of the South to the North and West was destined almost exclusively for urban places. There has been some dispersal of blacks into rural areas outside metropolitan cities or associated with military bases or other institutions, but it is slight. Rural blacks are concentrated in the Coastal Plain from Maryland to eastern Texas and, to a lesser extent, in the Piedmont. There were still eighty-one nonmetropolitan counties in 1980 in which blacks constituted a majority of the population, although this is only about three-tenths the number of such counties at the beginning of the century. At the extreme, there were eight nonmetropolitan counties in 1980 in which blacks comprised over 70 percent of the population.

Many of the conditions that prompted rural blacks to depart have ended, such as mechanization of cotton and other row crop farming or legal racial segregation, or else have greatly improved, such as having political participation or access to occupations not previously open to blacks. The rate of decrease in the southern rural black population in the 1970s (7.5 percent) was less than half that of the 1960s (17.0 percent), although some of the reduced loss may have resulted simply from better enumeration in the 1980 Census. Some growth in the movement of blacks into nonmetropolitan communities from metropolitan areas has taken place. Whereas the 1980 Census showed 354,000 nonmetropolitan blacks who had lived in a metropolitan area five years earlier, the 1970 Census showed 234,000.[1]

The discussion of historical trends is presented for the most part in terms of urban and rural, for these categories can be applied to the earlier censuses. As of 1980, the nonmetropolitan black population of 5,017,000 was considerably larger than the rural population (see Table 11.1). Particularly in the South and the Midwest, the number of blacks living in nonmetropolitan urban places is larger than the number in outlying rural parts. This is not true of whites, except in the West. This difference reflects a greater propensity for blacks to urbanize, even in small cities, plus the

---

1. Strict comparability of these numbers is not possible, because metropolitan areas were somewhat more liberally defined in 1980 and because nonresponses to the migration question were not allocated in 1970. These differences work in offsetting ways, however, and it is my view that the trend indicated is real and not overstated.

Table 11.1 Race and Spanish Origin of Population, 1980

Race or Spanish Origin	Metropolitan			Nonmetropolitan		
	Total	Urban	Rural	Total	Urban	Rural
Total (thousands)	169,431	145,443	23,988	57,115	21,608	35,507
White	138,064	115,719	22,335	50,307	18,602	31,705
Black	21,478	20,405	1,073	5,017	2,189	2,828
Indian, Eskimo, Aleut	696	558	138	724	182	542
Asian and Pacific Islander[a]	3,198	3,087	111	302	175	127
Other[b]	5,994	5,674	321	764	459	305
Spanish origin[c]	12,795	12,084	711	1,814	1,050	764
Total (percent)	100.0	100.0	100.0	100.0	100.0	100.0
White	81.5	79.6	93.1	88.1	86.1	89.3
Black	12.7	14.0	4.5	8.8	10.1	8.0
Indian, Eskimo, Aleut	.4	.4	.6	1.3	.8	1.5
Asian and Pacific Islander[a]	1.9	2.1	.5	.5	.8	.4
Other[b]	3.5	3.9	1.3	1.3	2.1	.9
Spanish origin[c]	7.6	8.3	3.0	3.2	4.9	2.2

[a] Japanese, Chinese, Filipino, Korean, Asian Indian, Vietnamese, Hawaiian, Guamanian, Samoan.

[b] Predominantly persons who wrote in any of various Hispanic entries in the race item. Also includes Asian and Pacific Islanders such as Thai, Pakistani, or Cambodian not listed in footnote a.

[c] Persons of Spanish origin may be of any race.

overwhelming presence of whites among people who disperse into the still rural but incipiently suburban territory around large urbanized areas. Expressed another way, within the total universe of nonmetropolitan or rural population, black representation is greatest in the nonmetropolitan urban population (10.1 percent), next largest in the nonmetropolitan rural population (8.0 percent), and least among metropolitan rural residents (4.5 percent).

Rural Hispanics

In the 1930 Census, Mexicans were enumerated as a separate racial category, a step that caused enough resentment to preclude its reuse in 1940. Since the count was limited to persons of Mexican birth or parentage, it was incomplete, for there were numerous people of early Mexican origin whose families had been in the United States for several generations by 1930, such as most of the "Hispanos" in the Upper Rio Grande valley.

By 1950, there was sufficient new interest that the census schedules in the five southwestern states of Arizona, California, Colorado, New Mexico, and Texas were inspected to identify white persons of Spanish surname. Although minor clusters of Mexicans were known to exist outside these states—often associated with industrial, railroad, or farm employment—it was commonplace knowledge that those five states contained the vast majority of persons of Mexican background. Some 770,000 rural Hispanics were identified in this manner, accounting for a little more than 1 percent of the U.S. rural population, but 12.6 percent of the rural population of the Southwest.

By 1970, the rapidly growing size and diversified character of Hispanics in the United States resulted in inclusion of a separate nationwide sample question on Spanish origin. This approach counted 1,160,000 such persons in rural areas, of whom 692,000, or 60 percent, were in the five southwestern states. Although statistical procedures in the 1950 and 1970 censuses differed, it is likely that the lower count of rural Hispanics in the Southwest in 1970 reflected at least some real decrease in population. Many of the rural and small-town counties having large numbers of Hispanics in 1950 had heavy out-migration over the next twenty years. There was a surge of urbanization among southwestern Hispanics, much like that of blacks in the same period. Some of the rather surprisingly high proportion of rural Hispanics counted in other

states appears invalid, associated with response problems stemming from schedule design, affecting people in the southern and
central states. But much of it is a product of the gradual diffusion
of Mexican-Americans into other regions, and of the rapid entry of
the Hispanics other than Mexicans into the country from 1950 to
1970.

In 1980, the same technique of asking about Spanish origin was
used in the Census, but on a complete count basis. A similar problem of spurious entries arising from misunderstanding of the question arose, giving somewhat inflated results in some areas, but this
problem is negligible in the national context. A total of 1,475,000
rural Hispanics was enumerated in 1980, an implied increase of 27
percent, far above the growth of 11 percent in the total national
rural population. Despite their rapid growth in the rural setting in
the 1970s, Hispanics were still only 2.5 percent of all rural
residents. Urban areas accounted for 90 percent of all Hispanics,
making them one of the most urban elements of the American people. Much Hispanic growth has come from immigration in recent
years. Although the presence of Mexican immigrants in farm work
is well known, especially as migratory laborers, Hispanic immigrants into the United States go in heavily disproportionate
numbers to metropolitan urban areas. Of Hispanics coming into
the country from abroad from 1975 to 1980, 94 percent lived in
urban areas in 1980, and 93 percent were in metropolitan areas.

Although only 2.5 percent of the rural population, Hispanics
nonetheless are so concentrated as to be the majority of the population in thirty-two nonmetropolitan counties (mostly in southern
and southwestern Texas). At the extreme, three counties are more
than 90 percent Hispanic—a higher degree of local "minority" dominance than in any of the black majority counties in the Southeast.

As with blacks, the nonmetropolitan population exceeded the
rural among Hispanics in 1980. Nonmetropolitan Hispanics numbered 1,814,000. In the dry Southwest, people of all races are typically more concentrated in towns than in the open country, but
within these states, this pattern is more true of Hispanics than
other races. Their comparative lack of participation in farming as
operators surely contributes to this pattern, although it is not a full
explanation.

The Hispanic rural or nonmetropolitan population is distinctive
for its continued high involvement in agricultural work. Some 28
percent of employed rural Hispanic men were in agriculture in
1980, far higher than the 12 to 13 percent found among whites and

blacks. However, only one-twelfth of the Hispanic men in agriculture were operators; the vast majority were hired laborers.

Rural Hispanics are also distinctive among racial and ethnic groups in that nearly half live in metropolitan areas. Many Hispanics live and work in large agricultural counties that have developed small metropolitan cities by the sheer volume of employment generated by the local scale of intensive farming, or that have large farming districts still surviving around growing nonagricultural urbanization. Examples are areas such as Phoenix, Arizona; Bakersfield, Fresno, Monterey, Riverside, and Tulare, California; Greeley, Colorado; Brownsville, Harlingen, and McAllen, Texas; and Yakima, Washington.

Two-thirds of the nationwide growth in the Hispanic rural population from 1970 to 1980 was registered in California and Texas, which also had a majority of the increase in urban Hispanics. Some of the increase probably derives from improved completeness of enumeration, but both states have had a heavy influx of Hispanic immigrants, both legal and illegal.

Nationally, Puerto Ricans and Cubans are the largest Hispanic population groups after Mexicans, amounting to nearly one-fifth of all persons of Spanish origin. They are an extraordinarily urban people, however, with only 3 percent living in rural areas. As a result, they constitute only 5 percent of all rural Hispanics.

Given the concentration of rural or small-town Hispanics in a rapidly developing region (the Southwest), plus the continued economic and demographic pressure for emigration from adjacent Mexico, the number and importance of Hispanics in the rural and related population will almost certainly grow further.

Indians and Alaskan Natives

In 1910, when a special Indian schedule was included in the census, 254,000 rural Indians were counted, representing an astonishing 95 percent of the total Indian population. Indians were then and remain now the most rural of the nation's major racial groups. In the century after the Revolutionary War, the assignment of Indian tribes to reservations and the forcible movement of many of them from the East and South to locations west of the Mississippi led to a greater degree of concentration of them in certain localities than otherwise would have occurred. But little urbanization occurred. The way of life was rural and often traditional.

Indians seem rarely to have been enumerated at similar levels of completeness in any two consecutive censuses in recent history, but since 1970 their number has risen rapidly, especially in the cities. Their total count in 1980 was 72 percent higher than that of 1970, making it all too obvious that improved enumeration, or heightened positive image of Indian origin, or other factors had produced a statistical increase that was far beyond the realm of reality. The growth from excess of births over deaths among Indians from 1970 to 1980 was very high (27 percent) but equal to only three-eighths of the total purported Indian growth. Immigration was insignificant, with only 2 percent of the Indian population being foreign born in 1980. Most of the enumerated increase was in urban areas, where a doubling of Indians is implied. As a result, over half of all Indians (53 percent) were found to be urban, the first census to show an urban majority. But a growth rate of 48 percent is implied in rural areas, where the Indian population rose from 437,000 in 1970 to 645,000 in 1980. This, too, is well beyond that possible from natural increase.

Much of the enumerated increase in rural Indians from 1970 to 1980 was registered in states with no reservations or other established Indian communities. In Arkansas, for example, persons counted as Indians in rural areas rose nearly sixfold, from 862 to 4,993. In Georgia, they quadrupled, from 731 to 2,854.

Four states reported at least 50,000 rural Indians: Arizona with 105,000, Oklahoma with 85,000, New Mexico with 75,000, and North Carolina with 50,000. Arizona and New Mexico together account for 28 percent of the national total. They contain most of the reservation area of the largest tribe, the Navajo, as well as several other sizable groups, such as the Apache, Papago, and the various Pueblo tribes. There is a wide range in degree of acculturation or proximity to the white-dominated urban culture in these states. But in general the major reservations contain rather few non-Indians, and the people persist in use of the native languages. For instance, 95 percent of the 100,000 residents of the Navajo reservation are Indian, and 92 percent of them speak the Indian language at home.

In Oklahoma, some tribes were native to that area at the time of white intrusion. In its prestatehood days, though, Oklahoma had the distinction of being the principal territory where tribes or portions of tribes were relocated from states to the east. It is perhaps best known as the home of five southeastern tribes—the Cherokee, Chickasaw, Choctaw, Creek, and Seminole. There were several smaller groups as well. Some of the resettled groups had much white and, to a lesser extent, black admixture. They were allowed a large measure of nationhood and self-government for a while; but unlike the lands of the large tribes of the Southwest, their lands were ultimately opened to white settlement and ownership, after the Indian families were allotted homestead-size parcels in individual ownership. Thus the major tribes lost collective tribal ownership of their former "nations," and the Indians lived in much greater propinquity to the rest of the population than was generally true in the Southwest or the Northern Plains.

The situation in North Carolina differs. There, the majority of the state's 50,000 rural Indians are people of uncertain origin, living in the Coastal Plain, whose tradition of Indian ancestry is strong, but whose language, religion, and other cultural identifiers were lost generations ago. The largest group is the Lumbee. Their existence was unknown, except locally, until the Civil War and Reconstruction period, when they came in conflict first with Confederate and then with Union authorities. Until the early 1950s they lacked any federal recognition. Their livelihood was based on farming, but, like other rural people in the area, most have now gone into other work.

Other principal locations of rural Indian settlement are the Northern Plains states (South Dakota, Montana, and North Dakota), with 76,000 in total, and California and Washington. Eleven U.S. counties have Indian majorities, five of them in South Dakota, where the rural Sioux presence continues to grow.

Other native minorities are the Eskimo and Aleut in Alaska, both of whom are still predominantly rural, and the Hawaiians in Hawaii. The rural Eskimo and Aleuts are both concentrated along the coasts. The Hawaiian population has become largely urban, by about a 4 to 1 margin.

Asians

Americans of Asiatic descent are exceptionally urban. Although much of the early immigration was for agricultural work, especially in Hawaii, by 1980, all of the largest six groups of Asian and Pacific origin were more than 90 percent urban. There are more than 250,000 of each group—Japanese, Chinese, Filipinos, Koreans, Asian Indians, and Vietnamese. With the exception of the Japanese, they were also more than 90 percent metropolitan. Only in Hawaii do they have any substantial rural demographic presence, where the Japanese and Filipinos between them account for three-eighths of the rural population.

Like urban residents, rural Americans are of diverse racial and national origins. They differ most from urban people in that rural areas contain a much smaller percentage of each of the three largest racial or ethnic minorities (blacks, Hispanics, and Asians plus Pacific Islanders). These three groups combined (including a negligible amount of double counting of Hispanics with the others) amounted to just 9.4 percent of the rural population and 12.5 percent of the nonmetropolitan population, whereas they were 18.9 of all urbanites and 22.1 percent of the metropolitan population. Further, the disparity is growing as blacks continue to register loss or little growth in rural and small-town settings, and Hispanics and Asians increase, but not nearly so rapidly as in urban areas. Thus social and economic issues related to the progress of these groups do not, on average, have the same proportionate immediacy and saliency in rural and small-town communities as they do in larger areas. But the geographic distribution of these minorities is so uneven that in most of the southern third of the nation, blacks and Hispanics constitute large fractions or even majorities of the rural populace. They are almost totally absent in many other areas. Hispanics seem to be making more of a gradual penetration of rural or nonmetropolitan areas beyond their original heartland than blacks.

The Indian population is a major exception to the dominant metropolitan urbanism of racial minorities. In 1980, for the first time, a slight majority of Indians lived in urban places, and this proportion is almost certain to grow; but the existence of reservations and the rural, even isolated, character of most of them ensures a continued rural base for Indians. It can still be said that a majority (about 60 percent) of Indians live in rural or nonmetropolitan America, whereas none of the other three minorities noted above has as much as 20 percent of its numbers outside metropolitan urban communities.

12

Notes on Visit to the Alabama Creek Indians

In early 1965, I was called by an official of the Bureau of Indian Affairs (BIA) who asked whether I had ever heard of a group of people in Alabama who claimed to be Creek Indians. No one at BIA knew of them, but the people insisted that they were descendants of Creeks who had managed to remain behind in Alabama when the federal government removed that tribe to Oklahoma in the 1830s. The Oklahoma Creeks had filed a claim for compensation for the land they lost when their ancestors were forced to move, and the Alabama people asserted that if an award was to be granted they should share in it.

I knew of the group and assured BIA that from what I had read of the community they were indeed authentic Creeks. I then quickly pulled together a brief account for BIA from records in the National Archives and a rereading of the published notes of a visit made to Alabama in 1941 by an anthropologist, Frank Speck. My curiosity was whetted, though, and later that year, I went to Alabama and, from April 26 through 30, I visited the Creek Indian descendants in Escambia and Monroe counties.

I flew to Mobile on the 26th and worked at the public library that evening. There I found several useful references from old histories plus more recent newspaper clippings. On the 27th I drove to Bay Minette, the county seat of Baldwin County, where I worked with Court House records of wills, marriages, and land titles for the period before 1870. That afternoon I drove over into Escambia County, located the Indian settlement from the directions given in Frank Speck's article,[1] and then drove over to Brewton, the county seat. The following day, Wednesday, I worked on the Court House records of Escambia County at Brewton for the period after 1870

Published here for the first time. Excerpt of full notes.
1. "Notes on Social and Economic Conditions among the Creek Indians of Alabama in 1941," *America Indigena* 7:3 (July 1947).

and interviewed the County Home Demonstration agent and a woman in charge of the office at the County Health Department. That afternoon I went back over to the Indian settlement, where I made contact with several families, including their so-called Medicine Man, Norman McGhee. Norman took me over to meet the Chief, Calvin McGhee, and I had a long conversation with him. The following day, Thursday, I spent mostly in Monroe County, where I checked Court House records at Monroeville, interviewed the county sheriff, who is an Indian, and visited several of the Weatherford descendants in the southern part of the county. That evening I came back to the Indian settlement, where the Chief had brought a number of families out to meet me. On Friday the 30th, I spent the morning with the Chief, other members of his family, and two women who had come up from Pensacola, Florida. In the afternoon I drove back to Mobile, taking Norman McGhee with me. Altogether, I saw about seventy-five of the Indians in Escambia County, meeting about thirty of them personally, and saw and visited with four Indians from three different households in Monroe County.

The Escambia County Indians

In Escambia County, Alabama, about 500 persons were enumerated as Indian in the 1960 Census. Almost all of them lived out in the country north of the town of Atmore. There are certainly other persons in the county of known partial Indian descent who were not enumerated as Indian in the census.

The country occupied by the Indians is generally among the most level and most suitable for agriculture of any of the sections of Escambia County. There is considerable cultivation of potatoes, rye, soybeans, and cotton. Although many of the Indians do some farming, few have enough land or resources to make their living full-time at agriculture. The men work at such jobs as cutting and hauling pulpwood, or doing manual work at industrial plants around Atmore, or even commuting to employment every day in Pensacola and Mobile. Speck, in his 1941 visit, found some of them working in the shipyard in Mobile, and this practice continues to the present day. Some of the women work at the textile mill in Atmore. In addition, the Indians have for many years engaged in agricultural labor. They pick potatoes down in Baldwin County, as well as in their local area, and also harvest pecans locally.

Furthermore, for many years they have done migratory farm work, following the potato and tomato seasons up north. Areas that were specifically mentioned were the eastern shore of Virginia, northern Ohio, and Wisconsin. The Chief and the Medicine Man have both done this. In recent years, some of the Indians have begun to take industrial work in various places up north that they have become familiar with from their migrant farm labor trips. Within the last three years, several of the McGhee families have moved to Antigo, Wisconsin. Housing among the Escambia Creeks varies from very poor to good. All of the homes that I saw were of one story and most of them were small, especially when one considers that their families are rather large.

Chief Calvin McGhee

The Chief of the group is Calvin W. McGhee. He is easily the dominant political and community leader of the Escambia County group, and has been so for many years. McGhee is sixty-one. His complexion is rather light, except where he is sunburned, but his features are very Indian-like, especially in profile. McGhee was a farmer and also worked, as many of the others have, as a farm laborer. He is poorly educated, having had only a grade-school education in a one-room school that did not meet more than three to six months a year. His speech, like that of most of the Indians, is that of a poorly educated white southern countryman. He apparently began to emerge as a leader in the group just after World War II.

Calvin McGhee's descent goes back not only to the half-breed Lynn McGhee, who was given land by Andrew Jackson for his help in the Creek War, but also to Sam Moniac, who was Alexander McGillivray's Creek interpreter, and his wife Elizabeth Weatherford, the sister of William Weatherford, who fought Andrew Jackson at the Battle of Horseshoe Bend in 1814. He is one of eleven brothers and sisters. His mother, who is now ninety, lives next door to him in a separate house and is now considered to be the oldest member of the group. She is a very pleasant and alert old lady who has neither hearing nor sight problems and who picked cotton last year. The Chief's wife is essentially white. Her maiden name was Ingram. She claims to have a small amount of Indian descent, but both she and her brother, who lives with the Chief, are entirely white in appearance.

Norman McGhee

The most interesting personage among the Alabama Creeks today other than the Chief would seem to be Norman McGhee, often called the Medicine Man. I had not made contact with the Indians for more than five minutes at Jackson's Grocery before Mrs. Margie McGhee, to whom I had been referred by the County Home Demonstration Agent, said, "Let's take him up to Norman," and then turned to me and said, "We have a Medicine Man, you know." So I drove Margie McGhee and her husband up to Norman McGhee's, on the old Lynn McGhee tract approximately half a mile west of the school. His house and its setting look like something out of Tobacco Road—small, dilapidated, overcrowded, with a sagging front porch, a small bare yard in the front, and maybe an acre of garden patch on the rear.

Norman McGhee is seventy-three. He is spry and mentally alert, without a trace of senility. He is rather dark and definitely Indian-like in appearance. His reputation as a Medicine Man comes from the fact that he collects herbs that have medicinal properties. These are not magical herbs, and I do not believe that there was any ritual connected with them. I asked Norman McGhee something about the herbs that he uses and the various ailments that he has treatments for, but frankly I forgot much of what he said on this subject by the time I had a chance to write it down. This discussion took place shortly after I met him and I did not want to take notes at the time. He did mention that he has a treatment for pyorrhea. He mentioned use of a plant that he calls "fever grace" or that is sometimes called "blue grace." He also mentioned ginseng, although I am not certain whether he implied that he was collecting it locally or obtaining it for use.

Norman McGhee is a widower, but his daughter and some of her family are with him. He worked a great deal as a migrant farm worker in the past. He lived in Cape Charles, Virginia, on the Eastern Shore for thirteen years. At that time, he was a contractor for black hired workers who harvested potatoes, tomatoes, and asparagus in particular. He often made good money as a contractor, he said, occasionally netting $100 a day.

Although he has been earning some money as a performing Indian in recent years, I found Norman a very straightforward person and very knowledgeable. On the way to Mobile, he explained how pulpwood cutting and hauling is arranged between the independent contractors, such as the Indians, and the mills. This included a discussion about prices and the hauling capacities of the trucks. Yet, like the other older people, he is a man with practically no formal education.

Cultural Survivals

I had the opportunity to question Calvin McGhee for perhaps half an hour about cultural survivals. I inquired about methods of hunting or trapping, and in this connection he gave me two interesting accounts. These are methods that to the best of his knowledge were used only by the Indians, although he does not pretend to be absolutely certain about this.

One account concerned trapping wild turkeys. A wild turkey is difficult to trap. He is very cagey and will not enter a pen or trap that is set out for him. He will simply go around it, although he may inspect it. The Indians would outsmart the turkeys in the following manner: They would set bait out and place around the bait just a few sticks or thongs that were eventually to enter into the construction of the pen/trap. These would not be numerous or imposing enough to alarm the turkey, and he would take the bait. At succeeding intervals they would place more bait and each time add a little bit to the construction of the pen. The changes from one time to the next were not sufficient to be perceptible to the turkey. Finally, they would complete the structure and set the bait and trap, and the poor turkey, who was accustomed to this structure and saw nothing unusual or alarming about it, would enter and be caught. This was certainly a method that required the proverbial Indian patience.

Another technique he described was a method of controlling crows. Crows were a great menace to the corn crop, especially when the crop had reached the stage of roasting ears and was ready for human consumption. It was next to impossible to get within shotgun range of them, for the crows would keep a scout who would caw and alarm the group whenever human beings began to approach. The Indians would build a blind or screen in the woods at the edge of the field. Two of them would then walk across the field to this blind. As they approached, the crows would alarm and fly away into the trees. The two Indians, armed with a shotgun, would go behind the blind. The crows would not come back into the field, being still uncertain about the location of the men. One Indian would then come out of the blind and walk back

across the field and away. The poor crows were not smart enough
to count and could not distinguish between the fact that two Indians had gone behind the blind but only one had come out. After
this one had gotten a safe distance away, the crows would then de-
scend again into the field and the Indian behind the blind would
have a good shot at them.

The Night Meeting at the School

At the end of our first meeting, Chief McGhee asked me if I could
come out to the area the next night. He said he would like to have
a few people come up to the school to meet with me. I agreed, but
with apprehension, aware that he wanted me to meet them as
someone from Washington and that there would be questions about
their land compensation claim against the federal government.

The next night I went to the school at about 7:30. I was
surprised to see how many had come. The Chief was rather apolo-
getic. Some of them, he said, had let him down; they had promised
they would be there, but had to do some overtime work in their
pulpwood hauling. Even so, about sixty people were there, of all
ages from about four to ninety.

The Chief introduced me around, especially to the men, and then
we all gathered in one of the classrooms. The Chief went over to
his car and got out his headdress, saying to me, "It wouldn't be an
Indian meeting if there weren't some feathers around." Apparently
he wears his headdress as a symbol of authority at meetings of this
type.

He opened the meeting by asking his brother Mace, who is a
Holiness preacher, to give an invocation. When those who were sitting did not stand up, the Chief said, in a tone that left no doubt
about his authority, "Now you all stand up," and everyone did so
with alacrity. He then introduced me and asked me to speak to
them and say just whatever I wanted to. It was obvious, despite
my entirely unofficial capacity, that he saw my visit as an
encouraging event and hoped it would boost the group's morale and
revive their faith in the prospect of an eventual settlement of their
claim.

There was actually nothing that I could tell them, but I
attempted to perform this role by expressing the good opinion that
I had of the officials at the Bureau of Indian Affairs and stating my
confidence that they were proceeding as quickly as their limited

staff and the volume of their duties would permit. I filled this out with some comments about my interest in Indian groups in the East and South and visits I had made to other groups. I also noted the fact that Indians are the most rural population group in the United States and spoke of the connection of rurality with problems of obtaining adequate education, adequate income, and employment. I talked for perhaps fifteen minutes, after which there were about twenty-five minutes of questions. Norman McGhee, who had asked me this question privately earlier, asked me whether I thought that there would ever be any money coming to them. I said yes, that I did. A very pretty young woman wanted to know whether or not the Bureau of Indian Affairs might establish a reservation for this area. Of course I said no and took the occasion to point out that the federal government had been trying for some years to close out reservations rather than to create new ones.[2]

---

2. **Author's Note:** The Alabama Creeks ultimately won a share of the Creek settlement, as I had predicted. Chief McGhee, however, died in 1970 and did not live to see the distribution of the money in 1972. Contrary to my expectations, the group also was federally recognized as a tribe in 1984, and 230 acres were declared a reservation in 1985.

13

Notes on Visit to the Warren County, North Carolina, Mixed-Racial Community

On April 27, 1954, I visited the mixed-racial community in Warren County, North Carolina. This group of people does not appear ever to have been mentioned in the literature on mixed-blood peoples. I first learned of them when more than 800 persons were enumerated as Indian in this county in the 1950 Census. From a subsequent inspection of the 1860 Census schedules, I inferred their names from a community of free people of mixed race who were listed at that time. I discovered they shared two names in common—Harris and Richardson—with the Gointown community of Rockingham County, and several names in common—Harris, Powell, Boone, Carter, Williams—with Lumbee and "Brass Ankle" groups further south.

I began my inquiries with the county superintendent of schools at Warrenton. He stated that some people in one part of the county were reputed to be part Indian but they had no special schools and were part of the colored population. Almost immediately, he raised the question of Sir Walter Raleigh's Lost Colony and expressed the hope that I could show them to be descended from the Colony. The superintendent, a Mr. Terrell, was apparently not entirely familiar with the people and suggested that I talk to the local newspaper editor, Mr. Jones.

Jones proved to be interested in my inquiry. His paper had published a story on the Indians, or "Issues" as the whites commonly refer to them, a few years ago, but he could not remember the date and hoped that I would not ask him to run it down. He was dubious of how much of the story, written by a Mr. Crockett, was truth and how much was not. At this point a lawyer, Mr. Taylor, who

Published here for the first time.

represents Warren County in the state legislature, came in and was brought into the conversation by Jones. It turned out that Taylor was the best informant I could have hoped to encounter because sometime last year he had been hired by a delegation of mixed bloods to do some research on their ancestry. Taylor had searched some old wills and deeds in Raleigh but had not arrived at any conclusions beyond the fact that the people were probably a triracial mixture. Both he and Jones were aware that this territory had been the home of the Tuscaroras before their migration to New York, and that the Robeson County Indians (Lumbee) have a tradition that some of their progenitors came from the area around the Roanoke River, which flows through Warren County. The Lost Colony was in the minds of Jones and Taylor, too, and they speculated upon how natural it would have been for the colonists to ascend Roanoke River from the original site of the colony. They had not heard of the Northampton County "Portuguese," who are thirty miles away.

Jones and Taylor testified that "Issues" did not commonly intermarry with Negroes, that some could pass for white, that some were quite Indian-like in appearance, and that they were good "citizens." If an "Issue" did marry a Negro, he became a pariah. Taylor suggested that I go down to the area where they are concentrated in Fishing Creek Township, about fifteen miles from Warrenton, and talk to some of their leaders. He gave me names of several men and suggested there was mutual benefit to be derived by the two of us; use of his name would guarantee me an interview and at the same time the "Issues" would think that he was still busy researching their history.

I interviewed only one person among the mixed bloods but spent about an hour and forty-five minutes with him. He was Bell Richardson, who like most of the others is a farmer. At the time I arrived, Richardson was supervising his son and another boy in plowing last year's cornfield with a tractor. Richardson is forty-four years old, with entirely Caucasian features. Where he was not sunburned, his skin was very light, but his face and hands were tanned a somewhat different shade than that normally observed among white people. His son and the other boy were brownish and could not have passed for white. Richardson in his countryfied manner was quite willing and even eager to talk. He quickly said that he was not white and did not pretend to be, but that there was no Negro blood in him. His father had told him that the Richardsons were white but that his mother was half Indian. Early in the

conversation he stated the humiliating social position of which his
people have become conscious, namely, that they do not know their
race. As he put it, "The newspaper will talk of events down here in
Fishing Creek Township and it will mention the white people, the
colored people, and the other. Now what are the 'other'?"

The Indians—as they will probably want to be known—know
that they have been free for generations and that some of their
ancestors were Confederate soldiers during the Civil War. Taylor
claims that some were even slave-holders. They have their own
churches—Baptist—but have to attend colored schools. However,
they are sufficiently concentrated that there are not more than five
or six Negro children in each of the two principal schools in Warren
County that they attend. I think their teachers are Negro. If they
want to attend high school, they must go to the Negro high school
in Warrenton. Richardson stated the children are "dogged" by the
Negro children about their race.

According to him, some of his people made an effort about forty
years ago to organize for the purpose of asserting a separate racial
status. It did not take hold, however, and Richardson supposed
this was because of the difficulty of communication in those days
and because with little interest in education there was little concern over the school question. In recent times, sentiment has
begun to crystallize regarding the desirability of "establishing our
nationality." As Richardson tells it, one Sunday morning after
church, about a year ago, a number of the men stood around talking about their problems. Someone made the suggestion that they
form a "club." The idea was well received and a community organization referred to as "the club" was formed. Although there is a
slate of officers and committees, the club has no formal name. The
members meet one night a month at the church and, says Richardson, so many folks turn out that it takes an acre of land to park the
cars. I could not determine what the club has done beyond its
efforts to learn through Taylor of the genealogy of the community
and to serve as a medium of group expression. These people have
learned through the newspapers of the Robeson County Indians
and of the special status and privileges they have obtained.
Richardson used the term *Croatan* to me in this connection and did
not regard it as derogatory. Several of the Warren County people
went down to Robeson County to look over the situation. I get the
impression that the Warren mixed bloods hope to establish blood
relationship to the Robeson group. Richardson was unaware of the

existence of the Person County Indians fifty miles away or of the Rockingham County group that contains people of his own name.

Repeatedly Richardson assured me that his people were not interested in passing as white. "We just want to be what we are," he said. Having to attend colored schools is perhaps the greatest source of irritation to them, but they are also unhappy about being identified as Negro on such personal records as drivers' licenses. (Taylor claims some public records list them as Indian.) Richardson also obviously felt a sense of frustration and shame over the eating arrangements necessary if one had to spend the day in town. They are not permitted in the white restaurants, and the colored restaurant owners make them feel uncomfortable if they come in for food.

Richardson did not know of many Indians in Warren County outside of Fishing Creek Township. A few families have moved into adjacent townships to obtain land and some are in Warrenton. Richardson, Jones, and Taylor all affirmed that many of the Indians are in Halifax County, probably "several hundred." I had counted about 250 in the 1950 Census in Halifax, mostly enumerated as Negro. But I did not check Brinkleyville Township, where Richardson and the others indicate that most of the Halifax group live. Thus, there may well be 500 in that county, as well as the more than 800 verified in Warren. Several families have also moved to Nash and Franklin counties. People from all four counties are participating in the club and in the effort to obtain a race name.

According to Richardson, there is not much movement away from the area, although he later stated that he had relatives in Washington, D.C. Many of the people, including Richardson, are landowners, and Richardson described the movement into Nash and Franklin counties and peripheral parts of Warren County as a continuing movement to acquire land. Warren is a cotton and tobacco county. Halifax is the same, plus peanuts. The important place of tobacco in the agricultural economy would seem to be a strong element in holding the population in the area. The homes of the people were intermediate in size and appearance between those of white and colored. None that I saw was in a ramshackle condition. The principal axis of settlement in the area I visited was on a paved road between Inez and Essex (in Halifax County).

At any rate, it is clear that after generations of indifference the mixed racial group of Warren and Halifax counties is emerging publicly as a separate-status group. They have numbers, leaders, incipient organization, and some money. All that would seem to be required now to duplicate the pattern of the Lumbee is a white sponsor and time.[1]

---

1. **Author's Note**: The group soon chose to call themselves "Haliwa" Indians, an Indian-like name coined from the names of the two counties in which they principally live, and gradually they achieved a general recognition as Indian.

Part III

Contemporary Rural America

Galesville, Wisconsin
(photo by Beale)

Grygla, Minnesota
(courtesy of Thomas Harvey)

As a wry irony it can be noted that if one wanted to point to the area of the United States in which incomes of female full-time workers most closely approach those of men it would be among blacks in the Mississippi Delta. They do so, however, not because women's income is so good, but because the earnings of black men in the area are so abysmal. (1985)

* * *

Retirement destinations are no longer limited to the popular stereotypes of Florida and the Southwest. Widespread in-migration has occurred in the Ozarks, the New England coast, the southern Blue Ridge, the Texas Hill Country, the Puget Sound area, the Upper Great Lakes, the Sierra Nevada foothills, western Oregon, east Texas, and the Tidewater areas of Maryland and Virginia. All of these locations involve dispersed settlement, and not merely aggregations of people in towns. (1985)

* * *

Because I am identified with the demographic work that documented the population turnaround in nonmetro areas, . . . I am increasingly asked to assess its impact on many areas of life. There is an unrealistic assumption that knowledge of the demography of the event makes one an authority on its implications. I wish that I did know what it means for residential and automotive energy use, for health services, for municipal and other local financing, for water and sewer needs, for schools, for gross national product, for land use issues, for U.S. economic policy, for rural law enforcement. Most of these are specific topics on which I have twice been asked to provide Congressional testimony this year. I have felt inadequate for the task except to offer common sense generalities. (1978)

14
The Revival of Population Growth in Nonmetropolitan America

The vast rural-to-urban migration that was the common pattern of U.S. population movement in the decades after World War II has been halted and, on balance, even reversed. During 1970–73, nonmetropolitan areas gained 4.2 percent in population compared to only 2.9 percent for metropolitan areas. In the eyes of many Americans, the appeal of major urban areas has diminished and the attractiveness of rural and small-town communities has increased, economically and otherwise. The result is a new trend that is already having an impact, one that modifies much of what we have taken for granted about population distribution.

The Old Trend

In the 1960s, the United States passed through a period of acute consciousness of the movement of people from rural and small-town areas into the metropolitan cities. This awareness was greatly heightened by the urban disorders that began in Los Angeles and Detroit and culminated in massive riots following the 1968 murder of Martin Luther King, Jr. There was thus a racial context to concern about rural-to-urban migration, although suppositions about the rural origin of rioters proved largely incorrect. The racial aspect in turn was part of a larger national focus on the extent and nature of urban poverty, and of a growing sense of increasing urban problems of pollution, crime, congestion, social alienation, and other real or suspected effects of large-scale massing of people.

Issued originally as Bulletin ERS–605 by the Economic Development Division, Economic Research Service, U.S. Department of Agriculture, June 1975.

Although there is usually some lag in public awareness of social and demographic movements, it is still rather remarkable that it took so long for concern to develop over rural-to-urban migration and the extensive impact this movement had on the nation's major urban areas.

Rapid rural out-movement had been occurring since 1940, with the beginning of the U.S. defense effort. It continued apace in the 1950s as farms consolidated and as the worker-short cities welcomed rural manpower. From 1940 to 1960, a net average of more than 1 million people left the farms annually (although not all moved to metropolitan cities), and a majority of nonmetropolitan counties declined in population despite high birthrates.

By the mid-1960s, this massive movement had drained off so much population previously dependent on agriculture and other extractive industries that the peak of potential migration was reached and passed. Yet, the impact of the movement had not been well recognized by cities or reflected in public policy. By the time that alarm over rural-to-urban migration arose around 1965, the economy of the nonmetropolitan areas and the social outlook and affluence of metropolitan residents were already changing in ways that would lead to a halt in the net outflow. Since 1970, changes in rural and urban population flows have occurred so rapidly that nonmetropolitan areas are not only retaining people but are receiving an actual net in-migration as well—an event not anticipated in the literature of the day.

The Rural Exodus

In the 1950s, a net of 5 million people left nonmetropolitan areas. In the South, farm population dropped by 40 percent in the decade, especially as a result of the mechanization of cotton harvesting and rapid abandonment of the cropper system of farming. By the mid-1950s, the Department of Agriculture began its advocacy of general rural development, urging communities to attract alternative types of employment. The emerging Interstate Highway Program began to shorten road travel times between places or entire regions. But only here and there in that decade were there actual population reversals from loss to gain in nonmetropolitan areas: the beginnings of revival in the Colorado slopes; the start of recreation and retirement in the Ozarks; oil-related development in south Louisiana; and the sprawling influence of Atlanta, Kansas City, or Minneapolis–St. Paul on accessible nonmetro counties.

In the 1960s, people continued to leave many of the areas of chronic rural exodus, such as the Great Plains (both north and south), the western Corn Belt, the southern coalfields, and the cotton-, tobacco-, and peanut-producing southern Coastal Plain, especially the Delta. However, closer examination of these losses reveals that, in a majority of cases, rates of net out-migration or decline had diminished compared with the 1950s. Indeed, about 250 nonmetropolitan counties in the South had net out-migration only in the black population, with the white population undergoing net in-migration into the same counties.

Harbingers of Change

A clear-cut and major reversal of nonmetropolitan decline occurred in two large upland areas of the South in the 1960s. One area stretched in an oval shape from St. Louis to Dallas, encompassing the Ozarks, the lower Arkansas Valley, the Ouachita Mountains, and northeast Texas. The other, of somewhat less dramatic size and reversal, was bounded by Memphis, Louisville, Atlanta, and Birmingham. Both areas were comprised heavily of districts with low previous income, low educational attainment, and low external prestige. Their reversal illustrated clearly the potential for rural turnaround in almost any part of the eastern half of the country once reliance on agriculture had been minimized. By 1960, only one-sixth of the labor force in these two areas was in farming, after a rapid decline in the 1950s. They were major beneficiaries of the decentralization trend of manufacturing that gathered speed in the mid-1960s. The Ozark-Ouachita area also had extensive development of reservoir-centered recreation and retirement districts.

The great majority of nonmetropolitan counties had greater retention of population in the 1960s than they had during the 1950s. Nonmetropolitan counties of that day lost only 2.2 million people by out-movement during the 1960s, a reduction of 60 percent from the 1950s. Population decline was more common than gain in most counties where a third or more of the employed labor force worked in any combination of agriculture, mining, and railroad work at the beginning of the decade. In such cases, only a rapid increase in other sources of work could fully offset continued displacement from extractive industry. But, because of this displacement, we entered the 1970s with far fewer counties depending primarily on the extractive sector of the economy. Thus, many more counties were in a position in 1970 to see future gains in manufacturing, trade, services, or other activity flow through to net job growth and population gain, without being offset by declines in traditional industries.

Our best single source of population data for the 1970s is the Bureau of the Census county estimates series published annually. Accurate local population estimates are not easy to make. In some counties it is difficult to be fully certain even of the direction of change, much less the amount. Nevertheless, the estimates of the Bureau for 1966 (the only county series in the 1960s) clearly caught the turnarounds of that period in the Ozarks, Tennessee Valley, Texas hill country, and Upper Great Lakes cutover lands, although they mistook the direction of trend in the Mississippi Delta. The subsequent improvement of techniques, the strength of the demographic changes now occurring, and the support of independent data series on employment bolster confidence in the current series, although no one would prudently interpret small changes for small counties literally.[1]

The Reversal

The remarkable recent reversal of long-term population trends is demonstrated by growth in nonmetropolitan counties of 4.2 percent between April 1970 and July 1973, compared with 2.9 percent in metropolitan counties (see Table 14.1, which sums counties by current metropolitan-nonmetropolitan status).[2] This is the first period in this century in which nonmetropolitan areas have grown at a faster rate than metropolitan areas. Even during the 1930s depression, there was some net movement to the cities. As late as

1. The 1973 estimates used here are being revised by the Bureau of Census to reflect additional data that have become available. But the revisions will not change conclusions reached here. They will show less increase in nonmetropolitan population retention in the western Corn Belt and the Wheat Belt than is implied in the data used here, but more such retention in a number of southern states and scattered other areas of predominantly nonmetropolitan character.

2. In general, Standard Metropolitan Statistical Areas—here called metropolitan areas—are designated by the government wherever there is an urban center of 50,000 or more people. Neighboring commuter counties of metropolitan character are also included in these areas. All other counties are nonmetropolitan.

Table 14.1   U.S. Population Change by Residence, 1970 and 1973

Residence	Population			Net Migration	
	1973	1970	Increase 1970–73 (percent)	1970–73	1960–70
Total	209,851	203,301	3.2	1,632	3,001
Metropolitan[a]	153,252	149,002	2.9	486	5,997
Nonmetropolitan	56,599	54,299	4.2	1,146	−2,996
Nonmetropolitan					
Adjacent counties[b]	29,165	27,846	4.7	722	−724
Nonadjacent counties	27,434	26,452	3.7	424	−2,273

Source: Current Population Reports, U.S. Bureau of the Census.
[a]Metropolitan status as of 1974.
[b]Nonmetropolitan counties adjacent to Standard Metropolitan Statistical Areas.

the 1960s, metropolitan growth was double the rate in nonmetropolitan areas.

Curiously, both metropolitan and nonmetropolitan classes had some net in-movement of people from 1970 to 1973. This is possible because the total population grew partly by immigration from abroad.

During the 1960s, nonmetropolitan counties of today were averaging a 300,000 loss per year from out-migration. Thus far in this decade, they have averaged a 353,000 in-movement per year, while metropolitan areas, in sharp contrast, have dropped from 600,000 net in-migrants annually to 150,000.

A common first reaction to these data and the basic change they indicate is to ask whether the higher nonmetropolitan growth might not just be increased spillover from the metropolitan areas into adjacent nonmetropolitan counties. To examine this logical question, nonmetropolitan counties were classed by whether or not they are adjacent to a metropolitan area. As might be expected, adjacent counties have had the higher population growth since 1970 (4.7 percent) and have acquired about five-eighths of the total net in-movement into all nonmetropolitan counties. The more significant point, however, is that nonadjacent counties have also increased more rapidly than metropolitan counties (3.7 percent versus 2.9 percent). Thus, the decentralization trend is not confined to metropolitan sprawl. It affects nonmetropolitan counties well removed from metropolitan influence. Indeed, the trend can be said especially to affect them. Their net migration pattern has shifted more than that of the adjacent counties, going from a loss of 227,000 annually in the 1960s to an annual gain of 130,000, a shift in the annual average of 357,000 persons. On a slightly larger base, adjacent counties have shifted from an average annual loss of 72,000 persons in the 1960s to an average gain of 222,000 from 1970 to 1973, an annual shift of 294,000 persons.

Increased retention of population in nonmetropolitan areas is characteristic of almost every part of the United States. As measured by migration trends, all states but three (Alaska, Connecticut, and New Jersey) show it, and two of the three exceptions are controlled by events in military-base counties. Nonadjacent counties have had some net in-migration in every major geographic division.

There were still nearly 600 nonmetropolitan counties declining in population during 1970–73, but this was less than half as many as the nearly 1,300 declining in the 1960s. The largest remaining block of such counties is in the Great Plains, both north and south. Former large groups of declining counties in the Old South and the Southern Appalachian coalfields have been broken up except in the Mississippi Delta.

Factors Affecting Growth

Major centers of nonmetropolitan population are found in counties with cities of 25,000–49,999 people. These counties contain a little more than one-sixth of the total nonmetropolitan population. Their growth rate for 1970–73 was 4.2 percent (Table 14.2), identical with that in all other nonmetropolitan counties. Thus, recent nonmetropolitan population growth has not occurred disproportionately in counties with the largest nonmetropolitan employment centers. Since these counties have a favorable age structure for childbearing, their rate of natural increase was higher than that of the rest of nonmetropolitan counties, but the rate of in-migration was lower.

At the other residential extreme are the completely rural nonmetropolitan counties that are not adjacent to a metropolitan area and have no town of even 2,500 inhabitants. Such counties have been subject to population decline in the past. In the 1960s they had considerable out-migration and declined by 4.5 percent in the decade. However, from 1970 to 1973 their population grew by 4.2

Table 14.2 Nonmetropolitan Population Change by Selected County Characteristics[a]

County Characteristic, 1970	Number of Counties	Population					Net Migration			
		Number (thousands)			Percent Change		1970–73		1960–70	
		1973	1970	1960	1970–73	1960–70	Number	Rate[b] (percent)	Number	Rate[b] (percent)
City of 25,000 or more	138	10,351	9,936	8,916	4.2	11.4	148	1.5	-74	-0.8
No city of 25,000	2,356	46,248	44,363	43,850	4.2	1.2	998	2.2	-2,922	-6.7
Entirely rural nonadjacent[c]	620	4,441	4,264	4,474	4.2	-4.7	123	2.9	-551	-12.3
10% or more net in-migration at retirement ages[d]	377	8,672	7,887	6,655	10.0	18.5	646	8.2	619	9.3
15% or more	214	5,310	4,728	3,764	12.3	25.6	509	10.8	642	17.1
10.0 to 14.9%	163	3,362	3,159	2,891	6.4	9.3	137	4.3	-23	-.8
Senior state college	187	8,852	8,369	7,419	5.8	12.8	265	3.2	78	1.1
40% or more employed in manufacturing	263	8,936	8,647	8,057	3.3	7.3	73	.8	-294	-3.7
35% or more employed in agriculture	193	916	919	1,039	-.4	-11.5	-12	-1.3	-201	-19.4
40% or more	104	398	402	463	-.9	-13.3	-8	-1.9	-100	-21.5
35.0 to 39.9%	89	518	518	576	(e)	-10.1	-5	-.9	-102	-17.6
50% or more black population	98	1,750	1,763	1,947	-.7	-9.5	-67	-3.8	-459	-23.6
10% or more military population	29	1,172	1,177	955	-.4	23.2	-66	-5.6	21	2.2

Source: U.S. Census of Population 1970 and Current Population Reports. U.S. Bureau of the Census.

[a] Metropolitan status as of April 1974.

[b] Net migration expressed as a percentage of the population at beginning of period.

[c] Nonmetropolitan counties not adjacent to Standard Metropolitan Statistical Areas.

[d] Counties with specified 1960–70 net in-migration rate for white persons 60 years old and over, 1970.

[e] Less than .05 percent.

percent. This reflects a definite reversal of the previous trend. Natural increase of population in the completely rural counties has been very low since 1970, because of the comparative shortage of adults of childbearing age (resulting from past out-migration) and the growth of older populations of higher mortality as retirement settlement spreads. The growth in these counties has come principally from in-migration, with a rate nearly double that of counties with cities of 25,000 or more people.

The decentralization trend in U.S. manufacturing has been a major factor in transforming the rural and small-town economy, especially in the upland parts of the South. From 1962 through 1969, half of all U.S. nonmetropolitan job growth was in manufacturing. However, population growth has not been high since 1970 in areas with heavy concentrations of manufacturing activity. Counties with 40 percent or more of their 1970 employment in this sector contained about 16 percent of the total nonmetropolitan population and grew by 3.3 percent between 1970 and 1973. This increase required some net in-migration and was slightly above the total U.S. growth rate, but it was well below the increase of 4.2 percent for all nonmetropolitan counties. Thus, although growth of manufacturing has been a centerpiece of the revival of nonmetropolitan population retention, the recent reversal of population trends has not been focused in areas already heavily dependent on manufacturing. Growth of jobs in trade and other nongoods-producing sectors has now come to the fore. From 1969 to 1973, manufacturing jobs comprised just 18 percent of all nonmetropolitan job growth, compared with 50 percent from 1962 to 1969.

A second and increasingly important factor in nonmetropolitan development has been the growth of recreation and retirement activities, often occurring together in the same localities. Recreational employment is not easily assessed, but by means of net migration estimates by age, it is possible to identify counties receiving significant numbers of retired people. Using unpublished estimates prepared by Gladys Bowles of the Economic Research Service in collaboration with Everett Lee at the University of Georgia, counties were identified in which there was a net in-migration of 15 percent or more from 1960 to 1970 of white residents who were age sixty and over in 1970. Migration patterns at other ages were disregarded and may have been either positive or negative. These counties, which had already become a source of nonmetropolitan population growth in the 1960s, are by far the most rapidly growing class of nonmetropolitan counties in the 1970s.

Although a number of the retirement counties are in the traditional Florida and southwestern belts, the spread of retirement settlement to other regions is a key characteristic of recent years. Clusters of nonmetropolitan retirement counties are found in the old cutover region of the Upper Great Lakes (especially in Michigan), the Ozarks, the hill country of central Texas, the Sierra Nevada foothills in California, and the east Texas coastal plain. In general, coasts, lakes, reservoirs, and hills are favorite locations.

"Retirement counties" is probably too narrow a label for a number of the counties described. In about five-eighths of the cases, in-migration rates were highest at retirement age and lower (or at times negative) at younger ages. But in the other three-eighths of the "retirement counties," in-migration was higher at some age under sixty than it was above that point. These areas often attract younger families because of climate, or amenities, or because manufacturing or other employment may have begun to flourish as well. Indeed the very influx of people into attractive areas for noneconomic reasons can stimulate follow-on types of job development—a case of supply creating demand. Further, it should be noted that, for many people today, "retirement" may at first mean simply an optional departure from a career job and pension system at a comparatively unadvanced age; for example, most federal government workers can retire at age fifty-five. Increasingly large numbers of such people then move to a different place where they may or may not reenter the labor force.

The nonmetropolitan counties with net in-migration of 15.0 percent or more of whites at age sixty and over grew by an average of one-fourth in total population in the 1960s. The pace of their growth has risen further, with a 12.3 percent population increase from 1970 to 1973.

The rapid growth of these counties suggested a look at counties with a more modest level of in-movement of older people. Counties of 10.0 to 14.9 percent retirement-age migration rates in the 1960s were examined and proved to have grown in population by 6.4 percent from 1970 to 1973. This is a little more than half the total growth rate for counties with higher retirement rates in the 1960s. The counties with modest retirement rates in the 1960s, however, have had a relatively more rapid buildup in their total growth trend since 1970. During the 1960s, their overall growth of 9.3 percent was well below the national average, but their growth since 1970 is well above the national average. The two classes of retirement counties have between them 8.7 million people in 377 counties, and they make up an increasingly significant part of the total nonmetropolitan population.

An equal number of nonmetropolitan people live in counties having senior state colleges and universities.[3] The expansion of these schools has been substantial since the end of World War II. Many have evolved from teachers colleges into major institutions. Some observers tend to denigrate the importance of nonmetropolitan population growth stemming from college growth, as if it were somehow less real or permanent in its consequences than other growth. But the rise of nonmetropolitan state schools has greatly increased availability and quality of higher education in nonmetropolitan areas and has also made the affected towns more attractive for other development. In fact, many new metropolitan areas over the last two decades have come from the ranks of college towns. From 1970 to 1973, nonmetropolitan counties containing senior state colleges and universities grew in population by 5.8 percent, well above the nonmetropolitan average, despite the slight national downturn in college enrollment rates that began at this time.[4]

Eventually these counties should experience a drop in students as the decline in the birthrate since 1960 affects enrollment. But towns and counties containing state colleges are unlikely to return to their earlier size or status. Perhaps equally important to nonmetropolitan areas has been the founding of numerous community junior colleges and technical education centers. These institutions typically do not have residential facilities and thus do not swell the local population with students, but they have made it much more feasible for nonmetropolitan residents to obtain post–high school education, and they are often able to cooperate with business firms in providing specific skills needed for new or expanded plants. More than 150 nonmetropolitan counties acquired public community colleges or college-accredited technical education centers during the 1960s.

Tabulations were also made for two types of counties known to have been highly susceptible to loss in the 1960s. Heavily agricultural counties, with 40 percent or more of their employment in farming, were the most vulnerable to population decline and out-

3. The lists of retirement counties and college counties are almost mutually exclusive. Only nineteen counties are in both categories.

4. Private colleges are omitted from this discussion because they are considerably smaller than state schools on the average and have had much less growth. Some private schools do, of course, exercise an effect on the nonmetropolitan population.

migration in the 1960s, losing jobs faster in the course of farm adjustments than other sources of work could be found. From 1970 to 1973, such counties declined by 0.9 percent in population, contrary to the general trend of nonmetropolitan population. But the more crucial statistic about these counties is that they have only 400,000 people, which is less than 1 percent of the nonmetropolitan population. Their trends now have little weight in shaping the national nonmetropolitan trend. Counties where 35.0 to 39.9 percent of all workers are in agriculture contained half a million people and were stationary in population from 1970 to 1973.

Heavily agricultural counties clearly are still different in population retention from the mass of nonmetropolitan counties and are not absorbing the equivalent of their natural population increase (their combined out-migration amounted to 12,000 people). Even so, they have been affected by the recent trend, for these same counties declined by 11.5 percent in the 1960s with a decade out-movement of 200,000 people.

Among the most uniformly heavy losers of population in prior decades were the nonmetropolitan counties of predominantly black population. They were once disproportionately agricultural and received less industrialization than the rest of the South. Further, their black residents had an impetus toward city migration that transcended what might have been expected from the dependence on farming or the slower pace of other job development. By 1970, ninety-eight predominantly black nonmetropolitan counties remained, although only one of them still had 35 percent or more workers in farming. These counties contained 1.75 million total population. From 1970 to 1973, they decreased by 13,000, or −.7 percent. Thus, predominantly black areas of the South have not yet shifted to growth. However, net out-migration has been reduced from an average of 46,000 people annually in the 1960s to 20,000 in the early 1970s. Some increased retention is evident.

Several other less numerous and less populated types of counties that had increased population retention can be identified, although no data are shown here for them. These include mining counties, counties with major prisons or long-stay hospitals, those containing state capitals, and counties with Indian majorities.

Increased retention is so pervasive that only one type of county could be found with diminished population retention. This type was military-base counties, defined as those where 10 percent or more of the total 1970 population consisted of military personnel. Military work was a major rural growth industry in the post–World

War II decades. Military bases were disproportionately located in nonmetropolitan areas, and they employed many civilians as well as armed forces. Since 1970, however, domestic military personnel have declined by about one-fifth. Nonmetropolitan counties with 10 percent or more of military personnel among their residents declined slightly in total population (−.4 percent), with a net out-migration of 66,000 people. By contrast, these counties grew rapidly during the 1960s (23.2 percent).

In summarizing categories of counties for which trends have been computed, highest rates of nonmetropolitan growth are found among retirement counties, counties adjacent to metropolitan areas, and counties with senior state colleges.

Geographically, several commonly recognized subregions have had rapid growth. In the three and one-quarter years after the 1970 Census, the Ozark-Ouachita area increased by 9.4 percent, the Upper Great Lakes cutover area by 8.0 percent, the Rocky Mountains by 7.1 percent, and the Southern Appalachian coalfields by 6.3 percent. The latter is a remarkable turnaround from a loss of over 15 percent in the coalfields in the 1960s. Each of the four areas cited is comparatively remote from metropolitan centers.

Residential Preferences

A change in attitudes may be of equal importance to economic factors in producing the recent reversal in migration. In the mid-1960s, we became aware of the great disparity between the actual distribution of the U.S. population by size of place and the expressed preferences of people. Millions of people presumed to have been happily content in their big-city and suburban homes said—in response to opinion polls—they would prefer to live in a rural area or small town.

When Zuiches and Fuguitt subsequently reported from a Wisconsin survey that a majority of such dissidents in that state preferred their ideal rural or small-town residence to be within thirty miles of a city of at least 50,000 people,[5] there was noticeable discounting by urban-oriented interests of the message of previous

5. James J. Zuiches and Glenn V. Fuguitt, "Residential Preferences: Implications for Population Redistribution in Nonmetropolitan Areas," in *Population Distribution and Policy*, vol. 5 of research reports of the U.S. Commission on Population Growth and the American Future, 1972, pp. 617–30.

polls. It appeared that basic trends were not being altered. Rather, only additional sprawl within the metropolitan areas was implied. The validity of the point established by Zuiches and Fuguitt was indisputable, especially when confirmed in a later national survey by the same researchers. However, in my opinion, a second finding in the national survey greatly modified the significance of the preference for a close-in rural or small-town location, although it received little notice. By a very wide margin (65 percent to 35 percent), the big-city people who preferred a nearby rural or small-town residence ranked a more remote rural or small-town place as their second choice, and thus as preferable to the big city.[6] Therefore, most of this group were positively oriented toward nonmetropolitan locations compared with their current metropolitan urban residence regardless of whether an opportunity arose to relocate within thirty miles of the city.

A second statistic foreshadowing the 1970–73 trends reported here appeared in another national survey done for the Commission on Population Growth and the American Future. This figure dealt with the likelihood that persons dissatisfied with their size of community would actually move to the type they preferred.[7] The commission found that three-eighths of the people expressing a desire to shift to a different type of residence declared that they were "very likely" to make such a move within the "next few years." An additional fourth thought they would eventually make such a move at a later time. The "very likely" group would have translated into a potential of about 14 million people of all ages moving from metropolitan cities and suburbs to smaller places and rural areas. The expectation of making a move was highest among comparatively young and well-educated persons (where migration rates in general are highest), and thus was not primarily a nostalgic hope of older people of rural origins.

I suggest the pattern of population movement since 1970 reflects to a considerable extent many people implementing a preference for a rural or small-town residence over that of the metropolitan city, quite apart from the fact that improved economic conditions in nonmetropolitan areas make such moves feasible.

Aside from demographic and opinion survey data, a variety of corroborative local information on the noneconomic aspects of

6. Glenn V. Fuguitt and James J. Zuiches, "Residential Preferences and Population Distribution," *Demography* 12:3 (August 1975).

7. Sara Mills Mazie and Steve Rawlings, "Public Attitude Towards Population Distribution Issues," *Population Distribution and Policy*, pp. 599–616.

current population distribution trends is now available in the form of newspaper and magazine stories and correspondence. The environmental-ecological movement, the youth revolution with its somewhat antimaterialistic and antisuburban component, and the narrowing of traditional urban-rural gaps in conditions of life all seem to have contributed to the movement to nonmetropolitan areas.

Effect of the Declining Birthrate

An additional factor contributing to higher nonmetropolitan population growth during a period of slower national and metropolitan growth has been the course of the birthrate. The decline of the birthrate since 1970 has basically occurred in the most metropolitan parts of the country. In the three and one-quarter years after April 1970, for which most of the population figures here are quoted, births numbered 5.2 percent less than for the previous three and one-quarter years in the Northeast (including Delaware, Maryland, and the District of Columbia), the North Central, and the Pacific states. On the other hand, in the South and the Mountain division of the West, they actually increased by 3.5 percent in the post-1970 period over the prior period. Although nonmetropolitan residents are a minority in both of these two super-regions, they comprise twice the proportion in the South and Mountain West than they do in the North and Pacific West (40 percent versus 20 percent). It is highly unlikely that this contrasting pattern in number of births could occur without being substantially associated with the large difference in proportion of nonmetropolitan population. It appears that the difference between average levels of metropolitan and nonmetropolitan fertility rates has somewhat widened since 1970, after three decades of convergence.

The 1970–73 population trends do not reflect effects of the more recent large increase in the price of oil and gas products. Inasmuch as rural people travel a greater average distance to work or for goods and services than do urban residents, and do not usually have public transportation alternatives, the higher costs of personal transportation could have a depressing effect on the future trend of population dispersal. It is too early to tell. However, the same shortage and higher price of fuels and energy-producing minerals has caused renewed mining activity for oil, gas, coal, and uranium, thus stimulating the economy of a number of nonmetropolitan counties, especially in the West. In a directly related manner, the agricultural economy is being operated in a greatly expanded way, primarily to serve export markets and balance-of-payment needs. This, too, generates some additional rural employment.

Future Impact

How long will the 1970–73 trend persist and what is its larger meaning? One doubts that we are dismantling our system of cities. However, except for Boston, all the largest U.S. metropolitan areas have had major slowdowns in growth. The eight largest areas, which contain a fourth of the total U.S. population, grew by less than one-third the national growth rate from 1970 to 1973, whereas they were exceeding the national growth in the 1960s. Small- and medium-size metropolitan areas have had increased growth and net in-movement of people since 1970 and thus are behaving demographically more like the nonmetropolitan areas than like the larger metropolitan places. The trend that produced the turnaround in nonmetropolitan population is primarily a sharply diminished attraction to the more massive metropolitan areas, and a shift down the scale of settlement—both to smaller metropolitan areas and small towns and rural areas.

Much is said in the literature of demography about the modern demographic transition. The process whereby nations go from high fertility and mortality through a period of rapid total growth as mortality drops, to a subsequent condition of low growth as fertility also falls, is seen to be accompanied by rapid urbanization. But in a nation where this process is essentially completed, another aspect of demographic transition may emerge, in which the distribution of population is no longer controlled by an unbridled impetus to urbanization. General affluence, low total population growth, easy transportation and communication, modernization of rural life, and urban population massings so large that they diminish the advantages of urban life—these factors may make a downward shift to smaller communities seem both feasible and desirable.

The trend in the United States since 1970 was not foreseen in the literature of scientific and public discussion of even three or four years ago. Its rapid emergence is basically the result of innumerable private decisions, both personal and commercial, that

collectively and subtly have created a pattern of population movement significantly different than before. Long-held social truths—
such as the view that the basic movement of population is out of
nonmetropolitan areas and into metropolitan areas—are not easily
cast off. But this one seems to have reached the end of its unchal-
lenged validity. Much new thought is needed on the probable
course of future population distribution in the United States,
uncolored either by value-laden residential fundamentalism or by
outmoded analytical premises.

15

Agricultural Communities: Economic and Social Settings

The agrarian ethic was long a dominant theme of American life. Yet even at its epic proportions in the homesteading era and in the sundering of the nation over an agriculturally based slavery, it was also a diminishing theme. Decade by decade, throughout the nineteenth century, industrialization and urbanization emerged. When finally in 1920 the urban population exceeded the rural for the first time, the shock was so great that Congress, for the only time in its history, found itself unable to reach any consensus on congressional reapportionment and ignored its constitutional requirement to reapportion. The debates of the time make it clear that distrust of urban society and disbelief in the permanence of the out-movement from farming were major factors in this failure.

After the onset of World War II, the farm population declined rapidly, being reduced by half in the period from 1940 to 1960. Factors impelling farm mechanization and enlargement, together with the lure of superior urban employment and income, produced this result. In particular, the agrarian component of the South was greatly reduced as the historic share-tenancy form of cotton, tobacco, and peanut farming was abandoned for procedures using fewer workers. Gradually, the fact that the farm population had become a small minority of the total population was accepted.

It has taken much longer to get the point across that farm people are also only a small minority of the rural population. We have 5.6 million farm population today (1983), out of the total of 59.6 million rural people. (There were 30 million farm people in 1940 out of 57 million total rural.) Farm linkages with other economic

Adapted from *Agricultural Communities: The Interrelationship of Agriculture, Business, Industry, and Government in the Rural Economy: A Symposium*, Committee Print, Committee on Agriculture, U.S. House of Representatives, October 1983.

sectors have increased as modern farming has required vastly higher purchases of equipment, fertilizer, pesticides, and services, and as we have moved to increased processing of many products before final consumption. But many of these linkages are urban based and/or do not necessarily involve a community of like interests with farmers. (For example, in the short run, what is bad for the farmer may not be bad for a buyer, shipper, or processor of farm products.)

Agricultural Dependency Versus Agricultural Production

There is no easy way of defining the limits of "agriculture" or "agricultural communities," and it is not my intent to do so here. But, no matter how these concepts are defined, agriculture as a direct or secondary employer is not the driving force of most of the communities of America today that are viewed as rural or small towns and that constitute the clientele of the Department of Agriculture for many federal programs. This does not derive from any contraction of agricultural output. Indeed, the central fact of American agriculture is the increase in its output despite the loss of three-fifths of its labor force in forty years.

The deagriculturalization of rural America results from a major expansion and diversification of the nonfarm rural and small-town economy, which has permitted the total rural population to increase despite the farm-sector losses. However, this growth has not been evenly spread. In general, it has affected the timbered and arid areas of the nation much more than the open plains and prairies of the midcontinent. In the northern plains, in particular, there are still counties in which the economy can be described as almost entirely agricultural. Other equally rural areas, however, either have almost no agriculture (for example, parts of the southern coalfields) or have retained an agricultural function, but have seen it overwhelmed in employment by such industries as manufacturing or mining (many parts of the South or West).

Today, there are only nineteen counties left in the whole country in which half or more of all employed people work solely or primarily as farmers or farm laborers. Thirty years ago, Kentucky alone had more than fifty such counties. Counties with one-fourth or more of their employment in farming—a level at which one can safely assume that agricultural interests still clearly dominate the economy—numbered 271 in the 1980 Population Census.

Most of these are thinly populated Plains counties and they contain only 8 percent of the total U.S. farm population. With some exceptions, their agriculture tends to be extensive farming of grain (usually wheat) or cattle ranching, requiring large acreages. Thus, we encounter the anomaly that none of the 100 counties most dependent on farming in the United States (as measured by employment) was among the 100 top counties in net value of agricultural output in the 1978 Agriculture Census (see Fig. 15.1).

The latter (top-producing) class of agricultural counties is more widely distributed. One major concentration is in California and Arizona. A second major group is in the more productive parts of the Corn Belt. Other counties are in Florida or the Columbia Basin. Many of them are characterized by irrigated farming, with its high value of output per acre. In sharp contrast to the high-dependency counties with their small populations, many of the ranking top producers are metropolitan counties (46 of 100), including the counties that contain such large cities as Los Angeles and its suburbs, San Diego, Phoenix, Honolulu, Sacramento, Miami, and Tampa. Much of our most productive farming is embedded in a metropolitan environment, in which the farm community is a small part of the total. The 3 percent of counties that constitute the 100 top producers yield 20 percent of the nation's total net value added of agricultural products.

The demographic contrasts between the high-dependency and high-production counties are substantial. In the high-dependency group (most of which have no urban population at all), the total population declined in the 1970s by 6.9 percent because of the lack of alternatives to farming. In the high-production group, where 87 percent of the people are urban, population grew by 20.4 percent. This is a level of growth far above that of the United States as a whole (11.4 percent) and one that unquestionably puts pressure on the price of farmland and its continued use for farming.

There is a gradient of social and economic conditions associated with varying degrees of agricultural dependence. In general, one can say that the higher the relative dependence on farming, the lower the overall levels are of education, income, minority race presence, and female labor-force participation, but the higher the average age and the percentage of children living with both parents (see Table 15.1).

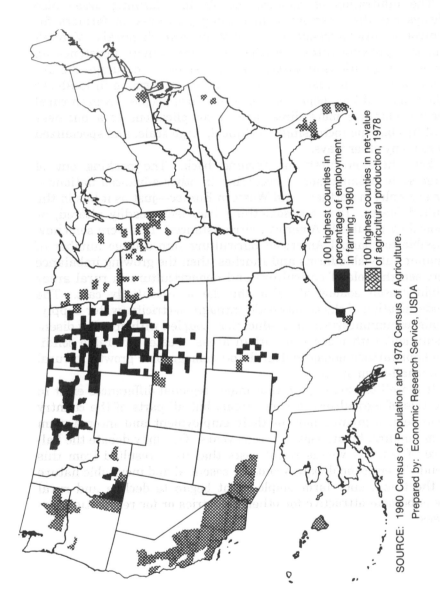

100 highest counties in
percentage of employment
in farming, 1980

100 highest counties in net-value
of agricultural production, 1978

SOURCE: 1980 Census of Population and 1978 Census of Agriculture.

Prepared by: Economic Research Service, USDA

Fig. 15.1 Leading counties in agricultural dependency and production

Table 15.1 Characteristics of Counties by Selected Levels of Agricultural Dependency and Production

County Characteristic	Percent of People Employed in Farming, 1980				Top Farm Production Counties
	33.3+	25.0–33.2	20.0–24.9	15.0–19.9	
Number of counties	104	167	150	238	100
Population, 1980 (thousands)	353	1,097	1,444	3,507	30,152
Rural farm (%)	35.9	27.4	23.7	15.8	1.8
Rural nonfarm (%)	61.4	61.7	53.7	49.2	11.3
Urban (%)	2.7	10.8	22.5	35.0	86.9
Ages 20–34 (%)	19.0	19.5	20.3	22.1	27.1
Ages 60+ (%)	22.2	22.5	22.0	19.0	15.1
Households with income					
Under $10,000 (%)	43.5	39.8	38.1	37.4	27.4
$30,000+ (%)	9.2	10.4	11.2	12.0	22.1
Children under 18, not with two parents (%)	7.7	9.0	9.9	12.6	20.3
Women 16+ in labor force (%)	38.2	41.0	41.8	43.9	51.7
Adults 18+ with 1+ years of college (%)	25.2	23.4	22.9	23.2	36.9
U.S. net value 1978 farm products sold (%)	2.4	NA	NA	NA	20.5

Source: Unpublished tabulations from 1980 Census of Population and 1978 Census of Agriculture.

Family Workers Versus Hired Workers

In the past, a major organizational feature that distinguished agricultural people and communities from one another was tenure status, especially the contrast between the South, with its extensive share-tenancy system, and the rest of the country. Today, the incidence (and importance) of full tenancy is greatly diminished and is actually somewhat less in the South than in the rest of the nation. There is another measure of organizational structure, however, that strongly differentiates agricultural communities and regions in the United States, and that is the comparative reliance on operator labor versus hired labor to do the work. At the time of writing, these data are not yet available from the 1980 Census. The pattern, however, can be reliably seen from the previous census.

In a large and basically contiguous area comprising the northern and central Great Plains, the Corn Belt, the midwestern Dairy Belt, the Ozarks, and much of Kentucky and Tennessee, the ratio of self-employed farmers to hired farm workers is more than 2 to 1. This region is dominated by commercial but family-scale operations. Some full-time hired labor is required on the larger operations, and there may be seasonal needs for extra help, but the main reliance is on family labor.

Adjoining this region and extending into the northern Rockies, the southern Plains, more of the upland South and the interior Northeast are many other counties where self-employed farmers are more numerous than hired workers, but not by a 2 to 1 margin.

At the other extreme are areas in which two-thirds or more of people in the production phases of agriculture are hired workers. These include most of the top-producing counties in California and Arizona, most of the Rio Grande area in Texas and New Mexico, most of the Florida Peninsula, a predominance of the Mississippi Delta, many counties around major cities, and Hawaii. Areas where hired workers are in the majority but are less than two-thirds of the farm work force fill in most of the rest of the West, the lower South, and the Northeast.

The character of agriculture in the two opposite types of areas differs greatly, on average. The area with the high percentage of self-employed workers is focused on the products whose surpluses, low prices, or policy problems seem chronically to dominate farm news; namely, wheat, corn, soybeans, and dairy products. This is also the area whose agriculture in recent years has become rapidly more dependent on export markets.

The areas that hire most of their farm work force, on the other hand, produce much of the nation's supply of vegetables, fruits, tree nuts, sugar cane, horticultural goods, and cotton. With the exception of cotton, they produce heavily for the American market. Producers are frequently large-scale and fewer in number than farmers in the area dominated by self-employment. Some of the areas of high use of hired workers are characterized by nearness to the Mexican border—providing a ready source of cheap labor—or by the previous existence of large plantations that once were farmed by tenants and now are too large for family labor operation, such as in the Mississippi Delta.

Although precise data have not been calculated, it is apparent from the location of the areas with a high ratio of hired work to self-employed work that they often—perhaps characteristically— have hired workers of different ethno/cultural and social-class background from the operators. Many are areas in which hired workers are predominantly Mexican-American, black, or, less frequently, Filipino or Indian, whereas the operators are usually white. Labor issues are prominent and in this context have racial and social-class overtones. In the operator-dominated areas, such farm labor is typically drawn more from the same social stratum as the operators, although some Mexican-American migrants are used and some of them have "settled out" locally.

Over the last decade both the relative and absolute importance of hired workers in U.S. agriculture has risen, while that of farm operators and other family labor has diminished. In 1970, hired workers averaged 28 percent of the farm work force; by 1982 this had climbed to 38 percent. Farming is still a preeminent source of self-employment, as compared with any other major occupation. Ironically, however, the numerical importance of the self-employed is decreasing in farming at the very time that self-employment has expanded rapidly in the nonagricultural population.

Although hired farm work is up, another and quite antithetical element in the farm community has also been growing, but for which little more than subjective evidence is available. I am referring to the "homesteaders" or "back-to-the-landers." This population has come into or back to the rural areas over the last decade or so. It has a strong ideology of the value of rural living, of self-sufficiency, and stewardship of the land. Some of its members want to be comfortable; others are antimaterialist. Their role in

farming seems to be typically small-scale, often with a focus on
organic farming, vegetables, or livestock specialties. Almost anything said of them lacks quantification, for it is difficult to identify
this population and thus estimate its size in regular data series.
The homesteaders probably account for the increase in small-scale
farms shown in the last census of agriculture. They seem to go
especially to partly timbered areas of marginal productivity where
the land was long farmed and a stock of farmsteads exists, but
where the land value in recent decades has been comparatively
low.

There was a time when it was possible to characterize farm people
and farm communities in terms of social disadvantage, as compared with the urban population. It was an obvious and relevant
thing to do. Striking contrasts were apparent in electrification,
education, quality of housing (heating, water supply, sanitation),
social security protection, income, transportation, and communication. Although residual levels of these deficiencies exist today,
modernization of rural life has seen a major convergence between
the material living conditions of farmers and others.

In the process of farm consolidation, many of the poorest people
in farming left or were displaced, with large numbers going to the
cities. For some years to come, many of the overall remaining
differences between farm and nonfarm communities will be shaped
partly by the size and character of the prolonged exodus from farming in the period 1940–c. 1965, and the continued, more gradual
decline since then. For example, until the farm population stabi-
lizes, it will continue to be an older-than-average population. However, social indicator comparisons that are age-specific show less
farm-nonfarm difference.

Within the farm population itself, there are major differences in
the extent to which:

1. Farm families depend on off-farm work (and thus the extent
    to which their problems can be addressed through farm pol-
    icy).
2. They and their interests dominate communities or are
    merely a minority social and economic segment within them.
3. Agriculture is practiced by the modern-day version of the
    yeoman farmer with his family labor, or by agricultural
    employers operating primarily with hired workers.

All classes of agricultural counties have been affected by the revival of population growth in rural areas. (Even those that are continuing to lose people are typically having much smaller losses than in the past.) I expect the diffusion of nonagricultural economic activity into rural areas to continue. I am not suggesting that farm people have or will become indistinguishable in values, attitudes, and life situation from everyone else. But it is hardly more than a truism to say that their economic and social setting is increasingly shaped by the complex forces of modern society and, indeed, by international trade and political factors as well. The internal variation among farmers may now be greater than their collective average difference from nonfarm America.

16

A Demographic Perspective on the Farm Population

The decline of the farm population from nearly 25 percent of all Americans in 1940 to just 2 percent by the mid-1980s is surely one of the most profound and dramatic changes in our national life. Agriculture is larger than ever in output, but only one-sixth as many people are on farms now (5 million) as were at the beginning of World War II (30 million).[1] Many millions of people moved from farm to nonfarm life, a movement impelled by mechanization and other changes in farming and made possible by opportunities in the nonfarm economy. With all the reduction in number of farm people that has occurred, however, an equilibrium has still not been reached. The size and characteristics of the farm population continue to be in flux. Here I review the most significant features and changes in current farm demography.

As late as 1940, 96 percent of all farm operators lived on their farms, as did 74 percent of all farm laborers. But increasingly, with better roads, more off-farm work by family members, multiple-tract operations, and fewer farmers keeping livestock, more of the operators lived away from their farms. There was also gradually less dependence on hired hands and a greater mutual preference for them to have their own nonfarm housing. By 1980, nearly one-third of all farmers and three-fourths of farm workers no longer lived on farms—higher proportions than I, for one, ever expected to see.[2]

Adapted from a paper presented before the Philadelphia Society for Promoting Agriculture, May 5, 1988. The author greatly appreciates the assistance of Margaret A. Butler, who prepared the charts.

1. Most of the farm population statistics cited can be found in Judith Z. Kalbacher and Diana DeAre, "Rural and Rural Farm Population: 1987," *Current Population Reports*, Series P–27, No. 61, U.S. Bureau of the Census, jointly with the Department of Agriculture, June 1988, or in earlier issues of the P–27 series.

2. If the farm population concept is limited to persons in households containing a farm operator or reporting receipt of farm self-employment income (regardless of where the household lives), there were 5.7 million people in such households in 1987, compared with 5.0 million people who lived on rural farms (regardless of occupation).

A second demographic change was the reduction in the birthrate of farm people. Farm families were always larger, on average, than urban families, and they still are to some extent. But because farm people have fewer children than they used to, the farm population is smaller today than it otherwise would have been.

From 1980 to 1987—the years of the recent farm crisis—the number of farm people dropped from 6.1 million to 5.0 million, a loss of one-sixth. This is a sizable loss, but not at all surprising given the severity and duration of the financial crisis that beset so many farmers during this period. What does surprise most people is that the average annual rate of farm population decline since 1980 (2.6 percent) is lower than that of any other recent decade. In particular, losses in the 1950s and 1960s were far higher (Fig. 16.1). And, since those earlier higher rates of loss occurred when the farm population was much larger, they involved many more people. The declines of the 1950s and 1960s did not take place without some public concern. But I will offer the opinion that there is a qualitative difference between the events of those years and the more recent period that distorts our perception of what the likely consequences of the recent crisis were for population. So much of the decrease in farms and farm people in the 1950s and 1960s was among small-scale farmers, especially tenants, whose operations were regarded as marginal to modern farming. For example, 95 percent of all black-operated tenant farms—about 350,000—disappeared between 1950 and 1970, with hardly a murmur of concern from the farm community. In the same period, there was a drop of nearly 70 percent—about 1,070,000—in white-operated tenant places, as these, too, became outmoded by mechanization or were rented by larger owner-operators to expand their farms.

In contrast, so many of the farmers who failed in the 1980s were well educated, technically efficient younger farmers, with farms that were presumed to be adequate in size. The 1980s crisis also involved financial institutions and local farm-community businesses more than ever before. The sense of community trauma was intense, and widespread decline in population was real after 1983, but the population losses did not match those of other post-World War II decades.

In 1950, the Midwest—the "Farm Belt" of popular image—contained only 32 percent of all farm people; the South had 52 percent. Today, the relative positions of the two major regions have reversed. Declines in the South have been so extensive compared

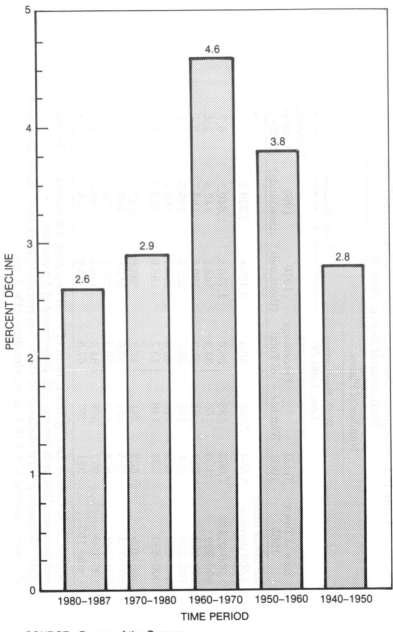

Fig. 16.1 Annual average rate of decline in U.S. farm population, 1940–87

with the Midwest that by 1987 the South had only 29 percent of the farm population, while the Midwest had a slight majority (51 percent) of the total. It seems fair to say that the Midwest has been the focus of most of the political and journalistic attention to the effects of the 1980s farm crisis. But the demographic trend of the period has been for continued, more rapid decline of the southern farm population. From just 1980 to 1987, the South's share of farm people dropped from 35.7 percent to 28.7 percent. I have no fully satisfactory explanation for this. But it is clear that although farming areas in the South are smaller and not as continuous as those of the vast prairies and plains of the Midwest, they, too, suffered great financial distress in the 1980s, aggravated throughout the Southeast by the intense drought of 1986. In addition, the highly labor-intensive growing of tobacco fell by two-fifths in acreage just from 1981 to 1986, as lower tobacco consumption and other factors reduced the U.S. crop. Thus, with limited public perception of the extent of the trend, the regional balance of farm people has shifted radically away from the South toward the Midwest and, to a lesser extent, the West.

As the number of farms declined over the last half century, the average age of farmers rose. This was the natural response in an occupation that no longer needed as many workers as it once did. By 1970, there were more than twice as many people solely or primarily self-employed in agriculture who were sixty years old and over than who were under thirty-five (Fig.16.2).[3] By contrast, among those self-employed in nonagricultural businesses, the number under age thirty-five equaled the number sixty years and over.

After 1970, however, more young people were drawn into farming, even though the total number of farmers continued to drop. In part, this reflected the fact that so many farm children were coming of age in the 1970s, as the Baby Boom children of the late 1940s and 1950s grew up. Thus, there was an ample supply of potential farmers. The decade saw several exceptionally good years for farm income, rising land values, and a frequently encouraging economic picture. In addition, the 1970s in general was a time of increased interest in rural living, and a number of "homesteader" types of urban background supplemented the farm-reared youth entering agriculture. Year-by-year the number of young farmers rose,

---

3. Data on age of self-employed people in agriculture are taken from January issues of *Employment and Earnings*, Bureau of Labor Statistics, U.S. Department of Labor.

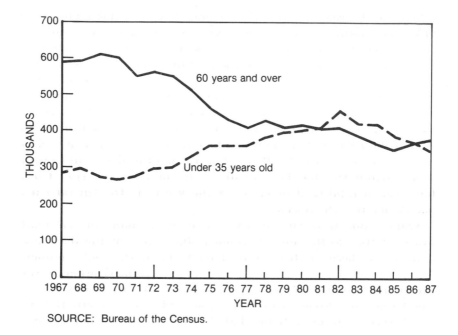

Fig. 16.2   Self-employment in agriculture,
by selected age groups, 1967–87

accompanied by rapid withdrawal of older farmers. By 1981, the
number of younger and older entrepreneurs had become equal in
agriculture.

It is likely that the number of young self-employed people in
agriculture would have begun to decline again in the 1980s, solely
as a reflection of the drop in the farm birthrate in the 1960s. But
the farm crisis of the 1980s guaranteed it, with its disproportionate
effect on younger farmers who had high debt-to-asset ratios.
Young farmers peaked in number in 1982, then decreased
thereafter. Since 1982, they have declined somewhat more rapidly
than farmers over sixty years old, with the absolute loss amounting
to about half of the 1970–82 growth. The median age of persons
solely or primarily self-employed in agriculture reached a high of
53.1 years in 1970 (Fig. 16.3). During the next fourteen years, the
figure fell to a low of 46.8 years in 1984. Even after young farmers
reached their numerical peak in 1982, the median age continued to
fall for another two years because of somewhat greater losses

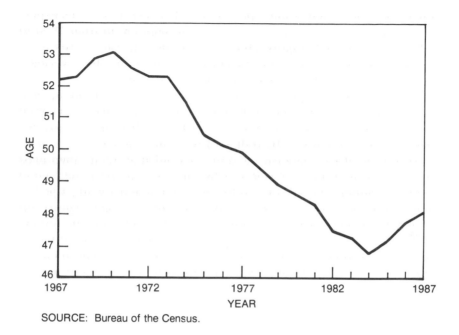

SOURCE: Bureau of the Census.

Fig. 16.3   Median age of self-employed persons in
agriculture, 1967–87

among older farmers. However, from 1984 to 1987, the median
rose each year, reaching 48.2 years in 1987. There are still more
young farmers whose principal work is agriculture than there were
in 1970, but this may not last without a more optimistic financial
prospect.

The decline in family size among farm operators is a demographic trend that in a quiet and scarcely noticed way is having a
marked effect on the potential future supply of farm-reared farmers. For at least three generations, most farm-reared children have
had to leave the farm for other careers. The existing number of
farms could not rationally be sustained under modern labor-saving
technology, and with the large average family size the supply of
farm children was too high to permit most of them to enter farming
anyway. But new farmers were drawn overwhelmingly from the
minority of farm children who elected to follow in their parents'
path. A national survey taken in 1973 showed that 81 percent of
male farmers twenty-one to sixty-four years old were the sons of

farmers.[4] The percentage may have declined somewhat since that time, but the great majority of new commercial farmers still have farm backgrounds. No other major occupation remotely approaches the intergenerational linkage of occupation found among farmers.

Farm families differ in the extent to which it is important to them to transmit their farm from one generation to another, or to see their children go into farming. But for many families an ultimate goal is to maintain a successful farm and see a son or daughter take it over. I think this is especially true of families whose home place has been in the same family for more than one generation, and whose operation is still basically a family-scale venture rather than a larger business with most work done by employees.

Obviously, an adequate supply of heirs is necessary to foster generational succession, although too many heirs can make it difficult to transmit a farm without breaking it up or putting a heavy debt load on the chosen heir who has to buy out any siblings. In 1960, the farm population averaged 85 children under fifteen years old for every 100 adults of prime work-force age (Fig. 16.4). This is a rather high ratio in American terms, and it reflects the Baby Boom of the previous fifteen years. It was the children from this group who, by and large, were drawn into farming in the 1970s, when young farmers increased. But as the birthrate among farm people dropped after 1960, the ratio of children to adults on farms fell rapidly—especially in the 1970s—and reached a level of 52 children per 100 prime working-age adults by 1980. By 1987, it had fallen further to 44/100, hardly half the level of 1960.

Farm men and women tend to marry earlier than nonfarm people and to have children somewhat earlier, too. But they no longer have or expect to have much larger families than do nonfarm people. For example, a national survey taken by the Bureau of the Census in 1987 showed that farm women eighteen to thirty-four years old expected to have 227 children ever born for each 100 women by the end of their childbearing period.[5] Nonfarm women expected 207 children per 100 women, just 9 percent fewer. By contrast, farm women who were forty to forty-four years old in 1960—and who had thus recently completed their potential child-

4. Unpublished statistics from data reported in David Featherman and Robert Hauser, *Opportunity and Change* (New York: Academic Press, 1978).

5. See Amara Bachu, "Fertility of American Women: June 1987," *Current Population Reports*, Series P-20, No. 427, U.S. Bureau of the Census, May 1988.

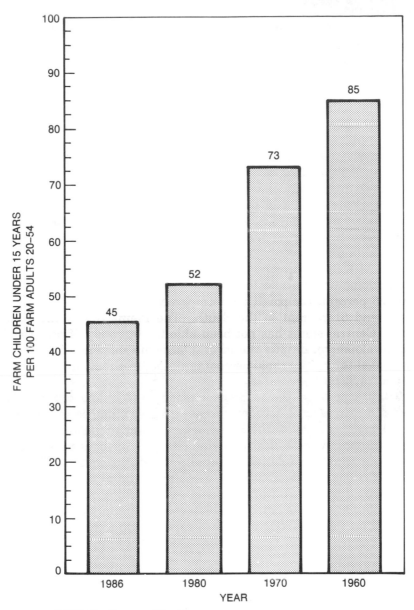

Fig. 16.4 Ratio of farm children to farm adults, 1960–86

bearing—bore 336 children per 100 women, compared with an average of 233 per 100 nonfarm women. The farm women of that period were averaging close to one-half more children per 100 women than were nonfarm women or than expected by today's farm women.

The current nearly urbanlike size of farm families means that somewhat more of them will lack a male heir, and many more will lack more than one male heir as compared with the past. As a result, unless the percentage of farm children who elect to enter the business increases substantially, the proportion of farm families who lack an heir interested in continuing to farm will rise. This in turn is likely to increase the amount of farmland that is sold in estate settlements. And sales often lead to fewer farms through use of the purchased land for enlargement of other operations. I have spoken of male heirs in order to deal with the realities of farm employment. There has been some increase in the proportion of women farmers, but in 1980 only 10 percent of persons employed solely or primarily as farm operators were women. It is conceivable that the smaller size of farm families may encourage more women to farm where there is no male heir available or interested. In any case, the decision by farm people to have fewer children is beginning to reshape and limit the pattern of father-to-son(s) continuity that has been so prominent in mainstream commercial agriculture.

Many aspects of the farm population have changed radically over the last several decades. Some of these changes offend our nostalgic attachment to the idea of a large, landed population with a traditional way of life, but the changes have been rational responses to implacable technological change, economic necessity, and the modernization of rural life. The size and composition of farm people are still in a dynamic state and will probably remain so, as forces such as emerging biotechnology and the increasing reliance on volatile foreign markets further affect the structure of agriculture.

17

The Role of Natural Resources in the Rural Economy

One of the most far-reaching changes in the American economy in the last four decades has been the drastic decline in the number and percentage of rural people engaged in farming. At the end of the Great Depression, nearly one-fourth of the U.S. population still lived and worked on farms, whereas the proportion today is barely one-tenth that high. Concurrently, the other major natural-resource industries of mining and forest products have failed to grow in employment with the rest of the economy. With modernization and the attendant advances in labor-saving technology, it

Adapted from Irma T. Elo and Calvin L. Beale, *Natural Resources and Rural Poverty: An Overview* (Washington, D.C.: Resources for the Future, Inc., 1985), chapter 1.

Coal stripping, Fulton County, Illinois, c. 1981 (photo by Beale)

has become a truism that natural-resource industries can maintain or increase output without additional labor force.

Fortunately for the welfare of rural people, the non-resource-based part of the rural economy has greatly diversified, especially in the last fifteen to twenty years. Manufacturing has decentralized and the quantity and quality of services and trade have rapidly increased. Coupled with a movement of people into rural and small-town areas that does not appear to be economically motivated, a revival of nonmetropolitan population growth occurred in the 1970s that was unprecedented in the modern history of the country. Thus natural-resource employment is now much more a part of (and in competition with) a broader rural economy than used to be the case.

This is not to say that the continuing role of natural-resource industries is insignificant. More than 1,000 nonmetropolitan counties can be identified in which at least 20 percent of employed people in 1980 worked in agriculture and food processing, mining, fishing, and forestry (including logging, wood products, and pulp and paper mills). Nationally, 16 percent of all nonmetropolitan employment was in these industries, compared with 19 percent in 1970.[1]

These natural-resource-industry categories are intended to reflect extractive production plus processing work largely done at or near the locality of raw-material production. They do include certain amounts of furniture production that are not closely linked to local timber production, and of food processing, such as bakery goods, which is more closely tied to location of people than raw materials. On the other hand, the categories exclude mineral smelting or refining, some of which is done near production sites and is directly dependent on continued local mining activity. For the purpose of statistical analysis in this overview, the categories are not perfect, but on the whole they are conceptually adequate for capturing natural-resource dependence.

We have not attempted to estimate jobs in the manufacture of natural-resource-industry equipment and supplies or in trade and

---

1. Employment in mining and in wood products industries is linked to business cycles and tends to slump severely during recessions. At the time the 1980 census was taken, employment in these industries was high, and not yet affected by the recession that soon began. Agricultural employment in March 1980 ran about one-eighth below that of the year as a whole because employment is usually greatest during harvest seasons. Thus average farm employment is somewhat understated in decennial census data.

services related to such industry.[2] Here we identify only those lines of natural-resource work identifiable from the intermediate industry detail of the census. Naturally, they also have a multiplier effect, which we cannot estimate.

Separate data for nonmetropolitan natural-resource employment for men and for women make clear the major difference that exists between them in direct dependence on this work. In 1980, 22 percent of employed nonmetropolitan men were engaged in natural-resource work, compared with just 7 percent of women. Accordingly, when mines or mills fail or crops do not pay, the effect is felt immediately by more of the male workers than female workers, because trends in the historically female trade, service, and government jobs are less sensitive to economic downturns.

Combined Role of Agriculture, Mining, and Forest Industries

To assess the extent of the rural and small-town economy dominated by the three traditional extractive industries (agriculture, mining, and forest industries), we identified those nonmetropolitan counties in which 20 percent or more of employment in 1980 was in agriculture and food processing; fishing; mining; and forestry, logging, wood products, and pulp and paper mills. This includes only direct employment and not that in manufacturing operations typically supplying equipment or services, or in the transportation or further processing or selling of goods.

Such counties numbered 1,051 in all, or 44 percent of all nonmetropolitan counties, and contained 15.3 million persons, or 27 percent of the total nonmetropolitan population (Table 17.1). Some three-fifths of the people in natural-resource-dominated counties lived in counties where no one resource activity was dominant, but where the combined employment in all types exceeded 20 percent. Somewhat more than one-fifth of the population (3.2 million) was in agricultural counties; one-eighth (1.9 million) was in mining

2. Attempts to do this for agriculture (e.g., John R. Groenewegen and Kenneth C. Clayton, *Agriculture's Role in the Economy of the United States*, Economics and Statistics Service Staff Report Number AGESS810407, U.S. Department of Agriculture, April 1981) sink into logical quagmires. They require estimates of person-equivalent workers (for workers in industries serving more than farming), and the categories become duplicative with other industries, rather than mutually exclusive. For example, a dealer selling phosphatic fertilizer could be treated as part of both agriculture and mining.

Table 17.1 Characteristics of Nonmetropolitan Counties, 1980
(absolute numbers in thousands)

Characteristic	Total Nonmetropolitan	Non-Natural-Resource Counties	All Natural-Resource Counties	Agriculture[a]	Mining[b]	Forestry[c]	Combination[d]
Population							
Total	57,115	41,763	15,352	3,239	1,904	1,040	9,169
White	50,357	36,637	13,720	3,050	1,776	939	7,955
Black	5,017	3,973	1,043	62	51	72	858
Indian[e]	750	540	210	45	26	22	118
Hispanic[f]	1,811	986	825	178	143	12	492
Percent high school graduates	59.0	59.7	57.0	60.6	50.3	60.9	56.6
Female labor force participation rate	45.1	46.4	41.7	41.2	33.5	43.7	43.3
Percent persons 16–64 with work disability	10.1	9.9	10.6	8.6	13.4	11.7	10.6
Percent unemployed persons in labor force, 1979[f]	18.2	18.7	16.9	11.9	19.7	22.0	17.6
Median household income, 1979 ($)	14,040	14,242	13,428	12,617	14,957	14,522	13,350
Percent persons in poverty, 1979							
Total	15.4	14.9	17.0	17.7	17.1	14.4	17.0
White	12.4	12.0	14.5	16.0	16.1	12.2	13.8
Black	39.0	38.1	42.5	55.6	32.9	40.4	42.4
Indian[e]	34.0	35.0	31.5	40.1	29.0	22.7	30.7
Hispanic[f]	27.3	26.0	28.8	37.7	20.8	22.0	28.0

| Percent with income below 75 percent of poverty level | 10.1 | 9.7 | 11.2 | 11.8 | 11.9 | 9.0 | 11.1 |

Source: Special tabulations from the *1980 Census of Population.*

[a] All nonmetropolitan counties in which at least 20 percent of all employment in 1980 was in agriculture.

[b] All nonmetropolitan counties in which at least 20 percent of all employment in 1980 was in mining.

[c] All nonmetropolitan counties in which at least 20 percent of all employment in 1980 was in forestry and logging, wood products, and pulp and paper mills.

[d] All nonmetropolitan counties in which no one resource activity was dominant, but in which at least 20 percent of all employment combined was in agriculture and food processing, mining, fishing, forestry and logging, wood products, and pulp and paper mills.

[e] Includes Alaskan natives.

[f] The Hispanic population may be of any race. Nearly three-fifths of all nonmetropolitan Hispanics reported themselves as white in the 1980 census. Most of the remainder were classed as "other races," but small numbers were black or Indian. Thus, the data shown by race are not mutually exclusive of data for Hispanics.

[g] That is, percentage of persons in labor force who experienced some period of unemployment during the year.

counties, and the remaining one-fifteenth (1.0 million) was in
forest-products counties.

In 1980, the region most thoroughly dominated by natural-resource employment was the Great Plains, where from north to
south the great majority of the nonmetropolitan counties were primarily agricultural, or, to a lesser extent, mining areas, or a combination of the two (see Fig. 17.1). The northern half of the West also
was heavily tied to natural-resource work, with timber industries
added to the mix.

The eastern third of the country showed few counties still
heavily reliant on the production phases of agriculture, but it did
have more combination counties when timber industries and food
processing are added in. A compact area of twenty-eight counties
in Kentucky, Virginia, and West Virginia was still heavily dependent on coal mining. What may seem surprising are the large
expanses of territory in the Carolinas, Alabama, and Tennessee, in
the Northeast, and in the eastern states of the Midwest, where few
or even no nonmetropolitan counties were resource-dominated in
1980. These areas have acquired such diverse economies of
manufacturing, trade, and services that they are no longer primarily resource-based, even though many counties within them
still have a productive agriculture.

The counties with a combination of natural-resource employment that exceeds 20 percent of all jobs, but with no one such
industry dominant, were rather scattered without any large groupings (see Fig. 17.2). A number of counties in the Northwest combined timber work and agriculture. In the southern Great Plains,
the usual combination was farming and oil and gas production. In
the Corn Belt, food processing added to agricultural employment.
A number of counties in the lower South had timber and agriculture. The pattern varied. The combination counties averaged
19,000 population each, much larger than the agriculturally dominated counties, but not as large as those focused on mining or
timber. The many counties with more than one natural-resource
activity make it clear that natural-resource counties cannot be adequately identified just on the basis of dominance by individual
industries.

To emphasize an earlier point, it should be noted that many
additional counties could have been identified as having more than
20 percent of their male employment in natural-resource industries. No attempt has been made to identify these counties, but
they would probably have numbered several hundred, with several

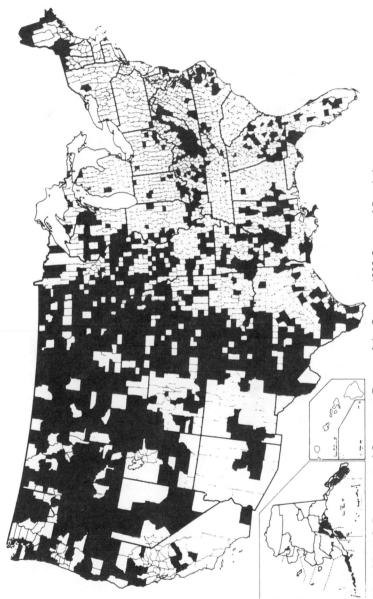

SOURCE: U.S. Department of Commerce, Bureau of the Census, *1980 Census of Population.*

NOTE: Includes all nonmetropolitan counties in which at least 20 percent of all employment in 1980 was in agriculture, food processing, mining, fishing, forestry and logging, and wood products and pulp and paper mills.

Fig. 17.1 Nonmetropolitan natural-resource counties, 1980

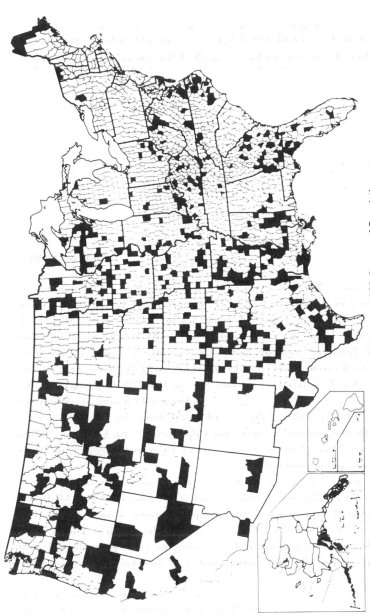

SOURCE: U.S. Department of Commerce, Bureau of the Census, *1980 Census of Population.*

NOTE: Includes all nonmetropolitan counties in which no one resource activity was dominant but in which at least 20 percent of all employment combined was in agriculture, food processing, fishing, mining, forestry and logging, and wood products and paper mills.

Fig. 17.2 Nonmetropolitan combination natural-resource counties, 1980

million population. In nonmetropolitan America, women numbered only about 17 percent of all natural-resource-industry workers but comprised 45 percent of the rest of the labor force in 1980.

Agriculture

Only 8.5 percent of employed rural people worked directly in agriculture in 1980. By counties, the percentage so employed ranged all the way from zero (in a few Alaskan areas, for example) to a high of 70 percent in one county of North Dakota. There were only 19 counties left in the whole country where at least half of all employed people worked solely or primarily in agriculture compared to thirty years ago, when there were close to 600 such counties. All told in 1980, some 442 nonmetropolitan counties containing 3.2 million people had 20 percent or more of their work force in agriculture. They averaged only 7,300 population per county, because agriculture is seldom dominant in partly urbanized or densely settled rural areas. Farm counties were concentrated in the Great Plains, and in the western Corn Belt, where three-fourths of the population in agriculturally dominated nonmetropolitan counties lived (see Table 17.2 and Fig. 17.3). As late as 1952, half of all farm people in the nation lived in the South. It is a measure of the diversification of the southern economy and of the extent of withdrawal of workers from farming that in 1980 only 0.2 million people lived in southern counties (outside of the Plains states of Oklahoma and Texas) that had 20 percent or more of their employment in agriculture and food processing.

Most of the farming counties are not among the top agricultural counties of the nation but rather lack other sources of employment. Their prosperity rises or falls with the interaction of agricultural costs, output, and prices.

As with other traditional extractive industries, the importance of farm employment in the rural economy is understated if one considers only its overall incidence. Farming is still an overwhelmingly male occupation, and is likely to remain so, even though the number of female farmers is growing. Among rural U.S. males, 11.7 percent were in agriculture in 1980. This is a closer representation of the percentage of all rural households that have some employment dependence on farming than is the figure on the percentage of all rural workers who are in the industry.

Table 17.2 Characteristics of Nonmetropolitan Agricultural Counties, 1980[a]
(absolute numbers in thousands)

Characteristic	Total	Region 1	Region 2	Region 3	Region 4	Region 5
Population						
Total	3,239	1,247	1,224	432	132	204
White	3,050	1,238	1,178	358	123	153
Black	62	2	1	12	0.2	47
Indian[b]	45	4	38	2	1	0.3
Hispanic[c]	178	4	13	143	11	8
Percent high school graduates	60.6	62.3	64.3	50.1	68.6	41.7
Female labor force participation rate	41.2	42.5	40.5	39.9	42.3	38.9
Percent persons 16–64 with work disability	8.6	8.5	7.8	9.0	9.5	12.3
Percent unemployed persons in labor force, 1979[d]	11.9	13.4	7.7	15.9	15.8	18.4
Median household income, 1979 ($)	12,617	13,323	12,372	12,366	13,297	10,449
Percent persons in poverty, 1979						
Total	17.7	14.7	17.2	22.6	15.9	28.9
White	16.0	14.5	15.9	19.3	14.9	21.1
Black	5.6	(e)	(e)	48.4	(e)	58.1
Indian	40.1	(e)	42.5	(e)	(e)	(e)
Hispanic	37.7	(e)	28.7	39.4	27.4	42.9
Percent with income below 75 percent of poverty level	11.8	9.5	11.7	15.2	10.3	20.0

Source: Special tabulations from the *1980 Census of Population.*

Note: Region 1: Iowa, Minnesota, Wisconsin, Missouri, Illinois. Region 2: North Dakota, South Dakota, Montana, Wyoming, Colorado, Nebraska, Kansas, Oklahoma. Region 3: California, Arizona, New Mexico, Texas. Region 4: Oregon, Washington, Idaho, Utah. Region 5: Census South, except Texas and Oklahoma.

a All nonmetropolitan counties in which at least 20 percent of all employment in 1980 was agriculture.

b Includes Alaskan natives.

c The Hispanic population may be any race. Nearly three-fifths of all nonmetropolitan Hispanics reported themselves as white in the 1980 census. Most of the remainder were classed as "other races," but small numbers were black or Indian. Thus, the data shown by race are not mutually exclusive of data for Hispanics.

d That is, percentage of persons in labor force who experienced some period of unemployment during the year.

e For base population less than 5,000, poverty rate is not shown.

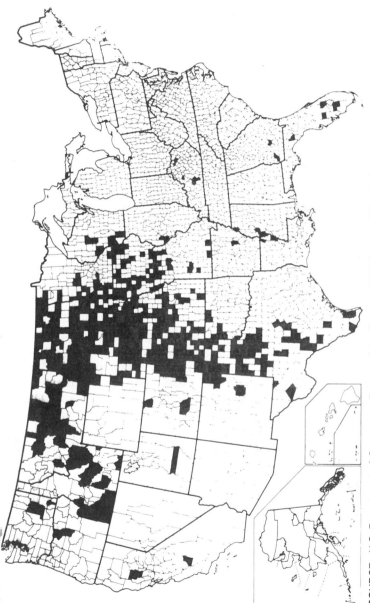

SOURCE: U.S. Department of Commerce, Bureau of the Census, *1980 Census of Population.*

NOTE: Includes all nonmetropolitan counties in which at least 20 percent of all employment was in agriculture and food processing.

Fig. 17.3   Nonmetropolitan agricultural counties, 1980

Mining

Mining employment peaked in the early 1920s after the rise of the automobile but before the erosion of the coal market for residential heating, steam-powered railways, and shipping. In 1920, 1.2 million workers were employed in the sector, most of them near the mine sites in rural areas and small towns.[3] Because of reduced coal demand, extensive mechanization, and increased use of imported metal ores, mining employment was cut in half to 0.6 million by the end of the 1960s, despite the intervening rise in oil and gas extraction.[4] After the first oil shortage of 1973, mining employment again rose, dominated by the response of oil and gas exploration to higher product prices and the increased use of coal for electric generation. By 1980, mining employment had again reached 1.0 million, and it further increased to 1.1 million in 1982 before slumping back to 1.0 million in 1984 with the recession in mineral use and lower prices.[5] The composition of the industry has greatly changed. Whereas sixty years ago about two-thirds of mining employment was in coal production, today more than half is in oil and gas. Coal has about one-fourth; metal and nonmetallic minerals (other than coal) one-tenth each.

During the 1970s, mining was a major rural growth industry, and a number of western counties that had rapid population increase through in-migration did so because of mining booms. Revival of mining was also an important contributor to the sharp population "turnaround" experienced in the southern coalfields. In rural areas, the 1980 census showed 2 percent of the labor force in mining, with the figure for men being 3.1 percent. Eighty-one counties had 20 percent or more of their employed population in mining. Most of these counties were in the coalfields of the Southern Appalachians, the oil and gas areas of Texas, and various metal, coal, and oil counties of the Mountain West (see Fig. 17.4).

Whether there will be a resumption of growth in mining employment is uncertain. Truly high prices for natural gas and oil could trigger renewed interest in coal-conversion plants, shale oil extraction, and deep oil and gas drilling. But events of the last several years have shown how susceptible all of these projects are to even

3. U.S. Department of Labor, Bureau of Labor Statistics, *Employment and Earnings, United States 1909–70*, Bulletin 1312–17 (n.d.), p. 4.
4. Ibid.
5. U.S. Department of Labor, Bureau of Labor Statistics, *Employment and Earnings* 32:3 (March 1985), p. 49.

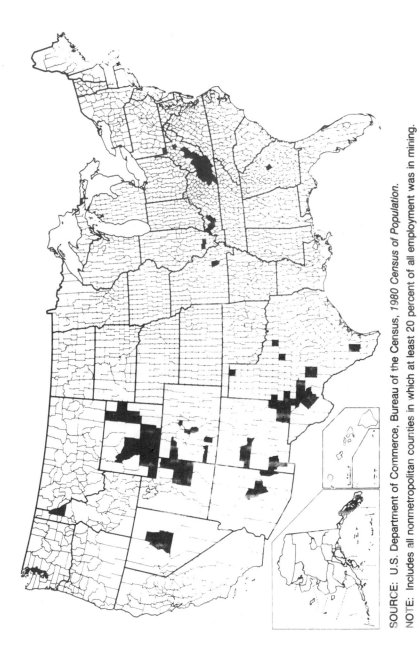

SOURCE: U.S. Department of Commerce, Bureau of the Census, *1980 Census of Population.*

NOTE: Includes all nonmetropolitan counties in which at least 20 percent of all employment was in mining.

Fig. 17.4   Nonmetropolitan mining counties, 1980

temporary market gluts and price slumps. Conventional coal-mining employment may also have difficulty recovering to 1980 levels as gains in production per worker continue to be made, and as metallurgical and export markets have dwindled in a manner that leaves their future in doubt. Further, the recession of 1981–83 demonstrated that copper production in developing nations is rather inflexible and unresponsive to lowered prices. The need of these governments for foreign exchange and labor peace and the continued availability of international credit all foster high output despite lack of markets. Most of the burden of reducing world copper production has fallen on the U.S. industry, which may be wary of reopening its more marginal mines. Even without re-sumed employment growth, however, the mining industry has a larger relative share of rural and small-town natural-resource jobs than it did in earlier decades before the decline in farm work.

Mining communities have long been among the most diverse ethnically of all rural communities. Workers in a given mining field were often recruited or attracted from various countries. English, Scots, Welsh, Irish, Yugoslavs, Finns, French, Italians, and Hispanics were all commonly found, in addition to native-born Americans. In newer western boom areas, the ethnic diversifica-tion continues, although now it is based on in-migration of workers from different regions of the country rather than on foreign in-migration. It is noticeable in the Southwest, however, that Mexican-American workers have become increasingly more likely than other groups to enter mining work, and the composition of a number of mining settlements there has become more Hispanic over the last generation.

Forest Products

In the nineteenth century, the rise of commercial timber operations resembled the mining industry: companies moved on to other areas as reserves were depleted, rather than operating on a sus-tained-yield basis. In the twentieth century, stabilization began. Historical employment statistics of a comparable nature are not as fully available for forest products as they are for agriculture and mining. However, in 1940, at the tag end of the depression, the census of that year counted 1.2 million workers in forestry, lumber, furniture, other wood products, and paper mills, with another 0.1 million unemployed. The number peaked in the 1950 census at 1.5

million and then had drifted down to 1.4 million by 1970, as labor-saving technology and market competition from other materials reduced the need for workers in logging and milling, although this was partly offset by growth in furniture and paper. By 1980, the figure was 1.7 million as employment expanded in every phase of the industry except paper.

Close to 3 percent of all rural employment was in forestry and wood products in 1980, with the percentage for men being 3.8. Although total employment is somewhat greater than in mining, it is much more dispersed in nature. Only forty-eight counties had more than 20 percent of their workers in forestry and wood products in 1980. A majority of them are in the Pacific Northwest (see Fig. 17.5).

Fishing

The number of people engaged in fishing has never been large in the national context. The peak of employment in census years came in 1930 at 73,000. By 1970, the total number of employed and experienced unemployed workers was only 40,000. By 1980, the number employed had risen to 62,000. The fishing industry has experienced much foreign competition and has undergone a process of increased capital requirements and larger but fewer operations—analogous to that in farming. Fishing is locally important in some coastal communities, but in no county does it directly employ as much as one-fifth of the work force.

Nonextractive Natural-Resource Activities

Recreation

The legitimatization and commercialization of leisure in twentieth-century society has been a significant source of rural employment growth related to recreational use of land, water, and scenic amenities. The proliferation of national and state parks, the creation of numerous dam reservoirs, the shortening of work weeks, the lengthening of holidays and vacations, the increase in early retirement, the influence of the environmental movement, and the growth of disposable income have all been causes or manifestations of this trend.

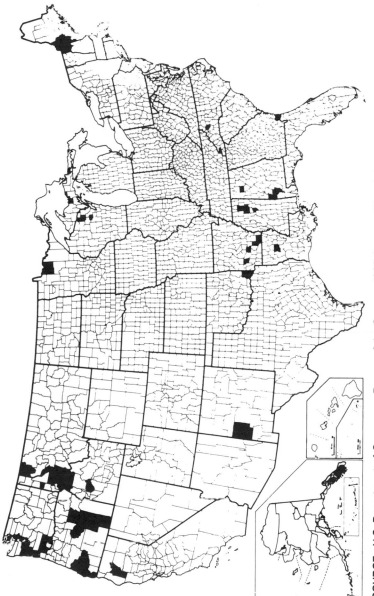

SOURCE: U.S. Department of Commerce, Bureau of the Census, *1980 Census of Population*.

NOTE: Includes all nonmetropolitan counties in which at least 20 percent of all employment was in forestry and logging, and wood products and pulp and paper mills.

Fig. 17.5 Nonmetropolitan forestry counties, 1980

Inherently, outdoor-based recreation is disproportionately found in rural and small-town settings. Its employment effects are somewhat difficult to measure precisely. Most recreation-generated jobs are not uniquely measured or characterized in employment data. Some are quite seasonal in nature and may never appear in the national census with its March employment reference. Basically, most forms of recreation generate employment in personal services (especially hotels and motels), retail trade (such as restaurants or gift shops), real estate (in second-home areas), or direct entertainment and recreation (such as golf clubs, amusement parks, ski resorts, and theaters). But a certain level of such activities occurs in almost all communities, and it is only a disproportionate level of employment in these categories that can be attributed to recreation.

If one considers nonmetropolitan counties in which 10 percent or more of all employment was in personal services, entertainment, and recreation in 1980, thirty-six such counties can be identified. This level of specialization in the two sectors most clearly related to recreation is nearly three times that of the nonmetropolitan United States as a whole. Most of these counties are readily recognized as having well-known resort areas, such as those in the Rockies (for example, counties containing Aspen, Vail, Sun Valley, Jackson Hole), Nevada gambling areas, the Hawaiian Islands, eastern coastal resorts (Nantucket, Key West), Appalachian Mountain resorts (White Sulphur Springs), or dam reservoir areas (Lake Powell, Lake of the Ozarks).

In most cases, the rate of poverty is below the national average and well below the nonmetropolitan average. (The median rate for the resort counties was 11.4 percent in 1980.) They tend to attract people as entrepreneurs and permanent residents of above-average education and income-earning capacity, although a number of low-skilled service jobs are also created, such as those in motels and restaurants. Work opportunities for women are usually high, with most recreation areas having over half of all resident women in the labor force. Some of the recreation counties are also retirement areas, but this is not typically true in the case of ski resorts. As a group, rural recreation areas have grown rapidly in population in recent times with many new residents of metropolitan origin.

Retirement

One of the commonest sources of population increase in nonmetropolitan America in recent decades has been the influx of retired people. Greater longevity, younger average age at retirement, and improved income levels of older people have all facilitated the apparent desire of a significant fraction of metropolitan residents to live in a rural or small-town setting in their later years. Although precise data of net movement of older people into nonmetropolitan counties are not available, it is estimated that 515 nonmetropolitan counties had growth of the population aged sixty years and over of 15 percent or more from net migration, 1970–80.[6] This amounts to one-fifth of all nonmetropolitan counties. The net in-movement was about 750,000 persons. Exactly comparable estimates for the 1960s are not available, but a more liberal procedure for that period showed 360 counties with net in-migration rates for older people of 10 percent or more. Thus, the demographic and economic importance of rural retirement grew during the 1970s.

Retirement destinations are no longer limited to the popular stereotypes of Florida and the Southwest. Widespread in-migration has occurred in the Ozarks, the New England coast, the southern Blue Ridge, the Texas Hill Country, the Puget Sound area, the Upper Great Lakes, the Sierra Nevada foothills, western Oregon, east Texas, and the Tidewater areas of Maryland and Virginia. All of these locations involve dispersed settlement, and not merely aggregations of people in towns. There is a marked tendency to settle around bodies of water—natural or artificial. Many of the numerous dams built over the last half-century primarily for power or flood control purposes have attracted rapid population growth of retired and younger people, as well as seasonal residents. A tally of nonmetropolitan townships and equivalents that border on dam reservoirs in twelve southern states showed a 26 percent population growth from 1970 to 1980, 8 percentage points higher than other parts of the same counties and 10 points above the national nonmetropolitan growth rate.

The economic impact of retirement on an area is difficult to state precisely. If the retired are at all numerous, additional employment is created to serve them, particularly in construction, retail trade, health, and other services. Labor-force participation rates among retirees themselves are very low—typically less than 10 percent, except among those under sixty-five. But the attraction of retired people serves as an "export" industry for communities as income in the form of pensions, social security, or other externally derived support is drawn into the community.

6. Unpublished estimates derived from the 1970 and 1980 censuses of population. Prepared by Calvin L. Beale.

Older migrants who come to nonmetropolitan communities from metropolitan areas have far lower poverty rates than do other older nonmetropolitan residents. The poverty rate among migrants sixty and over who moved into nonmetropolitan counties from metropolitan areas between 1975 and 1980 was only 10.1 percent. This is barely half the rate for all other nonmetropolitan residents of the same age (19.4), and even below the national average for persons of all ages.[7]

Thus, in the case of both the recreation and retirement counties, the use of attractive rural natural-resource features for these purposes has generally led to an income-resource transfer to the affected areas. In an absolute sense, there are more poor people in rural America today than there would be without the migrants who have come to recreation and retirement areas, but the relatively low proportion of poverty-level incomes among these older people has served to lower the overall percentage of rural poverty.

---

7. Nina Glasgow, "The Rural Elderly," unpublished paper, Economic Research Service, U.S. Department of Agriculture, 1984.

18
Varieties of Minority Rural Poverty

Minorities bear the worst brunt of poverty in rural areas. The depth and persistence of poverty among blacks, Hispanics, and Native Americans reflect historical legacies of injustice and also contemporary transformations under way in rural economies. Beyond these three groups, one must also recognize a fourth distinctively rural "minority"—hired farm workers—whose lives also are marked by poverty and disadvantage. The following sections

Adapted from Irma T. Elo and Calvin L. Beale, *Natural Resources and Rural Poverty: An Overview* (Washington, D.C.: Resources for the Future, Inc., 1985), chapters 3 and 5.

Father and child (courtesy of UNICEF)

trace the varied historical and contemporary circumstances that produce the poverty of rural minorities.

Blacks

The dynamics of change in the American black population have been highly varied and quite rapid over the last half-century. It would be difficult to point to any change that has been more central and far reaching than the exodus from farming. Although for a generation now we have thought of the black population as being concentrated in metropolitan central cities, it was more rural than the white population in all earlier periods of U.S. history. The economic justification for slavery was the use of blacks as agricultural labor, and emancipation did little to alter this basic pattern. With World War I and the postwar years, the urbanization of blacks advanced. Nearly two-fifths (39 percent) of all blacks, however, still lived on farms in 1930.

It is fruitless to try to apportion the causation of the out-migration thereafter between displacement from farming and the lure of the cities. Both factors operated. Three-fourths of all black farmers had been tenant farmers, most commonly in cotton and tobacco. They had no control over their destiny in farming once the mechanization and chemicalization of agriculture destroyed the logic of the family labor tenant system. At the same time, knowledge of job opportunities and the better life in the cities, away from the controls and chronic poverty of the rural South, convinced many blacks to leave the farm before actual displacement occurred.

Today, 94 percent of the black farmers are gone.[1] The flight of the owners was only relatively less than that of the tenants. There was no real land reform after the Civil War, and blacks who eventually acquired farms typically had small units not suited for the mechanized farming of the post–World War II era, which relied on large acreages, volume production, and smaller profit margins. By 1978 there were only about 57,000 black-operated farms left, and the median age of the farmers was high (57.5 years), reflecting the failure of young people to enter the business.[2]

---

1. U.S. Department of Agriculture, *Report of the USDA Task Force and Black Farm Ownership*, September 1983, p. 8.
2. U.S. Department of Agriculture, unpublished figure derived from special tabulations of the 1978 Census of Agriculture.

By 1980 fewer than one in 200 blacks nationwide lived on farms. For some years now, the primary role of blacks in farming has been as hired workers rather than as operators. On the large plantations, a minority of the sharecroppers were converted to paid year-round workers when the tenant system was abandoned. But further labor-saving innovations in farm technology continued to erode the amount of work available. Blacks continue to play a critical role through their labor in the conduct of agriculture in the Delta and certain other areas. But the generally low wages paid for hired farm work and the seasonally limited nature of much of the work are not conducive to good income and adequate levels of living. This is not to say that living conditions of black farmers and hired workers have not improved over the years. They have. But on average they lag far behind societal standards.

In the process of leaving the land, many black land-owning families sold or otherwise lost their land. The amount of land owned by black farmers fifty and sixty years ago was considerably more than that owned by all blacks—farm and nonfarm alike—today. (This considers land in plots of an acre or more and does not include smaller house lots.) The large number of heirs per family, the distant dispersal of heirs, the lack of wills, the clouded nature of titles, and other circumstances have led to the loss of black ownership of at least 5 million acres of land.[3]

There has been a recurrent sense of concern in parts of the black community over the future of blacks as farm operators and the ownership of rural land, reflected most recently in a report of the Civil Rights Commission.[4] But in a time when the number of commercial farms continues to decline because of poor farm income, the reentry of blacks into full-scale agriculture seems doubtful unless a stronger motivation for farm life develops among young people and unless a substantial program of financial and technical assistance is organized well beyond what is presently available. An increase in small farms that combine part-time farming with off-farm work is not out of the question though. Such farms are increasing in number nationally. Whether blacks are participating in this trend is not currently known.

Blacks are the only major racial group in which nearly as many residents are employed in timber industries (including manufacturing) as in agriculture. Some 6.9 percent in 1980 were so en-

3. U.S. Department of Agriculture, *Report of the USDA Task Force*, pp. 13–14.
4. U.S. Commission on Civil Rights, *The Decline of Black Farming in America* (Washington, D.C.: Government Printing Office, 1982).

gaged. The location of rural blacks has with minor exceptions always been in the timbered South, whereas large numbers of whites, Indians, and Hispanics live in unwooded areas of the prairies, plains, and the semiarid West. Blacks have long worked in timber cutting, turpentining, and sawmills.

In the past, the role of timber work did not remotely compete with farming in the number of blacks employed. But this work has not diminished to the extent that farm work has. The South, with its mild climate, is ideal for rapid growth of trees and has a wide variety of wood-processing industries. Blacks have a proportional employment in these industries, but not a proportional ownership of the forests. Counties with a high participation of blacks in wood industries have substantial rates of black poverty, but typically not to the extent as those in areas that are or were the most intensely involved in plantation agriculture. It may well be that in the future the welfare of rural blacks will come to depend somewhat more on wood industries than on farming.

Comparatively few black workers are in mining. Black miners have been an element in the coal mining industry in parts of eastern Kentucky and southern West Virginia and have some role in sand and gravel operations and oil and gas drilling. By and large, however, rural areas inhabited by blacks have not been richly endowed with minerals, and only limited migration to mining work elsewhere took place.

As with most other segments of rural poverty, it is possible to have either an optimistic or pessimistic view of the condition of the rural black population. This population is remarkably better off today than it was twenty or thirty years ago in housing, education, political enfranchisement, access to public facilities and programs, entry to manufacturing and other employment, and relief from the semithralldom of sharecropping. But American standards of well-being have also changed, and if one wants to quote shocking statistics on current poverty, there is no need to look beyond those pertaining to rural and small-town blacks.

In 1983, 43 percent of nonmetropolitan black residents lived with poverty level incomes, even after counting cash income received from public assistance. Many conditions of the black population militate against widespread achievement of adequate earned incomes. These include the continued low level of education compared with general standards (especially among people over forty), the unusually low rates of work duration and male labor-force participation (reflecting a high incidence of discouraged workers), concentration of much of the work force in low-wage industries, the lower degree of economic diversity in the Coastal Plain and Delta counties, where black rural poverty is the worst, the high and growing proportion of children and women in female-headed families, and large family size.

These conditions disproportionately affect rural blacks generally, but they are most serious in areas such as the Mississippi Delta and the Black Belt, where the former plantation agriculture system was most dominant, and where blacks form the highest percentage of the total population. Subjectively, blacks do not appear to evaluate these areas as bleakly as they did in the 1950s and 1960s, when the majority of each young adult cohort quickly moved away after leaving school. Although some population out-migration occurred in the 1970s, it was much reduced, and for the first time in recent history a number of rural counties had an increase in the black percentage of their population. The disparities between whites and blacks in these areas continue to be major, however.

But how does one address such conditions? To some extent, it is difficult to know which are causes and which are effects of long-term poverty, or indeed, whether they might not be a mixture of both. To work depends upon work being available or creatable. While economic development programs have broadened the employment base for blacks in many rural areas, the growth of non-farm employment opportunities during the last decades has been limited in rural areas that have the most persistent and intractable problems of poverty. Many of these are areas of the Deep South with a high concentration of rural blacks. To broaden the economic base in these areas, public and private sector efforts to increase the availability of capital and technical expertise are essential for the creation of private sector employment opportunities in these communities.

Hispanics

The Hispanic minority has by far the strongest commitment to natural-resource work of any of the major rural and nonmetropolitan groups. In 1980, 30 percent of employed rural Hispanics were in natural-resource jobs, a clear level of dominance. Among rural Hispanic men, the figure reached 38 percent.

The strong Hispanic dependence is largely attributable to the key role of that ethnic group in agriculture, mostly in California and Texas, and particularly in irrigated farming. By a margin of 8 to 1, Hispanics in agriculture were hired farm workers in 1980, rather than farm operators or managers. In the urban part of the nonmetropolitan population, the data suggest a hired worker-to-operator ratio of as much as 20 to 1.

At any given time, these workers are subject to competition from low-wage illegal aliens, usually from Mexico. Some such workers are counted in the numbers just given if they were in the United States at the time of the census, were successfully located, and were not treated as temporary visitors. Many, however, move between this country and Mexico on a seasonal basis or as they earn a stake and return home for a while. By the very nature of their clandestine entry, their precise numbers are unknown. It is known that about 100,000 are apprehended each year in agriculture, and one researcher has estimated their typical total annual number at 350,000.[5]

Hispanics also have a somewhat higher than average representation in mining, with 5.5 percent of their nonmetropolitan workers so employed, more than twice the proportion for non-Hispanics. They have become prominent in metal-mining operations in the Southwest and in oil and gas production in Texas, in some places constituting a majority of the work force. Mining work has been an avenue of upward economic mobility for many of the Hispanics engaged in it. Especially in the metal mining areas of Arizona, New Mexico, and Colorado, poverty rates are much lower for Hispanics than elsewhere, although the rates still are higher than those for white people in the same counties.

Native Americans

Historically, Native Americans (including Alaskan natives) have been one of the poorest segments of the nation's population. Today, they number slightly over 1.5 million people, of whom about 60 percent live in rural and nonmetropolitan areas. Only slightly over 22 percent of all Indians continue to live on reservations. The largest

5. Leslie Whitener Smith and Robert Coltrane, *Hired Farmworkers: Background and Trends for the Eighties*, Rural Development Research Report 32, U.S. Department of Agriculture, September 1981, p. 8.

concentrations of Native Americans are found in the Southwest, the Northern Plains, and the Pacific Northwest.

The incidence of poverty among nonmetropolitan Indians (30.4 percent) continues to be well above the national average for all nonmetropolitan residents—with the rate being even higher among reservation Indians (40.7 percent). Regionally, the highest incidence of poverty among Native Americans is in Arizona, South Dakota, Utah, and New Mexico, where poverty rates ranged from 43.5 percent to 49.8 percent in 1979. These rates largely reflect conditions among the Navajo and the Sioux, the two largest tribes with high rates of poverty.

There are also large numbers of rural Indians in portions of the South, especially in Oklahoma and North Carolina. Their poverty rates (averaging 27 percent) are substantially lower than those in the Northern Plains and the West but still are well above those of rural whites.

In 1980, only 14.7 percent of Native Americans living in rural areas were employed in natural-resource industries. This is somewhat less than the U.S. total of 16 percent for all rural workers. This percentage may seem low, given the wealth of natural resources found on many Indian lands. But even among the Navajo, whose reservation contains substantial mineral resources, only about 12.5 percent of employment was in natural-resource industries. Among these industry categories, agriculture and food processing employed the largest percentage of all rural Indians, 6.7 percent. Employment in forestry and fishing was somewhat above the average for all rural workers, as fishing plays an important role in the economy of Native American tribes in the Pacific Northwest. Mining employed 3.1 percent of rural Indians. At the same time, manufacturing accounted for only 18.0 percent of their employment in contrast to the service sector and government, which together employed 43.5 percent of all Native Americans in rural areas.

Several aspects of the labor-force participation pattern of nonmetropolitan Indians serve to lower their income. Almost 30 percent of all employed rural Indians (inclusive of Alaskan natives) had experienced some unemployment in 1979. At the same time, Indians have low rates of male labor-force participation, as well as female; for example, over 21 percent of nonmetropolitan males in the prime labor-force years (twenty-five to fifty-four years old) were neither working nor looking for work in 1980. Some of them were "discouraged workers" (to use the Department of Labor's term) who would have wanted work if they thought it was available, but believed it futile to look. Among nonmetropolitan white men of comparable age, only 7.6 percent were not in the labor force.

Employed nonmetropolitan Indians work fewer hours on average per year than do other groups. In 1979, somewhat less than half of employed Indian males had fifty weeks or more of work, compared with 65 percent of white males. Of Indian males who experienced unemployment during the year, the average duration of lack of work (17.8 weeks) was considerably longer than that for whites (14.6). Comparable evidence of more limited participation in employment could be cited for women, but the disparity between Indian and white nonmetropolitan women is not as great as that for men.

Further complicating the low-income problem of so many Native Americans are the large family size and rapid rate of population growth. The recent level of childbearing approaches a biological doubling of population in each generation, and that creates comparatively low per capita income levels even where wages and employment availability are average.

Contributing factors to the high incidence of poverty, high unemployment, and low labor-force participation rates undoubtedly are the lack of economic diversification, the employment opportunities available, and the low skill and educational levels of the group as a whole. Only 46 percent of all rural Indians had completed high school, and only 17 percent had attended one or more years of college. In addition, reservation economies traditionally have lacked a diversified economic base and private-sector employment. The federal government has limited its role to supporting services and has not invested its resources in the development of a private, productive sector of the reservation economies. Tribal governments in turn have lacked capital and technical know-how to expand the base. What private-sector development has occurred has been mostly limited to low-wage manufacturing. In addition, natural-resource extraction has occurred on reservations where such resources are located. However, resource extraction on Indian lands has not brought many employment opportunities for Native Americans, and much of the wealth generated has left the reservations.

Farm Workers

Over the last generation, the farm-resident population has come increasingly to be composed of farm operators and their families.

Hired farm workers are now much more likely to live off the farm than on it. In 1980, only 18 percent of hired farm workers lived on farms, compared with 55 percent in 1950. Because hired workers no longer typically live on farms and are the poorest group of people in farming, their removal from the farms has also been a factor leading to a reduction in the poverty rate of farm residents. But it increasingly means that rural farm data are representative only of the operator class. It should be noted that some farm workers receive noncash perquisites such as housing. Even so, allowance for such benefits would not significantly eliminate the disparity between the incomes of farm workers and persons in most other occupations.

Hired farm work has long been one of the lowest paid, least protected, and least prestigious of occupations. The work is often seasonal, with intermittent unemployment. Formal educational requirements are minimal (although some real skills are required if the work is to be done properly). The occupation was among the last to be protected by Social Security and Unemployment Compensation legislation. It draws disproportionately from disadvantaged ethnic groups and illegal immigrants.

In no other major occupational group is the incidence of poverty as high as among hired farm workers. Precise poverty data for hired farm worker households are not available. However, an approximation of the poverty level from 1981 income data yielded an estimate that 31 percent of hired farm workers were in economically disadvantaged (poverty) households. The estimate ranged from 25 percent for white farm workers to more than half for blacks.[6]

The plight of migrant farm workers is familiar to the public, usually because of attention given to poor conditions in the camps where they live. But this group is a small part of the total hired farm-work force. National surveys consistently show only about 200,000 persons who do migratory farm work in the course of a year (exclusive of foreign nationals who were back in their home countries at the time of surveying).[7] This is only 8 percent of hired farm workers. The vast majority of farm workers are local persons.

---

6. Leslie A. Whitener, "Hired Farm Labor Data from the Decennial Census: Limitations and Considerations," unpublished paper, Economic Research Service, U.S. Department of Agriculture, August 1983.

7. Susan L. Pollock and William R. Jackson, Jr., *The Hired Farm Working Force, 1981*, Agricultural Economic Report 507, U.S. Department of Agriculture, November 1983, p. 3.

Nearly half are primarily students, housewives, or retired persons who engage in seasonal work to supplement their income, often for less than 25 days a year, and are of average social and economic status.

The regular hired workers, who do 150 days or more of work annually, tend to be poorly educated, however, with 44 percent having only eight years or less of schooling.[8] The regular workers have a large Hispanic and black or other nonwhite race component (35 percent). Among the regulars, major differences exist between the whites and the minority groups. The whites are much better educated: Only 24 percent have just a grade-school education compared with 74 percent of the minority workers. In addition, the groups tend to do different work. Whites are disproportionately found in grain, other field crops (such as potatoes, peanuts, hay, sugar, seeds), dairy, and livestock work. A majority of Hispanics work in vegetables, fruits, nuts, and cotton; while blacks are heavily employed in tobacco, vegetables, fruits, nuts, and cotton.

For years, hired farm work was a declining occupation, as mechanization reduced the need for hand labor in farming, but since about 1970, the number of persons who do such work has stabilized. Although national agricultural income policy is largely directed to supporting farm-operator income and building export markets, the most serious and difficult poverty issues in the industry by far are those related to hired workers whose social condition often bears little relation to the condition of farm operators.

How to elevate the condition of hired farm workers is an old and ubiquitous problem, seemingly independent of time, place, or political systems. Poverty levels among hired farm-worker households have been high throughout history.

Most farm worker jobs have been effectively stigmatized by society, being among the very last deemed worthy of conventional social protection programs. Wage levels have been such as to attract few people with educational claims to better-paid employment. In vegetable, fruit, and irrigated farming in general—where farm laborers have been drawn heavily from disadvantaged ethnic groups—there are decided elements of class conflict in operator-worker relationships. Hired farm work is particularly important for rural Hispanics, among whom it provided nearly a fourth of all jobs for men in 1980.

---

8. Ibid., p. 30.

Part of the problem is the unavoidable seasonality of so many farm tasks and the difficulty of providing workers with year-round work. Migrancy is, in effect, one logical response to this problem; but it is then attended by the evils of poor housing and sanitation in the labor camps and the costs of special education and other programs for the children and families involved. Some labor tasks have become more demanding of formal technical skills as machinery has become much more complex and expensive and as chemical aspects of farming have become more widespread. Farm wages have advanced rather steadily and have kept pace with inflation, but some of this growth merely reflects the declining extent to which employers furnish housing or other perquisites in lieu of wages. Farm wages are still barely half the level of industrial wages.

Although there is a core of workers who persist in the work for years, surveys have shown a high degree of transiency and impermanence. From the farmer's point of view this is undesirable, even though it tends to keep wage costs low. It seems to be a rare farmer who does not complain about the scarcity of good farm labor. Nevertheless, given the high poverty rates among households containing farm workers, it may be just as well for the departing workers that they seek jobs elsewhere.

No other occupation in America is so subject to competition from immigrant workers, both seasonal and year-round, legal and illegal, government sponsored or unsponsored. It would appear almost certain that this inflow reduces the wage levels that otherwise would prevail. Yet it seems equally certain that large segments of perishable crop agriculture would not have enough capable and willing domestic workers for the arduous or dirty jobs of the industry, unless much higher wages were paid. The use of foreign workers—mostly Mexican—will undoubtedly continue.

The voices of farm labor employers are clearly heard in the federal government, both in the executive branch and in Congress. This has been demonstrated in the lengthy deliberations over protection of the foreign farm labor supply in drafting the new immigration act (subsequently enacted as the Immigration Reform and Control Act of 1986). The workers themselves have also organized somewhat in the last decade, but largely just in irrigated areas and not in the grain and livestock region with its more year-round domestic-origin workers. Still, political power among the group for economic and social gain remains weak, often overshadowed by employers and other interests competing for federal and state assistance.

There may be no full "solution" available to the farm labor aspect of rural poverty. Conditions have improved through better educational levels, the forces of the marketplace, elimination of some of the worst tasks by labor-saving innovations, and governmental and societal intervention on behalf of the workers. Farm workers have more societal protections now than in the past. But because of inadequate earned income from employment, improvement in the economic well-being of the group as a whole requires continued governmental assistance and protection.

19

Subregional Contexts of Rural Poverty

Almost every area has an aspect of its economy that is linked to natural resources. The very notion of what is a natural resource, however, varies from one time to another within a given area. A resource is not a resource until someone wants it and is willing and able to bear the cost of extracting it or using it. For example, the huge reserves of sub-bituminous coal in the northern Great Plains or the deep natural gas reserves of western Oklahoma did not become resources in development terms until the rising costs of other energy sources made them so in recent times. In addition, historical and cultural circumstances within an area structure the presence (or absence) of poverty and natural-resource linkages in ways that have to be understood if effective approaches to remedial policies are to be taken.

The dependence of communities on the natural-resource industries of farming, mining, and forest products and the levels of poverty vary by region, type of employment, and ethnocultural background. No matter what the nature of the activity, natural-resource areas in the South typically have poverty rates well above the national average and far above those in most of the West. These problems are particularly serious in the Southern Appalachian Plateau country, the Mississippi Delta, and analogous old plantation areas of the Lower South. In addition, certain areas of the Southwest and northern Great Plains also exhibit poverty and natural-resource linkages.

The three examples described below illustrate different ways in which natural resource use—past and present—has shaped current poverty conditions. The cases described are (1) the Southern

Adapted from Irma T. Elo and Calvin L. Beale, *Natural Resources and Rural Poverty: An Overview* (Washington, D.C.: Resources for the Future, Inc., 1985), chapters 3 and 5.

Appalachians, where both mining and farming have long been embedded in a high incidence of poverty, low education, poor health, and generally inadequate levels of living among a white population; (2) the Mississippi Delta, where although the great majority of blacks are no longer in natural-resource work, the legacy of deep poverty derived from earlier generations as sharecroppers and slaves persists in stark income contrasts between blacks and whites; and (3) the Texas High Plains, where development of irrigated farming has changed the population composition through introduction of a growing minority of Hispanics who have perceived an advantage in coming to the area, but whose poverty rates reflect the failure of agricultural industry to yield them adequate incomes.

Southern Appalachians

The deeply dissected Cumberland Plateau country of southern West Virginia, eastern Kentucky, and smaller parts of Virginia and Tennessee has been the classic area of white poverty in the United States. Initially, the Cumberland Plateau was settled by comparatively poor settlers who saw its timber, water, game, and cheap (even free) hilly land as ideal for their desire to have land of their own and a place removed from authority, slavery, and the wealthier classes. Ultimately, after the Civil War, some of the timber in the area became commercially valuable and the area was affected by its cutting. About the same time, coal was found in the region, and mining began with the attendant acquisition of large land holdings by outside investors, a pattern that continues to the present day.

Although mining brought new employment opportunities to area residents, the early history of mining in the region was characterized by exploitation of workers, low wages, and company towns.[1] The region became a clear case of the development of a rich natural resource failing to produce prosperous communities or equitable distribution of wealth. Labor strife, often violent, has been almost constant in the mining industry. And, especially since the introduction of strip mining, parts of the subregion form a textbook case of environmental abuse.

---

1. See, for example, John Gaventa, *Power and Powerlessness: Quiescence and Rebellion in an Appalachian Valley* (Champaign: University of Illinois Press, 1980).

In the twentieth century, the mining industry has brought intermittent growth and decline in employment with the boom-and-bust cycles typical of the industry as a whole. The most recent boom in mining occurred in the 1970s, when the energy crisis precipitated expansion of coal mining in the United States.

When mining began in the region at the turn of the century, people in the area already had high rates of poverty, and in the Census of 1900 the region (and related parts of the southern Blue Ridge Mountains) had the highest incidence of white illiteracy anywhere in the United States, except for equal levels in French Louisiana. However, while incomes have improved and poverty rates have declined in the region since then, the area remains as a whole one of the poorest in the nation.

In the 1970s, as a result of the energy boom, mining jobs more than doubled in the major coal mining counties in eastern Kentucky, and new trade and service jobs also appeared. During the same time, poverty in the area also declined. The pace of reduction in poverty in the poorest areas of the Southern Appalachian region (the tristate coalfields) was in fact the most rapid found in any region or sector of the nonmetropolitan United States from 1970 to 1980. Poverty rates in the 1980 Census were more than 40 percent lower than those ten years earlier. This was far better than that observed among other rural groups with chronically high poverty, such as Delta blacks, southwestern Hispanics, and western Indians. Nevertheless, despite these impressive gains, poverty rates in the mining counties still average over 20 percent, well above the national average and the average for all nonmetropolitan counties, whether or not natural-resource related.

Although the gains made during the 1970s are impressive, the instability of the mining industry makes these gains tenuous at best. Already, since 1980, coal production and income have declined as a result of the recession, and unemployment in the coalfields still averaged 23 percent during the first half of 1983. A disappointing feature of the employment boom in the mining counties during the 1970s was, in fact, the absence of development in other industries whose creation will be necessary to maintain the employment and income gains made in the area when mining declines. For example, from 1970 to 1980, when mining jobs doubled in the major eastern Kentucky mining counties, manufacturing employment actually declined by 4 percent in the same counties. In sharp contrast, a contiguous group of nonmining counties achieved a better than 60 percent increase in manufacturing work during the same period. This lack of economic diversification in the mining region makes long-term improvements in employment and income difficult as few alternative job opportunities are available in the area during the downturns so common in the mining industry.

It is also important to note, however, that rural poverty in Appalachia is not limited to the mining counties. In fact, poverty rates tend to be higher in the noncoal parts of the subregion than they are in the most highly commercial coal counties. In central southern Kentucky, county poverty rates regularly run from 20 to 35 percent, but with only 1 or 2 percent of employment in mining of any kind.

A historically small-scale tobacco and livestock agriculture in these counties and neighboring Tennessee has been supplemented with low-wage manufacturing, most notably female work in clothing plants. Thus, Southern Appalachian rural poverty extends beyond the mining region itself and is also associated with subsistence small-scale agriculture and low-wage manufacturing work.

Much of the income gain achieved during the 1970s in the Cumberland Plateau country reflects growth in earned income, before welfare assistance. Educational levels have risen, and in the nonmining counties there has been growth in manufacturing, professional services, and other nonextractive industry jobs. On the other hand, some of the poverty reduction has been accomplished only through welfare income supplements and other transfers. Most of the Appalachian counties with natural-resource-dominated economies are in the top national county quintile of per capita public assistance payments. And, despite growth in manufacturing employment, transfer payment income is often the leading single source of personal income outside the major mining counties.

Given the combination of conditions in the Southern Appalachians (difficult topography, intensely rural and very small-town character, the absence of high-wage businesses, high rates of work-limiting health disabilities, and limited educational levels among the older half of the labor force), it will be difficult to achieve an economy that lowers poverty levels to those of the rest of the country. Many issues of equity, taxation, safety, health, environment, and wages continue to surround the coal industry, all of which have consequences for the level of poverty. But equally important to the future of the region is the question of whether mining employment will grow, or even manage to regain its 1979 to

1981 levels. Perhaps metallurgical, export, and utility coal markets will revive, but barring further energy crises, they may not in the near future. The instability in the coal mining industry is particularly troublesome because of the lack of other employment opportunities in the mining counties.

The same problem of declining employment faces the small-scale tobacco and livestock farming pursuits that characterize the high-poverty counties of the outer parts of the region. Supplementing the economy with low-wage female textile jobs has made a contribution, but only additional forms of better-paid work for both men and women have the prospect of reducing work-related poverty any further.

The Mississippi Delta

The alluvial flood plain of the Mississippi is the richest farmland in the lower South, stretching about 500 miles from the Missouri Boot Heel to southern Louisiana. Yet it has been an archetype of the "Rich Land, Poor People" syndrome (borrowing the title of Stuart Chase's old book). From the beginning of settlement prior to the Civil War to its fuller development in the twentieth century, the Delta was preeminently the home of the plantation. Large-scale farms were operated first by slaves, next by sharecroppers, and more recently by hired workers. With exceptions, the area has been characterized by white capital and black labor.

With the modernization of farming after 1940, heavy out-migration of blacks took place. Nonfarm development has been inadequate and the population has declined—even in the 1970s—despite a relatively high birthrate. Poverty rates in the Delta are among the highest in the nation. (It has one of the two counties remaining in the United States where the total poverty rate was still above 50 percent in 1980.) Why should this be so when the quality of the soil and water resources is equal to most parts of the Midwest, where equally heavy farm dependence and out-migration are not accompanied by widespread poverty?

Aspects of the situation are puzzling, but clearly the racial aspect is central. Poverty rates run better than 50 percent for blacks in most all Delta counties, but seldom more than 12 to 16 percent for whites. This is an enormous difference. The Delta has long served the white elite well. In 1900, literacy rates among Delta whites were comparable to those in the Midwest and better than almost anything found in the South Atlantic states. But blacks have had almost negligible control over resources (and have not fared especially well where they did have, as in Mound Bayou). The legacy of sharecropping, exploitation, and the era of white supremacy is very much present in the Delta.

Even so, this does not explain one Delta riddle. Why is it that black poverty rates in the Delta are consistently 10 to 15 percentage points higher than those for blacks in other counties of the same states—counties that are distinctly poorer in their agricultural base? Have the non-Delta counties industrialized more? Perhaps, but not all that much. Is it because the proportion that blacks comprise of the whole population is higher in the Delta? And if so, why does proportionate massing of blacks lead to greater rural black poverty? (The same situation is observed in Alabama, where blacks in the black Belt have higher poverty rates than those outside of it.) Perhaps one factor is that in counties with a low-to-moderate percentage of black population, the presence of higher-income whites provides more employment in trade and service work for blacks than is available in counties where poor rural blacks are a majority of the population.

It could be argued that a logical but radical reform in the Delta would be land redistribution or some form of agricultural profit sharing for the workers. There are many plantations large enough to be subdivided into viable smaller units. Yet today, the percentage of blacks still working in agriculture in the Delta is too small for agricultural reform to solve the bulk of the Delta's poverty problems. Although in 1950 fully three-fourths of employed blacks in the Delta worked directly in agriculture, by 1980 only 14 percent did so—a truly extraordinary change in thirty years.

A major problem is the low level of labor-force participation by black men and the lack of year-round work for those who are employed. In the whole Delta, only 53 percent of black males sixteen years and over were in the labor force in 1980, compared with comparable national figures for nonmetropolitan males of 72 percent for whites and 60 percent for blacks. Furthermore, in the great majority of Delta counties, less than 30 percent of black men who had some income had year-round work. By contrast, in no county did less than 40 percent of white men with income have year-round work.

Labor-force participation rates were not at all low by national standards for black women, nor were the income levels of fully employed black women radically out of line with those for white women. But as a group, black Delta men have low participation in the work force, very low frequency of full-time work, and much lower pay than whites when they do have full-time work. As a wry irony, it can be noted that if one wanted to point to the area of the United States in which incomes of female full-time workers most closely approach those of men, it would be among blacks in the Mississippi Delta. They do so, however, not because women's income is so good, but because the earnings of black men in the area are so abysmal.

In addition, certain structural features of the black population there make any development approach difficult. Less than half of all black children under eighteen in the Delta are living with two parents, even when stepparents are counted as parents. The female-headed family with children seems to be the most vulnerable to poverty of all family units. Most such women lack adequately remunerative employment, and research seems to show comparatively poor social performance by children in such families.

In sum, the Delta is an example of a rural region with an outstanding land base for farming where there has been great stratification of society and a total failure to translate enviable resources into broad-based prosperity and social stability, or to make a successful transition from labor-intensive farming to a diversified economy with adequate employment.

Many of the same comments could be offered about the Black Prairie area of Alabama and Mississippi (often called the Black Belt). The land base there is not as desirable in the postcotton era as the Delta. But there, too, the descendants of black plantation workers, whose comparative isolation, repressed state, and backwardness were well known in the past, seem to be stranded in an area where they have demographic dominance and some local governmental control but lack land ownership or adequate nonagricultural development.

Texas High Plains

An emergent rural poverty situation closely linked with resource development has come to the Texas High Plains. Here I shall focus on a nineteen-county area in western Texas. The High Plains of this region are level to gently rolling and have good soils that are very productive when they have sufficient water. This was the last part of Texas to be settled.

As late as 1900, no more than 15,000 people inhabited the entire area. Ranching developed first, followed in the 1920s by rapid settlement of farmers using dry farming techniques for cotton (where the climate was warm enough) and wheat. For the most part, this was successful. The settlers were almost all Anglo whites, typically coming in from areas of Texas and Oklahoma to the east. A comparatively classless society developed (prosperous except during the 1930s droughts) that was more like midwestern rural society than anything else in the South. The standard of living as measured by modernization and conveniences, as well as farm mechanization, was far above the other areas of the South.

In the 1940s irrigation began, setting off new boom times and greatly altering agriculture. This change has only recently reached what appears to be its limits. It was found that the great underground reservoir that underlies the area (the Ogalalla Aquifer) could be profitably tapped. Irrigation greatly increased the yields of the traditional wheat, cotton, and sorghum crops. In addition, it made possible the introduction of corn, and even soybeans and sugar beets. The new abundance of feed grains led to cattle feeding and formation of some of the largest feedlot operations in the country. In turn, the process was further integrated by establishing meat packing. One indication of the magnitude of change can be seen in the amount of irrigated cropland, which went from 350,000 acres in 1944 to 3,800,000 acres in 1978.[2]

The irrigated farming required much more labor—much of it sheer drudgery—than had previously been required on individual farms. The feeding operations also led to more demand for farm labor. The local supply of people able or willing to do this work was insufficient. The solution was to bring in hundreds and ultimately thousands of Mexicans and Mexican-Americans (and much smaller numbers of blacks). For these people, the work prospects were clearly better in the High Plains than in the areas they came from. The ethnic composition has changed to a major degree. In the nineteen counties here considered (which consist of those having 100,000 irrigated acres or more in 1978, excluding Lubbock), the Hispanic population went from 7,000, or 4 percent of the population in 1950, to 68,000, or 29 percent of the total in 1980.

---

2. U.S. Department of Commerce, Bureau of the Census, *1950 Census of Agriculture*, vol. 1, part 26 (1960) Texas, county table 1a; and *1978 Census of Agriculture*, vol. 1, part 43 (1979) Texas, county table 3.

The poverty rate in these counties in 1979 was 20 percent—well above the the U.S. nonmetropolitan average. Even so, the rate for whites was just 11 percent, while that for Hispanics was 38 percent. Although the overall poverty rate in the area decreased somewhat during the 1970s—a time of general prosperity and increasing transfer payment supplements to the income of poor people—the decline in poverty was definitely less than the average decline for the U.S. nonmetropolitan population. In three of the counties, the poverty rate actually increased during the decade.

The addition of the water-resource development to the previous form of land use has sharply increased the value and volume of agricultural production. It also has transformed a relatively equalitarian society into one that has a large (albeit progressing) underclass, based on the utilization of a poor ethnocultural minority for unskilled labor.

East of the High Plains is an equally large area known as the Rolling Plains. This area is not as well suited to farming as the High Plains. The topography is not as level and there is not nearly as much irrigation water available (only 100,000 acres total). But other than some oil and gas there is little else to the economy. So the population has been dropping in most counties for the last forty to fifty years, including the 1970s. In the past, the area showed somewhat lower scores on income and other socioeconomic measures than did the High Plains. It is clearly under stress because of the inadequate employment opportunities associated with the current state of its natural-resource-based economy. Yet because of the high poverty rates among the Hispanics of the High Plains irrigated counties, the Rolling Plains now show a lower incidence of poverty than do the High Plains (17.6 percent versus 20.3 percent). Each area has a serious resource-related economic problem, but the comparative presence or absence of irrigation has shaped the problems differently.

20

Americans Heading for the
Cities, Once Again

After 1980, the exceptional rural and small-town growth of the previous decade ended. The 1980–83 nonmetropolitan population
increase (0.83 percent per year) was once again less than the
annual metropolitan rate (1.10 percent), and the number of nonmetropolitan counties with population decline had risen to 720,
more than half again as high as the 1970s low. Yet, the 1980–83
numbers still looked good compared with the 1950s and 1960s.

Adapted from *Rural Development Perspectives* 4:3 (1988): 2–6.

Virginia farm lane (courtesy of J. Norman Reid)

Only in contrast with the 1970s did they show less growth. More nonmetropolitan counties, especially in the West and in the Southern Plains, were still growing at above national average rates than declining.

From 1983 to 1986, however, nonmetropolitan ability to retain or attract people rapidly deteriorated, despite the ongoing economic recovery in the national economy. In this period, the nonmetropolitan population increase dropped to 0.42 percent per year, only half as high as the 1980–83 rate. Annual metropolitan growth rose slightly to 1.12 percent (see Fig. 20.1). The low growth of nonmetropolitan population from 1983 to 1986 is the most striking feature of post-1980 trends.

In assessing post-1980 nonmetropolitan population trends, I looked not only at the aggregate growth patterns but also at individual types of counties and at growth in the early 1980s versus growth in the middle 1980s. In sum, 1,306 nonmetropolitan counties (55 percent) lost residents between 1983 and 1986. The average loss per county was not large, but the incidence of loss was as widespread as when farm consolidation was at its peak in the 1960s (when 53 percent of the nonmetropolitan counties lost population) and the 1950s (54 percent).

There are two bright spots in the nonmetropolitan trend. Retirement counties still continue to attract new residents, not just older people but the younger workers, too, who provide services and goods to the retired population. These counties annually grew by more than 1.78 percent from 1980 to 1986, nearly double the national rate. Nonmetropolitan counties with a fourth or more of their residents commuting to jobs within the metropolitan area grew by 1.13 percent per year in 1980–86. That is a little faster than the national growth rate, although a sharp comedown from their 1.92 percent annual growth in the 1970s.

Population Change Linked to Industrial Trends

Population decline in the 1970s was confined chiefly to farming areas in the Great Plains, western Corn Belt, and Mississippi Delta. From 1980 to 1983, the losses in the Plains were less than in the 1970s, partly because of oil and gas activity and probably because the farm crisis occurred later in the wheat and range livestock areas than in the Corn Belt (see Figs. 20.2–20.4). Declines became much more common in the Corn Belt during the early

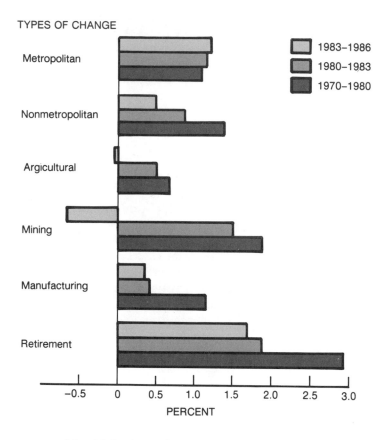

Fig. 20.1   Annual rates of population change

1980s, especially in the eastern part, where farming often coexists
with older manufacturing industries that were hard hit by the
recession. Scattered losing areas appeared in the West, usually
linked to cutbacks in mining or timberwork. Elsewhere, many new
small clusters of decline appeared in the lower South, the Ohio Valley, the central Appalachians, and in Michigan. But, although
decline was more common than it had been, population change in
1980–83 was still characterized by vast nonmetropolitan areas
with growth more rapid than that of the nation as a whole. This
was particularly true in the West, Oklahoma, Texas, and Florida,
all areas that had grown rapidly in the 1970s.

After mid-1983, nonmetropolitan counties with any growth at all
were a rarity throughout the Great Plains, Corn Belt, and central
and northern Appalachia. In Iowa, the quintessential farm state,

Nonmetropolitan population change, 1970–80

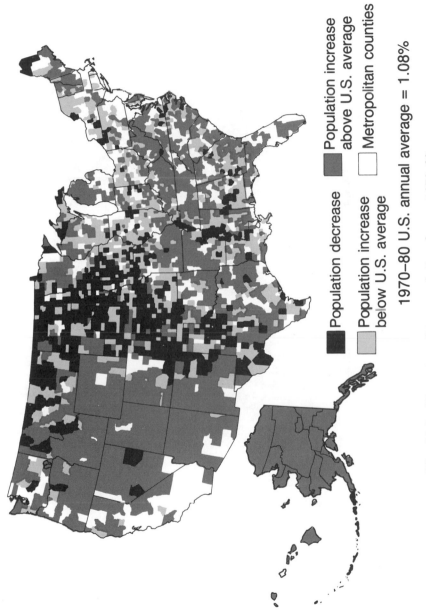

■ Population decrease

■ Population increase above U.S. average

▨ Population increase below U.S. average

□ Metropolitan counties

1970–80 U.S. annual average = 1.08%

Fig. 20.2   Nonmetropolitan population change, 1970–80

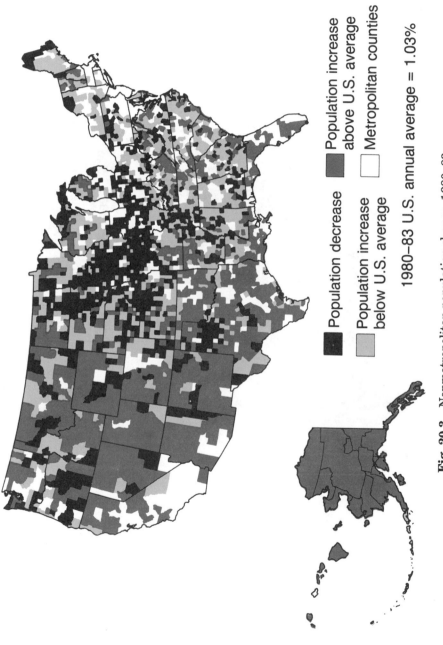

Population decrease

Population increase above U.S. average

Population increase below U.S. average

Metropolitan counties

1980–83 U.S. annual average = 1.03%

Fig. 20.3 Nonmetropolitan population change, 1980–83

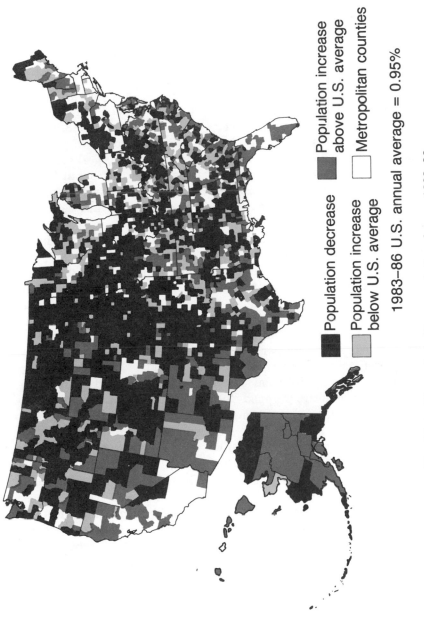

Population decrease

Population increase
below U.S. average

Population increase
above U.S. average

Metropolitan counties

1983–86 U.S. annual average = 0.95%

Fig. 20.4   Nonmetropolitan population change, 1983–86

eighty-four of eighty-eight nonmetropolitan counties lost population from 1983 to 1986, as out-movement more than offset any excess of births over deaths. Losses were also common in the lower South and penetrated some western regions where rapid growth had come to seem normal, such as eastern Utah and western Colorado.

In attempting to understand these changes, it is useful to look at trends in different types of areas. Mining counties, in particular, shifted from growth to decline in 1983–86. Whereas they had an overall increase of 1.47 percent per year from 1980 to 1983, which was higher than national growth, they annually lost 0.67 percent in population during the next three years. Total U.S. workers in oil and gas extraction rose by 13 percent from 1980 to 1983, but fell by 26 percent from July 1983 through June 1986, as world oil prices dropped. Employment in coal mining and metallic minerals also fell in 1983–86.

Agricultural employment responded only belatedly to the farm crisis. After holding steady in 1980–83, it dropped by 200,000 jobs in 1983–86. Only after several poor years in a row did people become discouraged enough to leave. Despite a drop in net farm income in 1980 of more than 48 percent from the previous year (inflation-adjusted), only in 1982, after two more years of low farm income, did farm real-estate values begin to plunge. From 1983 to 1986, the average value per acre of farmland dropped by about a fourth, after rising slightly from 1980 to 1983.

An extraordinary infusion of federal price-support loans and payments to producers propped up farm income in the middle part of the decade. Farmers used much of their income to reduce debt, however, rather than spend it for consumer or producer needs. Farmers cut their debt (both real estate and other) by $39 billion (19 percent) from 1980 to 1986, an amount larger than the direct government payments they received. They also reduced their cash expenditures by $16 billion (14 percent) from 1984 to 1986. Those measures helped raise their incomes but had a depressing effect on business in farm towns. The total number of people employed in agricultural counties did not grow at all during 1983–86. As a result, there was a slight (0.02 percent per year) population loss from 1983 to 1986 in farm-dependent nonmetropolitan counties, after an annual growth rate of 0.5 percent from 1980 to 1983. Three-fourths of these counties lost population from 1983 to 1986. Those with small urban centers were more likely to hold onto their population.

Nonmetropolitan manufacturing counties are not more numerous than agricultural counties, but they are much more densely settled and contain about two-fifths of the entire nonmetropolitan population. They have an average population of 33,000 compared with just 11,000 for agricultural counties, and thus are more urbanized and have larger labor markets. Manufacturing counties, therefore, are more stable and less likely than agricultural counties to have rapid rates of population change, either growth or loss.

Manufacturing was a major source of rural job growth and diversification in the 1960s and 1970s. The recession of 1980–83, however, was chiefly a goods-producing recession, with national employment in manufacturing falling by 11 percent from its 1979 high to 1982. Total employment in nonmetropolitan manufacturing counties dropped by 4.4 percent in the same period, a greater loss than in any other type of county. Manufacturing employment began to recover in the spring of 1983, but by spring of 1985 was sagging again (and has never reattained its 1979 level). Construction, trade, and service activity, meanwhile, continued to move ahead. Recovery and expansion in these other sectors were enough to push up total employment in manufacturing counties by 7 percent from 1982 to 1986. Even so, annual population growth was somewhat slower in these counties in 1983–86 than in 1980–83 (0.32 versus 0.4 percent), although the 1983–86 sag was less than in any other class of nonmetropolitan county. Population growth in manufacturing counties for 1983–86 was only about five-eighths as large as the excess of births over deaths, implying an out-migration of about 100,000 people.

Nonmetropolitan Retirement Counties Continue to Attract New Residents

Offsetting this pattern of low growth or population loss in areas dependent on farming, mining, or manufacturing was the growth of rural retirement areas. Nearly 500 nonmetropolitan counties in 44 states drew in significant numbers of older people in the 1970s. Concentrated in Florida, the upper Great Lakes, the Ozark-Ouachita area, Texas, the Southwest, and the far West, these counties were the most rapidly growing class of nonmetropolitan county during the "rural turnaround" years of the 1970s and have continued to be so since 1980. Population in these areas grew by 1.78

percent per year from 1980 to 1986, far above the 1 percent nationwide rate.

Given the older average age of the population in retirement
counties, such growth can be achieved only through substantial in-
migration, for the birthrate is somewhat low and the death rate
somewhat high. From 1980 to 1986, there was an estimated net
migration of nearly a million people into nonmetropolitan retirement counties. Not all of them were older people. Many retirement areas also offer recreational and other natural amenities that
attract younger residents. Furthermore, a large population of
older people creates a demand for trade and service jobs filled by
younger people, people of working age.

Retirement counties were probably the least affected by the
recession because the income of a large segment of their population
was shielded from unemployment, wage cuts, or other hardships of
the business slump. Even though some retirement counties are
also agricultural, manufacturing, or urbanizing areas, all of which
were in some way affected by the recession, most retirement counties experienced a smaller drop in their population growth in the
1980s than other types of counties.

The annual growth rate in retirement counties was 38 percent
lower in 1980–86 than it had been during the 1970s, while other
nonmetropolitan counties' annual growth rate was 67 percent
lower than in the 1970s. A closer look shows that the slowdown
was about the same for retirement counties and other nonmetropolitan areas in 1980–83. In those years, both types of counties
grew about three-fifths as rapidly per year as they had in the
1970s. However, from 1983 to 1986 population growth sank to
nearly zero outside retirement areas as losses spread in mining
and farming areas. Growth in the retirement counties, however,
remained near its 1980–83 pace.

Thus, the picture is mixed. The growth slowdown for retirement
areas was about the same as for other areas in the first three years
of the decade, but from 1983 to 1986 retirement counties were
much more successful in maintaining growth than were other nonmetropolitan counties.

Commuting Brings Growth, but Not as Much as Before

Another factor often associated with the growth and development
of nonmetropolitan counties is proximity to metropolitan areas.

Rural communities have a better chance of retaining their population or attracting new residents if they are within commuting range of metropolitan jobs. Consequently, counties adjacent to metropolitan areas have typically had somewhat more rapid population growth than those not adjacent. This was not the case, however, from 1980 to 1983, when both adjacent and nonadjacent counties had similar rates of change. In that period, many northern nonmetropolitan counties next to metropolitan areas and containing industrial cities of 20,000 people or more were hurt just as much by the business recession as their metropolitan neighbors, and lost population.

On the other hand, many remote counties in the Great Plains and West still retained the growth they acquired during the energy boom of the early 1980s. After 1983, however, that boom's collapse and the worsening farm crisis led to out-migration from scores of small remote nonmetropolitan counties, while northern industrial centers experienced some recovery. As a result, nonmetropolitan counties adjacent to metropolitan areas resumed their usual pattern of higher population growth rates than nonadjacent counties. Although metropolitan adjacency is a commonly used characteristic in nonmetropolitan research, it is only an approximate measure of metropolitan access. Some nonmetropolitan counties have only a nominal and distant adjacency to a broadly bounded metropolitan area, whereas others may lie much closer to a central city. For example, in the Southwest, central-city counties often contain several thousand square miles or more, whereas in parts of the East and South they have fewer than 400 square miles. Or, despite adjacency, highway connections to the central city may be poor in one case and excellent in another. The worker commuting rate is a good measure of whether a county is meaningfully adjacent to a metropolitan center. As might be expected, nonmetropolitan counties with a substantial percentage of workers commuting to adjacent metropolitan areas have somewhat higher rates of population increase than those with less commuting. At any given time, some of these high-commuting counties are incipiently suburban and will gradually become metropolitan counties through settlement sprawl if the nearby metropolitan areas continue to grow.

There are more than 100 nonmetropolitan counties from which 25 percent or more of the employed residents commuted to adjacent metropolitan central counties in 1980. Population in these commuter counties rose by 1.13 percent annually from 1980 to 1986, faster than the national average and slightly above the metropolitan rate. Adjacent counties with under 25 percent commuting averaged 0.77 percent annual population growth, with only minor difference between those with 15 percent or more commuting and those with under 5 percent. Low commuting nonadjacent counties were comparable in growth to most adjacent groups from 1980–83, but had almost no growth in 1983–86. In the latter years, the effect of adjacency and commuting was more evident, as high-commuting counties grew twice as fast as adjacent low-commuting counties, which in turn grew faster than the nearly stationary nonadjacent group.

One point of interest: Every commuting level of nonmetropolitan counties has grown more slowly in the 1980s than in the 1970s. Even though the U.S. metropolitan population has grown slightly faster in the 1980s than in the 1970s, this has not prevented the adjacent nonmetropolitan counties with high-commuting links from undergoing a major slowdown in their average growth rates. Whether that arises from a diminished vitality in their local economies or a lessening of long-range metropolitan sprawl, they are acquiring additional residents at a slower pace than the metropolitan areas, in contrast to the trend of the 1970s.

Lower Birthrate Another Factor in Slower Growth

Lower birthrates also make nonmetropolitan areas more susceptible today to population decline. During both the 1950s and 1960s, the nonmetropolitan birthrate was considerably higher than the more recent rate. It averaged more than 20 per 1,000 people during the 1960s, with a death rate of less than 10 per 1,000, leaving a potential annual population increase of more than 1 percent per year. Thus, net out-migration from a typical nonmetropolitan area had to exceed 1 percent before the population fell.

Since then, childbearing has declined significantly. The nonmetropolitan birthrate averaged only 15.6 per 1,000 people in 1980–86, a drop of approximately one-fourth since the 1960s, while the death rate has remained about the same, at 9.6 per 1,000. Gains in life expectancy were counterbalanced by the increased average age of nonmetropolitan people, which was partly the product of an influx of retirees. This left a yearly average of just 0.6 percent from births minus deaths, which would be offset by any net out-migration rate of more than that amount. As a result, many counties and some entire states with only moderate out-migration rates had a slow decline in population from 1980 to 1986. If they had had the higher birthrates of the 1960s, these areas would have grown. Altogether, some 1,517 nonmetropolitan counties, or 64 percent of the total, had a net out-movement of people from 1980 to 1986. In 555 of these cases, the excess of births over deaths was large enough to offset the migration loss. But, in all others, the natural increase was too small to do so and the population fell.

Regional Contrasts in Migration

Events of 1980–86 precipitated a net out-migration of 600,000 people from the nonmetropolitan Midwest, with Iowa having the largest exodus, 103,000. An almost equal number, 570,000, however, moved into the rural and small-town parts of Florida, Texas, California, and Arizona. Within the period, major shifts in the regional trend took place. The Mountain West (exclusive of Arizona) experienced a net in-movement of 103,000 in 1980–83 but lost a net of 87,000 in 1983–86. In the three oil states of Louisiana, Oklahoma, and Texas, a nonmetropolitan net in-movement of 263,000 people in 1980–83 reversed to a 75,000 outflow in 1983–86. Nonmetropolitan America as a whole still had a small net gain of 100,000 people from in-movement from 1980 to 1986, despite the adverse trends of 1983–86. Metropolitan areas received 4 million net in-movement over the same years. Both types of areas can have gains because of immigration from abroad. Despite the well-known use of immigrants, especially Mexicans as farm workers, most immigrants settle in and around large cities.

Where Do People Want to Live?

Residential preference surveys began to appear in the mid–1960s and yielded some surprising information. In an overwhelmingly urban nation, at a time when people were moving to the cities, a majority of those polled said they would prefer to live in a rural area or small town. If asked where they would like this place to be, most said they would prefer it to be within thirty miles of a large city. But an even more remote location was likely to be the second choice for such people rather than the city. Such preferences obviously provided motivation and philosophical support for the sizable move in the 1970s toward the countryside and its small towns. It was common in rural surveys during that decade to find large numbers of newcomers who had sacrificed urban income to move to smaller communities in hopes of finding a better quality of life.

An obvious question for the 1980s, when nonmetropolitan growth has dwindled, is "Have residential preferences changed?" Is there something more than economic problems that has brought about the recent nonmetropolitan demographic stagnation? The Gallup organization has continued to take occasional polls of the subject. The results are mixed.

In surveys using the categories "city," "suburban," "small town," and "farm," there was an increase from 13 to 19 percent between 1972 and 1983 in people who said they preferred to live in a city, but there was no drop in the percentage who wanted to live in a small town or on a farm. The offsetting loss came from the suburban category.

	1972	1983
City	13%	19%
Suburban	31	23
Small town	32	31
Farm	23	26

In other years, the Gallup Poll used different terms. Using the concepts "large city," "small city," "town or village," and "rural area," Gallup found a definite trend toward greater preference for large cities between 1978 and 1985 (from 14 to 23 percent), with a reduced inclination for rural areas (from 32 to 25 percent). There was no loss of support for town or village living.

	1978	1981	1985
Large city	14%	18%	23%
Small city	32	28	29
Town or village	20	20	23
Rural area	32	34	25

The two series of polls are consistent in the increased preference for the "city" and "large city" locations but give inconsistent results for "farm" and "rural area." These two terms are not synonymous, but it is difficult to accept the validity of an increasing farm preference without a corresponding rise in rural preference, especially during a farm crisis.

The two series of polls are consistent in the increased preference for the "city" and "large city" locations but give inconsistent results for "farm" and "rural area." These two terms are not synonymous, but it is difficult to accept the validity of an increasing farm preference without a corresponding rise in rural preference, especially during a farm crisis.

Two points seem to be conclusive from the surveys. The cities have come to be viewed more favorably in the 1980s, thus probably reducing the likelihood of city-to-rural moves. Nevertheless, whichever survey one uses, there are still millions of Americans not presently living in a small town, village, farm, or other rural area who say they would prefer to do so. If and when nonmetropolitan economic conditions rebound, we may see another burst of rural growth.

Wary Optimism

The worst may be over for nonmetropolitan areas in terms of loss of population associated with the poor economic conditions of the early and mid-1980s. Farm income reached an all-time high in 1987, albeit heavily supported by federal government subsidies, and the 1988 level of income is expected to be second only to that of 1987. With the debt burden reduced, farmers' net worth has stabilized. The farm export market has improved and surpluses of major commodities have been reduced. There, positive factors do not presage an increase in the farm population, for there is no need for additional farmers. But if the improved conditions are sustained, they should lead to resumed local investment and spending and greater retention of population in farm counties. Unemployment rates have dropped significantly in nonmetropolitan areas since mid-1987, although they are still well above metropolitan rates, especially when one accounts for part-time workers and discouraged workers (those who want work but are not actively looking for it). The decline in mining and manufacturing employment has ended. Under these circumstances, there may be no further drop after 1987 in the overall nonmetropolitan population growth rate or spread in the occurrence of outright decline.

In any event, the demographic trend in rural and small-town communities in the 1980s has proved to be as unexpectedly different from that of the 1970s as that decade was different from the 1960s. We learned in the 1970s that there are indeed conditions under which small-scale areas can retain their natural increase and also attract new residents. But we see now that major recessions in production industries can still have widespread and disproportionate effects on the population-supporting capacity of nonmetropolitan counties.

Bibliography

Sole Author

1950

"Increased Divorce Rates Among Separated Persons as a Factor in Divorce Since 1940," *Social Forces*, Vol. 29, No. 1, October, pp. 72–74.

1952

"Some Marriage Trends and Patterns Since 1940," presented at D.C. Sociological Society Meeting, Howard University, Washington, D.C., May 3.

1954

"Demographic Characteristics of Indians in the United States," paper prepared for the Third Inter-American Indian Conference held at La Paz, Bolivia, August 2–12. Published as "Características Demográficas de los Indígenas de los Estados Unidos de América," *América Indígena*, Vol. 15, No. 2, April 1955, pp. 127–137.

1955

"Population Trends and Distribution in Rural Areas," in *Rural Education—A Forward Look*, National Education Association of the United States, Washington, D.C., pp. 299–306.

1956

Characteristics of Farm-Operator Households by Number of Young Children, U.S. Department of Agriculture, Agricultural Marketing Service, AMS–118, Washington, D.C., June.

1957

"Farm Population as a Useful Demographic Concept," *Agricultural Economics Research*, Vol. 9, No. 3, July, pp. 105–111.

"American Triracial Isolates: Their Status and Pertinence to Genetic Research," *Eugenics Quarterly*, Vol. 4, No. 4, December, pp. 187–196.

1958

"Census Problems of Racial Enumeration," in Edgar T. Thompson and Everett C. Hughes (eds.), *Race: Individual and Collective Behavior*, The Free Press, Glencoe, Ill., pp. 537–540.

"Negro Farm Operators: Number, Location, and Recent Trends," unpublished version of a talk given at the Fourth Annual Agricultural Finance Seminar, Prairie View Agricultural and Mechanical College, Prairie View, Tex., June 17.

1962

"Causes of Population Growth in Rapidly Growing Rural Counties," paper presented at annual meeting of the Rural Sociological Society.

"Current and Foreseeable Trends in Rural Population," *Family Economics Review*, December, pp. 26–30.

1963

"Population and Labor Force Trends Relevant to Weed Control Activities," paper presented at annual meeting of the Southern Weed Conference, January 16.

1964

"Rural Depopulation in the United States: Some Demographic Consequences of Agricultural Adjustments," *Demography*, Vol. 1, pp. 264–272.

1966

"The Negro in American Agriculture," in John P. Davis (ed.), *The American Negro Reference Book*, Prentice-Hall, Englewood Cliffs, N.J., November 1966, pp. 161–204. An updated revision published as "The Black American in Agriculture," in Mabel M. Smythe (ed.), *The Black American Reference Book*, Prentice-Hall, Englewood Cliffs, N.J., 1976, pp. 284–315.

1967

"State Economic Areas—A Review After 17 Years," *Proceedings of the American Statistical Association*, Social Statistics Section, 1967, pp. 82–85.

1968

"Rural Minorities, Rural Fertility, and Their Relation to Rural-Urban Migration," *Agricultural Policy Review*, Vol. 8, No. 3, July–September, pp. 10–11.

"Rural-Urban Migration: Viewpoints, Issues and Facts of Life," unpublished lecture, University of Missouri, November.

1969

"The Relation of Gross Outmigration Rates to Net Migration," paper presented at annual meeting of the Population Association of America, Atlantic City, N.J., April 10–12.

"Demographic and Social Considerations for U.S. Rural Economic Policy," *American Journal of Agricultural Economics*, Vol. 51, No. 2, May, pp. 410–427.

"Natural Decrease of Population: The Current and Prospective Status of an Emergent American Phenomenon," *Demography*, Vol. 6, No. 2, May, pp. 91–99.

"Structure and Trends of the Rural Population Pertinent to Migration and Development Policies," statement before the Subcommittee on Urban Growth, House Committee on Banking and Currency, June 24, and published in committee print, *Population Trends, Part 1*, pp. 473–508.

1970

"Population and Environment," in *Increasing Understanding of Public Problems and Policies, 1970*, Farm Foundation, Chicago, pp. 104–111.

1971

"Needed Rural Population Research," in Abbott L. Ferriss (ed.), *Research and the 1970 Census*, Southern Regional Demographic Group/Oak Ridge Associated Universities, Inc., Oak Ridge, Tenn., pp. 139–143.

"Population and Migration Trends in Rural and Nonmetropolitan Areas," statement before the Senate Committee on Government Operations, April 27. Hearings published as *Revitalization of*

Rural and Other Economically Distressed Areas, Government Printing Office, Washington, D.C.

"Rural and Urban Migration of Blacks: Past and Future," *American Journal of Agricultural Economics*, Vol. 53, No. 2, May, pp. 302–307.

1972

"Rural and Nonmetropolitan Population Trends of Significance to National Population Policy," Chap. 5 in *Population, Distribution, and Policy*, in *The Commission on Population Growth and the American Future*, Part V, Government Printing Office, Washington, D.C., pp. 665–678.

"Demographic Trends in Tobacco Producing Areas," Chap. 14 in A. Frank Bordeaux, Jr., and Russell H. Brannon (eds.), *Social and Economic Issues Confronting the Tobacco Industry in the Seventies*, College of Agriculture and Center for Developmental Change, University of Kentucky, Lexington, February, pp. 243–250.

"Origins of the Population Distribution Problem," paper presented at the annual meeting of the American Association of Geographers, Kansas City, Mo., April 26.

"An Overview of the Phenomenon of Mixed Racial Isolates in the United States," *American Anthropologist*, Vol. 74, No. 3, June, pp. 704–710.

"The Nature and Significance of Recent Population Trends in the South, with Particular Reference to Nonmetropolitan Areas," report prepared for the Office of Economic Opportunity, July.

1973

"Implications of Population Trends for Quality of Life" and "Rural and Nonmetropolitan Population Trends of Significance to National Population Policy," both papers published in *Where Will All the People Go?*, a report of the Subcommittee on Rural Development of the Senate Committee on Agriculture and Forestry, Washington, D.C., October 23.

"Small Towns: Their Status and Recent Trends," paper for conference on The Future of the Small Town, sponsored by Southern Newspaper Publishers Association Foundation, Oak Ridge, Tenn., October 28–31.

"Migration Patterns of Minorities in the United States," *American Journal of Agricultural Economics*, Vol. 55, No. 5, December, pp. 938–946.

1974

"Rural Development: Population and Settlement Prospects," *Journal of Soil and Water Conservation*, Vol. 29, No. 1, January-February, pp. 23–27.

1975

"Quantitative Dimensions of Decline and Stability Among Rural Communities," Chap. 1 in Larry R. Whiting (ed.), *Communities Left Behind: Alternatives for Development*, Iowa State University Press, Ames, 1975, pp. 3–21.

The Revival of Population Growth in Nonmetropolitan America, U.S. Department of Agriculture, Economic Research Service, ERS–605, Washington, D.C., June.

"Recent Growth of Nonmetropolitan Population," statement before the Subcommittee on Housing and Community Development of the House Committee on Banking, Currency and Housing, September 4. Hearings published as *National Growth and Development*, Government Printing Office, Washington, D.C.

"Renewal of Population Growth in Nonmetropolitan Areas of the United States," statement before the Subcommittee on Census and Population, House Committee on Post Office and Civil Service, November 11. Hearings published as *Population*, Serial No. 94–65, Government Printing Office, Washington, D.C.

1976

"A Further Look at Nonmetropolitan Population Growth Since 1970," *American Journal of Agricultural Economics*, Vol. 58, No. 5, December, pp. 953–958.

1977

"The Recent Shift of United States Population to Nonmetropolitan Areas, 1970–75," *International Regional Science Review*, Vol. 2, No. 2, Winter, pp. 113–122.

"Recent Rural Population Trends of Significance to the Professional Agricultural Workers Conference," paper presented at the Professional Agricultural Workers Conference, Tuskegee Institute, Ala., December 5.

1978

"Internal Migration in the United States Since 1970," statement before the House Select Committee on Population, February 8.

Hearings published as *World Population: A Global Perspective*, Government Printing Office, Washington, D.C.

"Recent U.S. Rural Population Trends and Selected Economic Implications," statement before the Joint Economic Committee, May 31.

"People on the Land," Chap. 3 in Thomas R. Ford (ed.), *Rural U.S.A.: Persistence and Change*, Iowa State University Press, Ames, July, pp. 37–54.

"Population Trends in the Northeast," *Journal of the Northeastern Agricultural Economics Council*, Vol. 7, No. 2. October, pp. 5–11.

1979

"Demographic Aspects of Agricultural Structure," in *Structure Issues of American Agriculture*, U.S. Department of Agriculture, Agricultural Economic Report No. 438, Washington, D.C., pp. 80–85.

1980

"Nonfarm Rural America," in *Farm Structure: A Historical Perspective on Changes in the Number and Size of Farms*, U.S. Senate Committee on Agriculture, Nutrition, and Forestry, Washington, D.C., pp. 36–48.

"The Changing Nature of Rural Employment," Chap. 2 in David L. Brown and John M. Wardwell (eds.), *New Directions in Urban-Rural Migration: The Population Turnaround In Rural America*, Academic Press, N.Y., pp. 37–49.

1981

"A Characterization of Types of Nonmetropolitan Areas," Appendix to Chap. 1 in Amos H. Hawley and Sara Mills Mazie (eds.), *Nonmetropolitan America in Transition*, University of North Carolina Press, Chapel Hill, pp. 54–71.

"Rural Development in Perspective," in *Implementation of the Small Community and Rural Development Policy*, a report from the Secretary of Agriculture to the President, January 15.

"Population Change in Rural America and Implications for Economic Development," statement before the Subcommittee on Economic Development, House Committee on Public Works and Transportation, November 19. Hearings published as *Projected Changes in the Economy, Population, Labor Market, and Work Force, and Their Implications for Economic Development Policy*, Government Printing Office, Washington, D.C., pp. 169–184.

1982

"Older Rural Americans: Demographic Situation and Trends," statement before the Senate Special Committee on Aging, May 19. Hearings published as *Older Rural Americans: Unanswered Questions*, Government Printing Office, Washington, D.C., pp. 22–28.

"The Population Turnaround in Rural and Small Town America," *Policy Studies Review*, Vol. 2, No. 1, August, pp. 43–54. Also published as Chap. 4 in William P. Browne and Don F. Hadwiger (eds.), *Rural Policy Problems: Changing Dimensions*, Lexington Books, Lexington, Mass., 1982, pp. 47–59.

"Rural America Today: Progress and Problems in Achieving Development Objectives," paper presented at the 1983 Agricultural Outlook Conference, Washington, D.C., November 29–December 1.

1983

"Agricultural Communities: Economic and Social Setting," in *Agricultural Communities: The Interrelationship of Agriculture, Business, Industry, and Government in the Rural Economy—A Symposium*, prepared by the Congressional Research Service, Library of Congress for the House Committee on Agriculture, October, pp. 90–104.

1984

"Poughkeepsie's Complaint, or Defining Metropolitan Areas," in *American Demographics*, January, pp. 28–31, 46–47.

1986

"Six Demographic Surprises," in *Increasing Understanding of Public Problems and Policies—1985*, Farm Foundation, Oak Brook, Ill., pp. 3–6.

1988

"Americans Heading for the Cities, Once Again," *Rural Development Perspectives*, Vol 4., No. 3, pp. 2–6.

1989

"Race and Ethnicity" (Chap. 5), "Fertility" (Chap. 7), and "Income and Poverty" (Chap. 11). Forthcoming in Glenn V. Fuguitt,

David L. Brown, and Calvin L. Beale, *Rural and Small Town America*, Russell Sage Foundation, New York.

"Significant Recent Trends in the Demography of Farm People," paper presented to the Philadelphia Society for Promoting Agriculture, May 5, 1988. Published in *Proceedings of the Philadelphia Society for Promoting Agriculture, 1987–1988*, pp. 36–49.

Co-Authored Writings

1953

Economic Subregions of the United States (with Donald J. Bogue), U.S. Department of Agriculture, Bureau of Agricultural Economics, Washington, D.C., Farm Population Census, BAE series, No. 19, June.

1954

"Future Trend of Fertility in the United States" (with Henry S. Shryock, Jr., and Jacob S. Siegel), paper prepared for the World Population Conference, held under the auspices of the United Nations Economic and Social Council, Rome, August 31 to September 10. Published in proceedings of that conference.

1961

Economic Areas of the United States (with Donald J. Bogue), The Free Press of Glencoe, New York.

"The 1960 Definition of Farm Residence and Its Marked Effects on Farm Population Data" (with Gladys K. Bowles), paper presented at annual meeting of the Association of Southern Agricultural Workers, Jackson, Miss., February 6–8.

1963

Recent Population Trends in the United States with Emphasis on Rural Areas (with Donald J. Bogue), U.S. Department of Agriculture, Agricultural Economic Report No. 23, Washington, D.C., January. Also published as "Recent Population Trends in the United States and Their Causes," in James H. Copp (ed.), *Our Changing Rural Society: Perspectives and Trends*, Iowa State University Press, Ames, 1964, pp. 71–126.

Farm Population Estimates for 1910–62 (with Vera J. Banks and Gladys K. Bowles), U.S. Department of Agriculture, ERS130, Economic Research Service, Washington, D.C., October.

1964

"Socioeconomic Differences Between White and Nonwhite Farm Populations of the South" (with James D. Cowhig), *Social Forces*, Vol. 42, No. 3, March, pp. 354–362.

"Relative Socioeconomic Status of Southern Whites and Nonwhites, 1950 and 1960" (with James D. Cowhig), *The Southwestern Social Science Quarterly*, Vol. 45, No. 2, September, pp. 113–124.

Characteristics of the U.S. Population by Farm and Nonfarm Origin (with John C. Hudson and Vera J. Banks), U.S. Department of Agriculture, Agricultural Economic Report No. 66, Economic Research Service, Washington, D.C., December.

1965

"The Rising Levels of Education Among Young Workers" (with James D. Cowhig), *Monthly Labor Review*, June, pp. 625–628.

Characteristics of the Population of Hired Farmworker Households (with Gladys K. Bowles), U.S. Department of Agriculture, Agricultural Economic Report No. 84, Economic Research Service, Washington, D.C., August.

The French and Non-French in Rural Louisiana: A Study of the Relevance of Ethnic Factors to Rural Development (with Alvin L. Bertrand), Bulletin 606, Louisiana State University Agricultural Experiment Station, Baton Rouge, December.

1966

Potential Supply and Replacement of Rural Males of Labor Force Age, 1960–70 (with Gladys K. Bowles and Benjamin S. Bradshaw), U.S. Department of Agriculture, Statistical Bulletin No. 378, Economic Research Service, Washington, D.C., October.

1967

"Vocational Agriculture Enrollment and Farm Employment Opportunities" (with James D. Cowhig), *The Southwestern Social Science Quarterly*, Vol. 47, No. 4, March, pp. 413–423.

"Impact of Socioeconomic Factors on Farm Labor Supply" (with Varden Fuller), *Journal of Farm Economics*, Vol. 49, No. 5, December, pp. 1237–1243.

236 BIBLIOGRAPHY

"Population Trends of Southern Non-metropolitan Towns, 1950 to 1960" (with James D. Tarver), in *Rural Sociology*, Vol. 33, No. 1, March, pp. 19–29.

"Relationship of Changes in Employment and Age Composition to the Population Changes of Southern Nonmetropolitan Towns" (with James D. Tarver), in *Rural Sociology*, Vol. 34, No. 1, March, pp. 16–28.

Farm Population by Race, Tenure, and Economic Scale of Farming, 1966 and 1970 (with Vera J. Banks), U.S. Department of Agriculture, Agricultural Economic Report No. 228, Economic Research Service, Washington, D.C., June.

Farm Population Estimates 1910–70 (with Vera J. Banks), U.S. Department of Agriculture, Statistical Bulletin No. 523, Economic Research Service, Washington, D.C., July.

"The New Pattern of Nonmetropolitan Population Change" (with Glenn V. Fuguitt), CDE Working Paper 75–22, August, presented at the Conference on Social Demography, University of Wisconsin, Madison, July 15–16. Also published in Karl E. Taeuber, Larry L. Bumpass, and James A. Sweet (eds.), *Social Demography*, Academic Press, New York, 1978, pp. 157–177.

"Population Trends of Nonmetropolitan Cities and Villages in Subregions of the United States" (with Glenn V. Fuguitt), CDE Working Paper 75–30, University of Wisconsin, Madison, September. Also published in *Demography*, Vol. 15, No. 4, November, 1978, pp. 605–620.

Population Change in Nonmetropolitan Cities and Towns (with Glenn V. Fuguitt), U.S. Department of Agriculture, Agricultural Economic Report No. 323, Economic Development Division, Economic Research Service, Washington, D.C., February.

1980

"Commuting and Migration Status in Nonmetro Areas" (with Gladys K. Bowles), *Agricultural Economics Research*, Vol. 32, No. 3, July, pp. 8–20.

1981

"Diversity in Post-1970 Population Trends" (with David L. Brown), Chap. 1 in Amos H. Hawley and Sara Mills Mazie (eds.), *Nonmetropolitan America in Transition*, University of North Carolina Press, Chapel Hill, pp. 27–54.

1983

"Socioeconomic Context of Nonmetropolitan Land Use Change" (with David L. Brown), in Rutherford H. Platt and George Macinko (eds.), *Beyond the Urban Fringe: Land Use Issues of Nonmetropolitan America*, University of Minnesota Press, Minneapolis, pp. 61–81.

1985

Natural Resources and Rural Poverty: An Overview (with Irma T. Elo), National Center for Food and Agricultural Policy, Resources for the Future, Washington, D.C.

"Metropolitan and Nonmetropolitan Growth Differentials in the United States Since 1980" (with Glenn V. Fuguitt), paper prepared for the General Conference of the International Union for the Scientific Study of Population, Florence, Italy, June 5–12. Expanded version also published as CDE Working Paper 85–6, Center for Demography and Ecology, University of Wisconsin, Madison.

1988

"The Decline in American Counter-Urbanization in the 1980s" (with Irma T. Elo), paper presented at the annual meeting of the Population Association of America, New Orleans, April 22.

Index

Selected List of RAND Books

Alexiev, Alexander R., and S. Enders Wimbush (eds.). *Ethnic Minorities in the Red Army: Asset or Liability?* Boulder, Colo.: Westview Press, 1988.

Builder, Carl H. *The Masks of War: American Military Styles in Strategy and Analysis.* Baltimore, Md.: The Johns Hopkins University Press, 1989.

Dorfman, Robert, Paul A. Samuelson, and Robert M. Solow. *Linear Programming and Economic Analysis.* New York: McGraw-Hill Book Company, 1958. Reprinted New York: Dover Publications, 1987.

Fainsod, Merle. *Smolensk under Soviet Rule.* Cambridge, Mass.: Harvard University Press, 1958. Reprinted Boston, Mass.: Unwin Hyman, 1989.

Gustafson, Thane. *Crisis Amid Plenty: The Politics of Oil and Gas and the Evolution of Energy Policy in the Soviet Union Since 1917.* Princeton, N.J.: Princeton University Press, 1989.

Horelick, Arnold L. (ed.). *U.S.-Soviet Relations: The Next Phase.* Ithaca, N.Y.: Cornell University Press, 1986

Hosmer, Stephen T. *Constraints on U.S. Strategy in Third World Conflicts.* New York: Taylor & Francis, 1987.

Kanouse, David E., et al. *Changing Medical Practice Through Technology Assessment: An Evaluation of the NIH Consensus Development Program.* Ann Arbor, Mich.: Health Administration Press, 1989.

Klahr, Philip, and Donald A. Waterman (eds.). *Expert Systems: Techniques, Tools, and Applications.* Reading, Mass.: Addison-Wesley Publishing Company, 1986.

Korbonski, Andrzej, and Francis Fukuyama (eds.). *The Soviet Union and the Third World: The Last Three Decades.* Ithaca, N.Y.: Cornell University Press, 1987.

Nerlich, Uwe, and James A. Thomson (eds.). *Conventional Arms Control and the Security of Europe.* Boulder, Colo.: Westview Press, 1988.

Nerlich, Uwe, and James A. Thomson (eds.), *The Soviet Problem in American-German Relations.* New York: Crane, Russak & Company, 1985.

Quade, Edward S., revised by Grace M. Carter. *Analysis for Public Decisions* (Third Edition). New York: Elsevier Science Publishing Company, 1989.

Ross, Randy L. *Government and the Private Sector: Who Should Do What?* New York: Taylor & Francis, 1988.

Williams, J. D. *The Compleat Strategyst: Being a Primer on the Theory of Games of Strategy*. New York: McGraw-Hill Book Company, 1954. Revised 1966 edition reprinted. New York: Dover Publications, 1986.

Wolf, Charles, Jr. *Markets or Governments: Choosing between Imperfect Alternatives*. Cambridge, Mass.: The MIT Press, 1988.

Wolf, Charles, Jr., and Katharine Watkins Webb, (eds.). *Developing Cooperative Forces in the Third World*. Lexington, Mass.: Lexington Books, 1987.